MW01631947

PC
TM
PEN CUSHION
PUBLISHERS

THE

BULL DOG

CREW

A STORY BY MIZ

PEN CUSHION PUBLISHERS
PO Box 85
New York, N.Y. 10019

This book is a work of fiction, Names, characters, Places, and events have been created by the author's imagination. Any resemblance to actual persons or events, living or dead, is absolutely coincidental.

Copyright © 2004 by MIZ
All rights reserved. No part of this book is to be reproduced in any form without permission from the publisher, except by reviewer who may quote brief passages to be printed in a newspaper or magazine.

Typeset in Times New Roman

ISBN#978-0-9764446-1-9

Written by: MIZ
Edited by: M. Adams/ O. Vaughan
Cover concept by: MIZ
Graphic Design by: Kevin Cosme
Cover Photography by: Kevin Cosme
Mallony Incorporated May 2007
Printed in Michigan

DEDICATED IN THE
MEMORY OF
MY BROTHER AND COMRADE
TYRONE "TEE ROCK" BAUM

"A BRANCH FELL BUT THE TREE WON'T FALL, CONTINUE TO LOOK OVER YOUR FAMILY AND FRIENDS, WE'LL CONTINUE TO STAND STRONG AND TALL."

MIZ ACKNOWLEDGEMENTS

First and foremost, I would like to send all Praise, Love, Respect and Honor to the Most High GOD. You make all things possible. I love and thank you for blessing me with the gift to reach and entertain others through my writing. The Bible says, "Honor your father and mother." That I do, and I would like to send a big thank you out to my father and mother, Alfred and Dot Adams. I love and honor you. You've created an author.

Much love to all my brothers and sisters: Lorraine, Freddy, Michelle, Nay, Cynthia, Shaborn("My Brother's Keeper". Keep writing those proper books you got as well), and my baby sister Niecy (My success is yours).

Much love to my twin cousin and co-publisher, Omar "OH!" Vaughan. After I wrote "BISHOP", I'm glad you saw the vision. Thanks for starting the company when I was unavailable to do so. Now lets get that paper! I can't wait till you drop your songs to show the world what you got and for

your little ones Jada & OJ. Big Kev stay focus, its time. What up Shim? Keep them hot beats coming! Shout out to the whole Adams, Browns, and Redding family. We are too deep to name all my nephews and nieces. It's DEFINITELY a lot of us. Now I must get a few of my comrades in here: White Owl, Kool-Aid, Prince, Fuji, Mel, Great god, his crimie Big Kurt, C-god, his brother Raleek, My man Rondu (Vandyke)< Kalief< Ashanti, Shawn, Mike(Harlem), Bajah (NA Rock), Pretty boy Bar from the Fort, Boxing Bar from Albany projects, Big Biz(E.N.Y), Doc, Knowledge, Ramel, DaQual and Shameek (Lefrak), K.B., Larry, Pezo, Drama, Askari, PB, Dorian, the big homie Lite Luch, Gutta Man, Bush, Swells, Berry, Rah Dollars, Stud Money, P.I., Tony, Marion, Jayme and the whole Venditto-Ross family, Cam, Du-Bar, Big Unique, General Stitchie, Umajesty, T.J.(Marcy projects, you been in the Feds a long time Money Grip, and though some have forgotten you, I haven't. You a real nigga), My boy Clay (Lo Life), and I know it's many names I have

forgotten to put down, but you're in heart. I'll catch you on the next book.

Much love to Stacia (I'm waiting to read those books), Baby girl, My sis Shani, etc. Too many to name.

To all the authors I love, look up to, or just wanted to shout out: Sister Souljah, My girl Teri "Motherfucking" Woods (Ha! Love you girl. Thanks for the support), Carl Weber, My girl Queen Pen (Keep pushing out those good books. Thanks for the support. BROOKLYN!!!), can't forget the blue print Mr. Dan Poynter, The "Bad Boy" Michael Baisden who encouraged me and others through your terrific show, starting our own business and work hard, Triple Crown Publishing(Vicky Stringer), the beautiful Crystal Lacey Winslow, Donald Goines, Ice Berg Slim, Terry McMillan, My boy Zach Tates " Lost and Turned Out" (Remember those rapping days? Ha!), The Twinz "Crime Pays" (Born and Shabee, that's fire! I'm sure you remember the Green Haven rapping days as well), and oh yeah, shout outs to the brother Bear "Thug Misses" and LD "My Side of the Story", and the MANY other authors who's work I've enjoyed. Big shout out to all independent authors who hit that street grind. Much success to Cricket and your magazine, "Street Talks" and those who I forgot, thank you and much love in your success.

Big thanks to all the websites, book stores, street vendors, hand to hand sellers, distributors, family and friends. Power 105.1 Ed 'Eddy Mack" Lover, Hot 97's Angie Martinez, DJ Enuff and The Heavy Hitters. Most importantly all the readers, purchasers, and fans who made it possible for "BISHOP" and now "THE BULLDOG CREW". Much love to everyone who are making this possible.

Now my list to my peoples who are no longer here.

R.I.P

Tyrone"Tee-Rock"Baum, Darry "Hommo" Baum, James "JR" Hamilton, Ivory "Nut" Davis, Myron "Wise" Hardy, Benjamin "Killer Ben" O'Garro,

Edward "Ju-Ju" Silva, "Sharod" Brown, Robert "Poo" Chance, Nate "NA", Carlton "C-Asiatic" Smith, Jimmy Dean, Belvue Troy, Ron-K, K-Sun, Demencio, Tracy "Tray" Washington, Eric "Terminator E", Sharod "Hot Rod" Joyner, Lil JayO and many more…too many to name. Last but not least: family:

Harold Redding, Myra "Nibeya" Redding, David "Shyne" Redding, Taren Adams, Jessica Smith, Prim Rose Adams and Della Adams.

After doing seventeen and a half years in prison, I promise not to disappoint any of you. Please keep supporting me and Pen Cushion Publishing. And I will continue to give you classic books, music, comedy sit-coms, movies and more.

Much Love!!!!!!

Chapter 1

The tension in Attica's yard was full with emotion and a tension that never ceased. It was always some kind of drama popping off in each yard, especially A-Block.

Every block had its own individual yard, and it was a regular routine to see someone getting cut, stabbed and even killed at times. Almost every inmate in the yard stayed close to their own individual cliques. The Muslims sat three tables deep in one area of the yard, the Bloods stood along the walls near the basketball courts, the Latin Kings and other Puerto-Ricans held one another down near the handball court while a few of them played a few games, the Jamaicans sat two tables deep chatting and banging on the table as some smoked their marijuana on the low, the White boys sat and stood around one table laughing and joking, and everyone else that belonged to no clique moved all around the yard freely doing whatever they did. Whether it was playing basketball, walking and talking, watching TV, talking on the phones, lifting weights, or doing pull-ups and dips to stay physically fit, there were no telling when something would jump off, so a person would have to definitely be ready for show time whenever it popped off.

The only inmates who enjoyed the music that played over the loud speaker in the yard were the White boys, being that the radio stayed on the Country or some other station that the other nationalities did not really care for. And this was odd indeed, considering the white inmate population only made up ten percent of the General prison population. But to be fair, sometimes you might catch a rap or something R&B you knew all the words to on the yards radio. More often than not, it would be some kind of country or hillbilly song playing, and the funny thing is that you would hear it so much, you would find yourself singing all the words to the song and maybe even liking it.

On this hot particular day, Light was standing near the TV disrespecting a stocky brown-skinned brother wearing a brown crown on his head. The guy was a Muslim, but Light didn't care about any of that. He was Big Light from the Bulldog Crew and that's all that mattered.

A group of A-Block's most dangerous inmates stood around the TV laughing at the inmate taking the verbal assault from Light. "You punk ass motherfucker," said Light. "You lucky I wasn't the nigga CB. Cause if your girl was looking all in my face on the visit floor, I would've bagged that bitch! But then again, that bitch is ugly. She look like a smoked out Daffy Duck, you bird ass nigga!"

All of the guys standing around laughed. Some laughed so hard, they were in tears. "Light is off the hook!" a few of them said.

The brown-skinned guy he was dissing said, "I'm saying though, she troop for a nigga. And I go down on the visit floor more than most of these niggas in this spot. Some of these niggas don't even know what the visiting room look like!"

The guys standing around knew he'd spoken the truth because some of them were the ones who never got visits.

"Motherfucker, my bitch troop too!" said Light with his face screwed up. "Plus I get trees nigga!"

"I'm saying," said the guy. "That's you. Drugs ain't my thing."

Light's friend CB knew Light long enough to know when he was still tight. He also knew Light was ready to put a steel shank in the boy. CB looked at Light and said, "Yo, come on man. Let's take a few laps around the yard before we work out. I need to talk to you anyway."

Light looked at the brown-skin guy he was dissing, and the guy knew he should've took Light's verbal assault quietly like most of the inmates did. When he looked in Light's eyes he saw danger, so he was glad that CB was successful in getting Light to walk away as he pulled his arm. Now he hoped Light would forget about the whole incident and not take it out on him at a later date.

"Yo man," said CB as they walked around the small yard, "you gotta chill out if you wanna go home. You should be on the low anyway. I mean, you just got that reversal on that 440.10, right? So, you might get time served. What did your lawyer say?"

"He said me and my crimies will get that appeal bail most likely," answered Light calming down. "And he said he believe they'll throw it out or something. I don't know. But once I get outta here, I ain't coming back to this shit! That faggot ass Governor got motherfuckers going to their 4th, 5th and 6th parole board in this bitch! Before I come back to this shit, I'm going out like my nigga Divine."

"No doubt," said CB. "I hear you. Shit, I feel the same motherfucking way."

Light was part of a small gang of notorious thugs called the "Bulldog Crew" and Divine was basically the founder of it. The name came about because whenever they did a hit, the .44 Bulldog handgun was always the gun of choice. Of course they would have some kind of automatic weapon on them as well for back up, but when it came to a simple hit, the .44 Bulldog was favored.

Divine was always a well known killer, but he wasn't seeing no real money until he met a church boy turned thug name Richard who everyone called Bishop. Richard got put on to the drug game by his wife Lisa's older brother Omar. Now Omar was a big drug kingpin, a multi-millionaire from Fort Greene Projects that helped Richard with anything he needed. He retired from the drug game and became a CEO of one of the hottest record labels out. Whatever Richard wanted to do, Omar backed him all the way, until Richard himself decided to leave the game alone as well. But before that happened, Richard saw it was the right decision to make Divine his lieutenant in his multi-million dollar drug operation. Not only did they become rich, but they also had terrorized the New York City streets when Divine started a small gang called the "Bulldog Crew" that consisted of six very dangerous gunmen including him self. Three of them had gotten killed: Tommy Guns, Big Dave, and little Murder Mike. Divine had also gotten killed, but not before killing Richard's worse and most dangerous enemy Shameek, and also one of the police most corrupted detectives to ever walk the Brooklyn streets, Detective Martin "Rambo" Harrison. Divine was remembered as a hero to many thugs in the streets of almost every major city. After Divine's death, Richard quit the drug game and became a preacher down south in North Carolina. The last three remaining Bulldog members: Light, Fats, and L, had just gotten a reversal on their conviction for killing a well-known Harlem drug dealer.

Light and CB stopped walking, and Light approached the small metal table and all seated gave him a pound.

"Much respect," said Light to the dread with a smile. "Who got that good shit?"

The dread looked around making sure the CO's weren't anywhere in the area as he gave Light another pound with three New York joints of weed in his hand.

"Good looking brethren," said Light as he pocketed the marijuana. "If you need anything, let me know."

"Cool," replied the dread as Light and CB continued walking around the small yard.

"Did you get the weed from your crimie?" asked CB.

"Nah," answered Light. "I'm good! Fats and L can keep that. When Kia come up tomorrow, I'll send them some more over there. But what they need to do, is get up outta D-Block and come over here."

"Oh hell no nigga!" smiled CB. "I can put up with L. But you and Fats together? Forget about it!"

"Come on man," said Light changing the subject. "Lets go work out. Get a little chest in."

They walked over to the weights along the wall, and the inmates lifting weights greeted Light and CB giving them enough room to work out.

"A yo, remember Karen from Kingston and St. Johns?" asked CB as Light put 245 pounds on the incline bench.

"Nah, I don't remember that bitch," answered Light. "The only one I remember from that block was Shanique."

"Damn, how you don't remember her? She had a crazy fat ass on her! But then again, she's older than you. She's my age."

"I still probably know her by face," said Light looking around for more weight. And then sitting down he said, "Come on spot me!"

Light laid back on the incline bench and pressed the 245 pounds ten times before getting up.

"Damn kid!" smiled CB. "You getting strong. You was always a little skinny nigga, now you beefing it up! Remember when you was like twelve and I was fifteen, and we had that fight in the game room? Yo, you a funny nigga. That day I had to put it on you," CB laughed as Light gave him a little smirk as he also remembered the fight they had when they were children.

"Arr man," continued CB laughing. "That shit was crazy! And you know I still got it," he said, throwing a flurry of punches at the air before sitting down on the incline bench. He then looked up at Light and noticed that something was troubling his friend.

"A yo man," said CB with concern. "Don't let that bird ass nigga you was beefing with near the TV get to you homie. I can see it all in your face. Come on, let's just get this work out over with, and then we can blow a bone or something."

"Yeah, you right," smiled Light as he spotted CB helping him take the weight out of the rack.

CB pressed the 245 pounds six times and then felt a sharp pain in his side. He felt it again as he yelled and dropped the weight on the ground just barely missing his left foot. He then saw Light walking away quickly. He looked down at his side and recognized that he was bleeding badly. As he grimaced in pain, he got up and started to go after Light, but a brown-skin stocky baldhead guy that was working out named Mont-Mont saw everything that transpired. He pulled out a sharp looking ice pick and told CB, "Don't blow it up bitch, take yours and heal up! If you try to walk behind 'em, I'ma kill you!"

CB thought about it for a second, and then walked towards the CO's bubble to let them know he'd been stabbed and was in need of some serious medical attention. He just couldn't believe that light had stabbed him. He knew Light his whole life, and wondered why he flipped on him and stabbed him up. But for now he just hoped he wouldn't lose too much blood as the CO's rushed him to the hospital.

Chapter 2

Fats and L walked around the yard in D-Block, and was making plans of what they were going to do when they got out of prison.

"The first thing I'ma do," smiled Fats, "is stick all of 'dem niggas up that's getting that drug money and rap money, except the nigga Omar."

"Man, we'll be back in jail faster than a motherfucker messing wit' them faggot ass rap niggas," said L. "They talk all that gangsta shit and straight pussy. And they got the game hot as a motherfucker right now wit' all that snitching on records. 'He shot me and so and so shot him'. Yo, I hate them faggots! That's why the Feds is watching everything right now. Even most of the rap niggas sign to Omar is pussy! The only ones I like, is the O.G.'s and that's it."

Fats laughed and said, "Man, fuck all them niggas. Shit, if Omar wasn't peoples, I'll get that nigga too!"

"Nah," said L. "That's family right there."

Then changing the subject he asked, "You heard why Light hit the nigga CB?"

"Yeah I heard," laughed Fats. "He sent me a kite about it. You know the nigga Light never got over the fact that CB duffed him out when they was kids and shit. He said the nigga CB had the nerve to mention the fight and throw a few flurries at the air, so he blew 'em!"

L busted out laughing as he stopped walking and held his stomach. He knew Light was a bug out, but damn! When he was back in control of his laughter, the two of them started walking again.

"That nigga Light is stupid!" said L.

"He's on the visit right now," replied Fats. "Kia came up, and when he come back he said he'll send us some weed over."

"Aiight," smiled L. "That's what I'm talking about. Yo, you know he put the nigga Mont-Mont down wit' us, right?"

"Yeah, he told me he's BDC now. But I don't mind, he's a good nigga and I heard he don't hesitate to let his gun go in the town."

"I'm feeling that. But I don't know homie to feel him though," confessed L. "But I know what your saying about letting that thang go. Fuck all that talking shit! Look what happened to Big Dave and Tommy Guns."

"Yeah," said Fats thinking about it. "You're right about that, man. You're right about that."

Big Dave, Tommy Guns and L, killed six Bloods in the Flatbush section of Brooklyn, as they came from visiting Tommy Gun's uncle. A little Blood kid who was looking for some kind of recognition, provoked the verbal exchange of heated words before Big Dave getting tired of shorty's mouth, pulled out and opened fire on the small group of Bloods. Of course the Bloods fired back, but they was outwitted and outgunned by the three dangerous Bulldog crew members. As the months passed, Big Dave and Tommy Guns found themselves visiting Tommy Gun's uncle once again. The rest of the bloods in the area, had heard they were inside of the apartment, and decided to make their move by standing in front of his uncle's apartment waiting for the two gunmen to come out.

Big Dave looked at Tommy Guns and said, "Yo, it's a lot of them niggas out there. Call Fats, Light and L and tell them niggas to get down here."

"I just tried to call Fats cell phone, but I'm not getting no answer. And you know they're all together."

Big Dave looked out of the window and said, “Aiight, this is what we gonna do. Them niggas got guns, but they ain’t pull out yet. So, just open the door and when I step out blazing, you follow behind me.”

“Aiight bet!” said Tommy Guns pulling a nine millimeter and .44 Bulldog hand gun from his waist. He and Big Dave carried the same guns that day, so together they had four guns.

“Give me one of them guns,” said Tommy Gun’s uncle in a voice like he had too much to drink, as he looked out of the window. “I’m going out there with y’all. Come around my house with this bullshit! I’ll show ‘dem muh’fuckers, you don’t fuck with my family. Oh, hell nah!”

“Chill out Unc! I got this,” said Tommy Guns looking out of the window. He then smiled when he saw a very familiar face. It belonged to a guy named Bo-Scagz, that was close to his family. Their mothers were like sisters, which made them like first cousins being they grew up together since childhood. Bo-Scagz was a well-known and respected leader of the Bloods, and when Tommy Guns saw him arguing with a few Bloods, he knew his cousin was speaking in his defense.

Tommy Guns left the window, looked at Big Dave and said, “Yo, I’m feeling your plan. But I don’t think we have to go out like that. My cousin Bo-Scagz is out there checking them niggas now. They scared of ‘em. He’s they leader or some shit.”

“Where’s Bo?” asked his drunken uncle. “Bo-Scagz out there?”

“We can just walk up out of here,” said Tommy Guns to Big Dave, not paying his uncle no mind. “Trust me, my cousin got them niggas in check.”

Big Dave didn't feel comfortable with Tommy Guns idea, because he was never a talker, and had no intentions of being one now. He also did not want to possibly get his boy killed with his plans either, so he tucked his guns back into his waist.

"Come on," he said "let's get this shit over with."

As soon as they walked out the door, almost all of the Bloods reached for their guns but none of them pulled out.

"Nobody better not shoot!" yelled out Bo-Scagz as he walked over and gave Tommy Guns a pound, and glancing at Big Dave with a funny look on his face.

Big Dave knew something wasn't right, and it was confirmed when he saw one of the Bloods slowly inching his gun out, and Bo-Scagz trying to lead Tommy Guns away from everyone else. Big Dave had then knew what time it was. It was not hard to see that Bo-Scagz had made a deal to give him up, and save Tommy Guns. But he wasn't going out like a chump! Before the Blood could get his gun out, Big Dave went for his own. He pulled out and moved so swiftly, he caught the Bloods by surprise as he fired his weapon hitting the Blood that was pulling for his gun in the head. He then saw a way out and went for it, but caught a bullet in the back of his head from Bo-Scagz gun. Before Bo-Scagz could turn around , Tommy Guns shot his fake cousin so many times it looked like he was doing the "Harlem Shake' dance. Tommy Guns had then tried to shoot it out with the rest of the Bloods and make a run for it, but got gunned down before he could let off a shot. He was dead before he hit the ground, and the Bloods ran in different directions because they all knew the police would be surrounding the area, probably before they could even get off of the block!

As the four dead bodies lay sprawled out on the concrete, Fats, L, and Light was torturing a well-known Harlem drug dealer in a Brooklyn basement. They already got the whereabouts of where his money was kept, but Fats and Light was having fun breaking all the bones in his body with two small sledge hammers! A big time drug dealer from out of Brownsville named Hook, had put the hit out on the Harlem drug dealer. Being that Light knew Hook for years, the Bulldog Crew took the hit. All Hook told them to do was kill the drug dealer so he could come home from jail, being that the drug dealer was the only witness against him, but Light and Fats had other plans for the snitch besides what Hook had paid them to do.

"Just shoot the nigga and get it over with!" said L tired of hearing the guy yell in pain, and tired of seeing him pass out only to be awakened again by the bone cracking blows of the hammers as Fats and Light laughed with every sickening blow they delivered. It was blood everywhere and the guy was unrecognizable to the point where his own mother would not be able to identify him

"Yo, just chill and try to call Big Dave and Tommy Guns back," instructed Fats.

"I just tried," said L. "I'm not getting no answer."

After being satisfied with the work they delivered to the dead drug dealer, they went to collect the money he would never need, as well as the money Hook was paying for their services. But when the Homicide police had discovered the murder victim, they knew it had to be the three remaining Bulldog Crew members that did the gruesome killing, so they paid a crack head off the streets to lie and say that he saw Fats, L and Light enter the empty apartment building dragging the drug dealer. However, after a few years, the crack head cleaning up his act and now becoming religious, felt that it was the right thing to do by recanting his statement and letting the truth be known that he did not see anything, and was paid by the police to say what he said that caused three men to be wrongfully imprisoned. And because of that, Light, Fats and L was soon to be sent back down to Rikers Island on a reversal of their case.

"Yeah, I agree with you," said Fats as he and L walked around the yard in Attica for at least the twentieth time today.

"From what Tommy Gun's uncle said," replied Fats, "they might've still been alive if they didn't go out there to talk to that faggot ass nigga Bo-Scagz. He lucky my boys killed him, before I could get my hands on 'em. Man, I would've tortured that boy so bad, they wouldn't be able to figure out was the nigga a human at one time or not."

"Yeah," said L knowing his friend had meant every word he'd spoken. Then changing the subject he said, "Yo, guess who wrote me yesterday."

"Who? Bishop?" laughed Fats.

"Yeah, how you know?" asked L, amazed at his guess.

"What is he talking about?" asked Fats with a smile, not answering his question.

"He always say I'm the more reasonable one out of all of us, because I'm the only one who writes him back," answered L. "He just sent me a bunch of 'Get in touch with Jesus pamphlets. You want one?"

"Hell no!" laughed Fats. "That's why me and Light don't answer that nigga letters. Nobody wanna hear that shit!"

L laughed and said, "He's a good nigga though. He just wanna save everybody. But I ain't try'na be saved, I just wanna get the fuck outta here!"

"No doubt!" said Fats. "Yo, I thought you was going down on a V.I. today. What happened?"

"Everything is cool," answered L. "I told this bitch Sonia from outta Queens to come next weekend. You want me to tell her to get one of her friends, to pull you down?"

"Nah I'm good," answered Fats as they continued walking around the small yard. "I ain't thinking about them bitches. A nigga just need some streets! And the nigga Hook said whatever cash we need to get outta here, he got us."

"Shit, that ain't no big offer", said L. "We got enough money individually to do that. All that money we made fucking wit' Divine and Bishop. But if the nigga Hook wanna give up some cash, fuck it I'll take it. A yo, what's up with your girl Denise? She ain't been up here in a minute."

"Man , I told you I'm not thinking about them bitches. Especially, that lying ass bitch! She's mad right now, 'cause I gave ten niggas in here her name and address. I'm saying, them niggas lie all fucking day and all her letters are lies, so I figured I'll just let them lie to each other."

L started laughing as Fats continued talking.

"The bitch is lucky, I ain't give them niggas the naked flicks she sent me."

L immediately stopped laughing and asked, "Word? You got naked flicks of her? Yo, bring them shits out tonight!"

Instead of answering, Fats just smiled as they continued walking around the small yard.

"The yard is closed!" yelled the CO over the loud speaker in the yard. "Line up near your company and prepare for the go back!"

All the inmates in the yard stopped whatever they were doing, and began to stand in certain areas of the yard. A few of them laughed and joked, some exchanged books of naked girls in yellow manilla envelopes as if they were trading top secret information, some stood against the wall with their faces screwed up in a gangster glare, and the very few booty bandits that had sex with other men looked around for a possible weak or willing victim they could make a move on at a later date. The scene was actually comical, as well as very dangerous.

L and Fats were on the same company, and after going inside and locking in, the CO walked down the tier taking a list of those who wanted to go to chow as well as rec. He came back and stopped at L's cell and then going to Fats cell telling them both to pack up because they were going back down to court early Monday morning!

"Yo Fats!" yelled L through the bars. "You got the news, right?"

Fats laughed and yelled through the bars, "No doubt! New York City next stop! It's on boy!"

The whole tier erupted in noise celebrating the reversal of those fortunate enough to give the white oppressive system their time back.

Chapter 3

"I don't know what the fuck you're talking about," said Denise as she entered her living room wearing nothing but a white towel.

"You know what I'm talking about!" exclaimed her best friend Tawanna, lying down on the couch as if she lived here in Denise's apartment.

"I'm talking about Fats," she continued. "You know he ain't no good, and you keep running upstate to see that nigga. Don't he got forever up in there?"

"I don't know," answered Denise. "He wrote me a while back and claimed he got a reversal on his case, and should be coming home soon. But you know them niggas in jail will tell you just about anything to keep your ass trooping that bid. But I ain't been up to Attica in months! But I'ma get up there soon. You don't know, me and Fats been through a lot of shit together."

"Yeah, but he ain't do a lot of shit for you," replied Tawanna.

"You know what?" said Denise dropping her towel and oiling her body, "You act like you're jealous of Fats or something."

Tawanna stared at her naked friend as if she'd lost her mind. "I 'm not hardly jealous of that nigga!" she said with her lip turned up.

Denise laughed and said, "When I go up there to see him, you might as well go with me. You can pull his friend L down. He'll like your slim pretty ass."

Tawanna was slim, brown-skinned and very pretty, with shoulder length hair. Her best friend Denise was light-skinned, thick in all the right places, with her short hair dyed a reddish color. Both were gorgeous!

"Don't even try it!" said Tawanna holding up her hand. "I'm not going up there with you, and I'm definitely not pulling his friend L down. I don't want nothing to do with them Bulldogs, German Shepherds…whatever the fuck they call themselves. Plus, them jail niggas can't do shit for me!"

"Yeah, but you're the first one to be all in they face when they come home," said Denise while slipping on her pink panties.

"So," responded Tawanna. "It ain't nothing wrong with that! Shit, I ain't the one that put'em in jail. When they come home we're on equal grounds, and whatever happens, happens."

Denise shook her head with a smile and said, "I hear you, but you can't always expect to share only the good times with a nigga and not the bad. Did you ever think that maybe guys shit on girls when they come home, is because the girls didn't keep it real?"

"Whatever!" replied Tawanna . "And you got some nerves, 'cause you definitely ain't keeping it real with Fats!"

Denise knew her friend had spoke the truth, but she also knew it was easier to say something, than actually doing it.

"Yo, let's go to Nostrand Avenue", continued Tawanna changing the subject. "You know Mikey and 'nem is down there."

"I ain't fucking with them niggas," said Denise. "Plus, I gotta go to East New York and see Poison."

Tawanna laughed and said, "Bitch, you ain't no good! A few minutes ago, you was talking like the faithful girlfriend of Fats. Now, you're ready to jet to East New York and suck Poison's dick!"

Denise smacked and licked her lips, causing Tawanna to go into a fit of laughter.

"Nah," said Denise. "Fats is my baby. He'll always be number one, but shit, he's in jail! I'm not gonna stop getting my groove on!"

"That's what I'm talking about girl," said Tawanna giving Denise a high five. "But I'm not going to lie, that nigga Fats is crazy! So if he is coming home, you better drop Poison quick, if you don't want him to come up dead!"

Denise threw on a white tee shirt with a picture of the late great rapper Big Pun on the front and pulled on her tight blue jeans, as she thought about Tawanna's last statement.

The thought of Fats actually coming home, excited her as well as frightened her. She knew he was a very dangerous gangster, and judging from the last visits she'd spent with him in Attica's visiting room, she knew from his demeanor that he had not changed one bit. He had not even become an 'old sometimer'. That's what Denise called old school gangsters that killed a lot of people back in the days, but after doing a lot of time, they were so scared to go back to prison that they would only carry their guns 'sometimes' giving them the name 'sometimers'. And of course it would lead to them being killed by a young boy who carried a gun every day that didn't care, or know the importance of staying out of prison. But Fats was different, and Denise knew it. The funny thing was that he was humorous and quiet, to the point of even being shy. However, he could sit down with you, laugh, talk and then blow your brains out without a second thought. It didn't matter whether you were a man or woman, his guns did not discriminate!

Yes, if it's true that Fats is coming home, she thought, she would definitely have to drop Poison and any other guy she occasionally had sex with in Fats absence. For some strange reason, Denise wished Fats stayed in jail. This way she could visit him whenever she had time, as well as get her freak on in the streets. She didn't know what it was about her, but she always been attracted to bad boys. Regular nice guys were too boring, because they did not possess that thuggish sensuality that turned her on. And it was sad, because when she reflected back on it, she realized all of her past boyfriends had either gotten paralyzed, killed or put in prison forever. She knew her choice in men were not healthy, but what could she do? It was either be in a boring relationship with a nice guy, or having fun living on the edge with a thug who possibly wouldn't be around too long. And many thugs were hollering at Denise because she was very pretty. She could easily take the spotlight from any video vixen that flaunted themselves in almost every rap video that aired on television. She was that pretty!

Denise stayed wearing the latest wears. She dabbled in credit card scams, and the few thugs she dealt with, while Fats were away, gave her money whenever she asked for it. The only thing she hated about being in relationships with thugs was that, as soon as one found out that she use to deal with one of their enemies, they would try anything in their power to get her to give up some information so they could be successful in their wars. Of course she would never participate in their problems, and that's one thing she loved about Fats. He never involved her in any of his beefs and street activities. And even though he talked to her in a disrespectful manner at times, she knew he loved her, and was not physically abusive like her ex-boyfriend Jimmy. She remembered when Jimmy put her head through a car window giving her a deep cut, causing her to receive ten stitches in the back of her head. But you couldn't see the scar because her hair covered it. And it was Fats who saved her from the physically abusive relationship she was in with Jimmy. She first saw him in the grocery store across the street from her house, and when he spoke to her, she tried to warn him that her boyfriend jimmy was waiting outside for her in front of the store and if he saw them talking, he would kill them both.

Fats just laughed and continued to press her.

"I don't give a fuck about that bird ass nigga", he said. "I'm saying, let me take you out to dinner or something, so I can get to know you a little better."

"You crazy?!" said a wide eyed Denise. "Jimmy will kill me if I went out with you! If he even knew I was talking to you in this store, he'll kill me."

Fats smiled, grabbed her hand and said, "Well I wanna take you out, so come on, let's go get the nigga's permission."

Denise thought either Fats was crazy or just plain old stupid! She was trying to get out of the relationship with Jimmy for the longest, but he had her so afraid, she actually believed it would be safer for her to stay in the relationship and just deal with the black eyes and busted lips he often gave to her.

When they walked out of the grocery store holding hands, Jimmy could not believe that she had disrespected him.

"What the fuck is this?!" asked Jimmy with his face screwed up, ready to punish Denise and the guy who was holding her hand.

"Shorty belongs to me now," smiled Fats. "And if you was a real man you wouldn't have to beat up on a woman…coward! Now break the fuck out!"

"What?!" yelled Jimmy. "Nigga, you better ask somebody who the fuck I am!"

Denise wondered how Fats knew that Jimmy was abusive. She had no visible scars and said nothing about the things he'd done to her. Little did she know, that Fats had watched her from a distance for quite some time before approaching her.

"No," smiled Fats. "You better ask somebody who I am."

"What?!" said Jimmy. "I don't give a flying fuck wha—"

"Bam!!!" Light smacked him in the back of the head with his .44 Bulldog handgun from behind knocking him out cold.

"Take that nigga to the car," ordered Fats.

Light dragged Jimmy to a brand new blue BMW and tossed him in the back seat.

Denise couldn't believe what had just happened. And all of this in broad daylight! Everything happened so quickly, no one even noticed that an assault and kidnapping had just occurred.

"Listen ma," said Fats to Denise. "When I told that clown you're mine, I meant it. Now go 'head home, and get ready for tonight. I'm taking you out to dinner."

"You don't know where I live," said a still shooken up Denise.

Fats smiled and said, "Yes I do." He then walked away, got in the back seat of the BMW with the knocked out cold Jimmy, and the car pulled away from the curb. That was the last time Denise had ever saw Jimmy!

"Denise! Denise!" yelled Tawanna. "Stop fucking day dreaming, and let's get up outta here!"

"Oh yeah," said Denise snapping out of her thoughts of Fats. "Let's get out of here. But I still want you to come upnorth with me to see Fats one day."

"I'll think about it," replied Tawanna.

"I definitely have to get up there, and curse his ass out for giving my fucking address out to them niggas in there!" said Denise as they walked out of the apartment.

Chapter 4

"Shut the fuck up, and lay down!" Whitey ordered the four Dominican drug dealers who had mistaken him to be a cop.

"And put your hands behind your backs!" he ordered.

They did as they were told, as Whitey held his nine millimeter handgun pointed in their direction. He searched them finding two guns, and then he snatched the blue nap-sack one of them had dropped to the ground when he first swung around the corner with his gun out and said, "freeze don't move." He smiled as he peeped inside of the bag and saw the kilos of cocaine, packaged up in brown paper and stacked together.

It was then that the drug dealers noticed that no other police had careened on the scene, and they were still un-cuffed, when they figured out that Whitey was no police officer and they were being robbed!

"You ain't no fucking cop!" said one of the drug dealers as they all stood up from the ground with angry looks on their faces. "You're a dead man!"

"Spare me the Scarface bullshit!" said Whitey. "No, I'm not a cop, and that makes me more dangerous. Now get the fuck outta here! Run!"

The Dominican drug dealers did not follow his order. They just stood there breathing heavily with frowns on their faces.

"Oh, y'all don't wanna run?!" asked Whitey before opening fire on the drug dealers hitting them in the legs and stomachs. He then quickly walked away to his car parked around the corner on 176 street and Davidson, up in the Bronx. He had been watching the drug dealers for nearly three weeks now, and knew they was getting a lot of money, because they were talked about on a regular basis as the ones to see if you wanted to cop some good quality weight.

Whitey was happy that he was able to pull off the robbery. Getting rid of the cocaine would be easy. All he had to do was go back to Brooklyn, and sell it all to a big time drug dealer named Big Lord for a reasonable price.

Big Lord was down with Omar when he was still in the game. But when Omar and Richard left the drug game alone, Big Lord took over their drug spots, becoming one of the riches drug dealers in Brooklyn. Actually, the only other drug dealer in Brooklyn known to have as much money as Big Lord, was Hook from Brownsville.

Whitey wished he still had his dangerous partner Moe-dog doing hits and robberies with him. The money came so easy with the two of them together, and plus certain jobs called for more than one person to pull it off. But Whitey definitely was not taking just anybody with him on jobs. That's how fools ended up dead or in prison, he thought to himself.

He drove back to Brooklyn taking the Major Deegan Expressway. He looked like anything other than a stick up kid and hit man. Here he was, a white guy with dark brown hair driving a brand new Maxima. He looked like a doctor, or to most drug dealers, an undercover police officer. He was happy that his looks had finally paid off for him in some kind of way, because his looks had always worked against him, growing up in Albany Housing Projects in the Crown Heights section of Brooklyn.

His family were the only whites in the projects, so he had to hear the white jokes and get picked on everyday! It came to a point where he had to literally, get a gun and prove that he could be just as tough and dangerous as any other thug in and outside of the projects.

After finally being accepted and recognized, life became much easier for him, but now he was so deep in the game, that it became mandatory for him to keep a gun on him at all times!

As Whitey hit the Brooklyn Bridge, his cell phone began to ring. He looked at the caller ID, and smiled before putting the caller on speaker phone.

"What's up Tammy?" asked Whitey as he got off of the Brooklyn Bridge and turned off of Flatbush Avenue.

"Ain't nothing," answered Tammy. After a slight pause she asked, "Where are you? I need to see you."

"I'm Downtown Brooklyn, and I can't get over there until later on. I have to go see my man Big Lord, and take care of some very important business."

"Can't you do that later? I haven't seen you in two days! What, you want me to fuck somebody else?"

Whitey sighed, looked at his watch and said, "I'll be there tonight. I gotta take care of this business. But I promise, I'll see you later tonight."

Before Tammy could say anything else, he hung up the phone. She was his girlfriend and he loved her to death, but he had a lot of things to do and she was too time consuming. All she wanted to do was have sex and spend money, and he knew if she had it her way, he'd be sexually drained and financially broke!

As Whitey headed down Lafayette Avenue, he inserted Jay-Z's "Black Album" CD into the sound system, and as he caught every green light down Lafayette, he rapped along with the song "What more can I say?". He liked Jay-Z, and wondered why he retired from the rap game. Especially now, with the game full of snitches and wack rappers. They were telling so much in songs, Whitey even heard his name being thrown around by rappers he didn't even know. And this was something he did not appreciate, because for one, it drew too much unwanted attention, and he also knew the police were listening to everything these rappers were saying!

'At least these punks can wait until I retire from the streets or go to jail, thought Whitey. After doing business with Big Lord, he figured he'd head straight out to Lefrak Housing complex in Queens to spend some quality time with Tammy. She was a freak and she had Whitey's nose wide open! He remembered how he first met Tammy, and had to smile at the memory. He was sticking up a drug stash spot in Jamaica Queens, and thought the two drug dealers were the only ones in the house as he handcuffed both of them to the radiator. He took all the money and drugs and was about to leave until he heard sounds coming from a back room. He pointed his gun towards the room and slowly walked in the direction the noise was coming from. He quickly pushed the door open and could not believe his eyes. The prettiest girl he ever saw, laid naked on a king sized bed moaning softly with her middle finger inserted inside of her, and her eyes glued to the pornographic movie on the big television screen. She was very much into the movie. She was dark-skinned, silky long hair, almond shaped eyes, and everything about her said sex! And not the ten minutes of trashy sex, but deep, intense, toe curling, freaky, sweaty, soul searching sex!

Whitey caught an instant erection and when Tammy looked up at him, she showed no signs of fear as she continued to get herself off.

"Are you Johnny's friend?" she asked indicating one of the guys handcuffed to the radiator in the front room.

Whitey put his gun away and without answering her question asked, "What are you doing here?"

"I'm little dick Johnny's girlfriend," she laughed. "That should explain why I have to please myself when I'm horny!"

Whitey could not explain why he was so attracted to this girl. He had sex with some of the most gorgeous women of all races, but none captivated him like the girl who lay before him.

"I never had sex with a white boy before," said Tammy with a seductive smile. "And you're cute too. But Johnny would kill you if he knew you were in here looking at me the way you're looking at me."

Whitey smiled, pulled the blue bag from his shoulder and said, "I got Johnny's money right here, and he knows I'm back here with you. In fact, I left him and his girlfriend handcuffed to the radiator."

It didn't take Tammy long to figure out what had transpired while she pleased herself with the door closed. Whitey expected her to show some kind of fear as he searched her eyes for some kind of reaction.

The loud laughter caught him off guard, and when Tammy had stopped laughing she said, "I can't believe them punk ass niggas let a white boy stick them up!"

Whitey was use to hearing such things, that is until he showed that he was everything but a regular ole' white boy.

Tammy looked on the night stand, grabbed a condom and threw it at whitey. "You done took everything else around here white boy," she said with a smile, "so you may as well take some of this good loving before you leave."

They both started laughing, as Whitey got undressed but keeping his gun near. Usually, he would never do something so dangerous and stupid, and he knew had Moe-dog was still doing hits and robberies with him, he wouldn't even consider doing what he was about to do. But Moe-dog was no longer with him, and lately Whitey had been feeling a bit daring.

"Give it to me white boy," said Tammy as Whitey slipped on the condom and walked over to the bed.

"The name is Whitey not white boy," he corrected as he lift one of her legs and entered her slowly.

"Oh yes!" moaned Tammy as he humped into her with one hand holding her leg up and the other hand under the pillow holding his gun.

The guy Johnny and his friend must have heard the moans and cries of pleasure from the front room, because as Whitey and Tammy were having sex, Johnny started yelling and pulling the handcuffs against the radiator as if he was trying to uproot it from the floor.

"Get the fuck off my girl!" yelled Johnny from the other room. "You cracker bastard! I'll kill your ass!"

Whitey stopped mid-stroke, looked at Tammy and said, "Damn baby, the punk didn't do all this yelling when I took his money from him."

Tammy laughed as Whitey got up and began to dress.

"Where are you going?" she asked.

"Home," he answered. "If you want, we can finish where we left off at my house. I can't fucking concentrate with that bitch in the next room screaming. What's up, you coming?"

Tammy got out of the bed and got dressed.

As they were leaving, the two of them had to laugh when they saw Johnny crying like a baby as his friend looked on with a stupid look on his face.

That was three months ago, and Whitey and Tammy had been together ever since.

Whitey pulled up in front of a big white house on Jefferson Street between Bedford and Nostrand Avenues.

Big Lord and four of his soldiers were standing out front, and a few of them reached for their guns when they saw Whitey's black Maxima pull up.

Big Lord had then recognized that it was Whitey and told his soldiers to relax as he walked over to the car. After getting in the car and giving Whitey a pound he asked, "What brings my favorite white boy through here?"

When Richard introduced Moe-dog and Whitey to Big Lord years ago, he decided that he would use the pair of dangerous thugs whenever he needed to, and when Moe-dog left the game and got with Omar's record label as part of the security team, Big Lord stayed in touch with Whitey.

"I got some keys for you," said Whitey passing the bag to Big Lord. "All I want is ten each!"

Big Lord looked in the bag and counted eleven wrapped up kilos of cocaine. He then asked, "Is this shit good?".

"Big Lord," smiled Whitey. "I'm no junkie. How the fuck would I know?"

"I'll tell you what," said Big Lord zipping up the bag. "Come see me tomorrow night, and I'll have the hundred and ten thousand for you. But first, I have to test this shit out.."

"Aiight," said Whitey as Big Lord got out of the car and quickly walked into the house.

He knew the cocaine was good because of the drug dealers he took it from. Their reputation would not allow them to possess garbage! They were known for having the best cocaine in the Bronx, and after watching their every move for so long, he knew when they were about to travel with a nice amount of drugs. He definitely did his homework on them.

Whitey drove off figuring he'd go and see Tammy. Instead of calling, he decided to surprise her. But the surprise came to him when his cell phone began ringing on the way to her house. He didn't recognize the number on his caller ID, but when he answered the phone, the voice on the other end was unmistakable.

"What's up Whitey?" asked Moe-dog with a chuckle. How's the street life treating you?"

"Moe-dog, what's up boy?!" asked Whitey excitedly. He hadn't heard from Moe-dog in over two years, and as he now heard his voice, he realized how much he had missed his comrade.

"I know everything is good with you," said Whitey. "As for me, I'm still getting this paper. I just made a deal with Big lord that should have me straight for a while. At least until I pull off another one of them thangs!"

Moe-dog laughed and said, "I see you're still spending your money faster than it comes."

"Yeah man, you know how it goes," smiled Whitey as he hit the Brooklyn-Queens Expressway. "So, how's your girl, and the little guy?"

"Oh yeah, Gina is good to a nigga. As for little Divine, he's a terror! We never met his father, but from what I heard about him , his son may very well follow in his foot steps."

At one time, Moe-dog and Whitey was paid to do hits for Richard, and being Gina and Richards wife Lisa were best friends, it was relatively easy for Moe-dog to step in the picture when Gina was mourning the death of her love, and un-born baby's father, Divine.

"But you know what?" said Moe-dog to Whitey. "I miss the streets, man. This working shit ain't about nothing! I got enough money to chill, but you know I can't sit around and do nothing. I miss putting in work. I did that my whole life! This security shit is garbage! Niggas not even violating, for me to get busy. Now tell me, when was the last time you bust your gun?"

Whitey smiled and answered, "A few hours ago!"

"That's what I'm talking about!" said Moe-dog excitedly. "It keeps you focused and on your toes. Fuck that, I'm getting back in the grind! Them faggot ass Columbian niggas got them hits on you?"

"Yeah," answered Whitey. "The last I heard anyway."

"Good," replied Moe-dog. "Let's get rid of them niggas. I'm back homie! Take this information down, and come over now and pick me up."

Whitey took all of the information down, and got off of the Brooklyn-Queens Expressway. The way things were looking now, he doubt if he'd see Tammy for another two days!

Chapter 5

Mont-Mont sat on his bed, in the small cell in A-Block. Everything was looking good for him now. He was about to go home in two weeks on his conditional release date and could not wait to get back on the grind. Like his boy Light, he vowed never to come back to prison ever again. When the police come for him, he would definitely have his .44 Bulldog handgun in his waist and his AK-47 in his hands. He thought this to himself many of times. Maybe had he made his first or second parole board, things might have been a little different. Due to the continuous parole denials, it only made him more bitter than he already was. And it didn't help any, when his aunt who raised him since he was a kid passed away after his second parole appearance. That had fueled his hatred even more. Mont-Mont did everything positive that the Department of Corrections had ordered him to do. He received his G.E.D., picked up a few trades under his belt, completed therapeutic programs, and a few other programs, only to be denied parole again and again. The Governor of New York had ordered the parole commissioners he had appointed, to keep denying parole, to show New York that he was tough on crime. All that did was make inmates more bitter, and then they were pushed back into society worse than when they first entered the system. For many, there were no jobs for those who really wanted to change. But Mont-Mont like many others was bitter at the system, and was the perfect example of what the Governor of New York produced!

"Yo, CO!" yelled Mont-Mont through the bars. "Open 27 cell! I put down for the motherfucking yard!"

"I'll let 'em know," said a dark-skinned stocky brother with dreads walking pass Mont-Mont's cell.

Mont-Mont was from Manhattanville in Harlem, and was well respected in his borough, as well as other places. He had a very bad temper and did not hesitate to bust his gun. He didn't care about another man's reputation. The way he saw it, a reputation was just something you did sloppy where witnesses saw what you did. So, he didn't care about a reputation, not even his own. That's why he got along with the Bulldog Crew so well, because they didn't do things with hopes of being seen. Just the way they moved, caused people to know they were not the ones to have any problems with.

Mont-Mont, also had a thing for Puerto Rican women. Of course, he loved his Nubian sisters equally, but it was just something about a Spanish Mommy that turned him on like no other. But for now, even they had to take a back seat in his life. His first mission was taking money, and showing Light, Fats and L that he was indeed Bulldog Crew material. He even suggested they all go back down to Flatbush Avenue and kill all the Bloods they thought that had something to do with Big Dave and Tommy Guns death. But L told him no, and to not even suggest it to Light and Fats, because they would be down to do it, and L believed that the police would just be waiting for them to do something like that.

Light, Fats and L had only been gone a week now, but to Mont-Mont it seemed as if it had been a month already. Their presence was definitely missed, but if all things went right, they would all be together again real soon. But this time it would be in New York City, stacking money and letting their presence be felt!

Mont-Mont's cell clicked open, and he grabbed his jug of water and workout gloves. He then bopped down the gallery with his smooth Harlem walk, as the other inmates piled out of the gate and headed for the yard. They were all rushing to get on the phone, play basketball or grab some weights to workout. But Mont-Mont took his time because he would be invited first to do all three as soon as he step foot in the yard. The other inmates would give him his props out of respect, or fear. Love was only for those he planned to see on the outside, or those he planned to look out for when he touched the outside.

As soon as Mont-Mont stepped into the yard, you could see disgust on his face. Everywhere he looked, he noticed the guys from New York City boroughs were separated in gangs or where they were from. He didn't see the Bulldog Crew as a gang. In his eyes, they were only a few real niggas that was out to get that money. And he definitely didn't care where you were from in the five boroughs. The way he saw it, there were only two types of people in the world: the real and the fake, and they were scattered all over the globe.

Mont-Mont was in jail for murdering a back in the days thug who thought his past reputation, entitled him to take the block Mont-Mont's little brother Joseph sold drugs on. The year was 1993, and a hot summer day in July, little Joseph and a few of his workers was making a killing on 143rd Street and Edgecomb. The old gangster Silk, came on the block with his gun in his waist and his face screwed up. As soon as little Joseph and his workers saw him approaching, they knew it was going to be problems.

Silk walked up to them and asked, "Yo, which one of y'all little niggas is Joseph?"

The workers were shook up.

"That's me," said Joseph also a little nervous. "Why, what's going on?"

Silk put his hands under his shirt, grabbed his gun without pulling it out and said, "I want you off this block!"

Joseph was about to say something, but he didn't have a gun on him and knowing Silk's reputation, the wrong words could get him killed so he remained quiet.

"You understand lil' nigga?" asked Silk with the Ice Cube ice grill on his face.

"Yeah," answered Joseph. "I understand."

Silk looked at his watch, and walked away as if he was giving them minutes to get off of the block.

"Y'all niggas stay here," Joseph told his workers as soon as Silk walked off of the block. "I gotta get in touch with my brother!"

Before he could even walk away to a phone booth, Mont-Mont was pulling up on the block in his blue BMW to check up on his little brother being that he hadn't seen him in a few days.

Mont-Mont knew something was wrong, because his little brother's workers kept looking up and down the street with worried expressions on their face instead of serving those who were waiting to buy drugs.

Joseph quickly walked to the car, got in the passenger seat and said, "I was just about to call you."

"Why, what's up?" asked Mont-Mont knowing something was wrong, and he did not play when it came to his little brother.

"I just got into it with that nigga Silk," answered Joseph. "He said I can't sell here no more, and I better be gone when he come back through. The nigga always starting some bullshit!"

Mont-Mont's face showed no signs of anger. He looked at his watched and said, "Fuck that nigga Silk. Go back out there and get that money. I'll be sitting right here in the car, and I'll see 'em when he come through."

"Aiight," said Joseph exiting the car feeling a bit safer. After about an hour of waiting, Silk walked up the block not believing the young boys did not follow his orders. He screwed his face up and headed in little Joseph's direction.

Seeing him, Mont-Mont quickly got out of his car and very quietly walked behind him as he approached Joseph.

"I see y'all little niggas don't listen!" said Silk as he reached under his shirt. "I see I'ma have to set an example! Y'all little coward ass—"

"Boom!!!"

The first shot hit Silk in the back of the head, and he fell to the sidewalk. He was dead before Mont-Mont shot him again in his back.

Mont-Mont than looked at Joseph and calmly said, "Yo, get these niggas off the block for a few hours!"

He put the .357 Magnum back into his waist and quickly walked back to his car and drove away.

A month later, he got caught for the body, and the one witness against him turned out to be one of Joseph's workers. At trial, the jurors acquitted him of murder, but convicted him of Manslaughter in the first degree. He was sentenced to five to fifteen years in prison. All through the trial, the witness knew he messed up when he looked into Mont-Mont's eyes. It was a look that told him if he ever got out of jail, the witness would die worse than anyone he had ever heard about! And now hearing that Mont-Mont was on his way home soon, the witness packed his bags and moved out of state never to be heard from again.

$

Mont-Mont looked around A-Block's yard, and decided not to work out today. He figured he'd get on the phone and call his little brother. Joseph was no longer the little boy Mont-Mont left in the streets. He was now the man in the drug game, but his team was still weak. He could tell from the war stories he'd been hearing about concerning his brother and enemies. It was a lot of shooting, with no one getting hit. All Mont-Mont felt he had to do was come home and show them boys how it suppose to be done.

"Yo Mont-Mont!" said a dark-skinned brother holding a phone up in the air. "You want this?"

"Yeah, yeah," he answered walking to the phone and taking it. "Good looking out."

He dialed the number and then his pin number, hoping he would be able to catch Joseph in the house.

The phone rung and then a female's voice said, "Your call is being—"

"Who the fuck is that?" Mont-Mont asked himself before the jail's recording came on.

"You have a collect call from 'Mont-Mont' at a New York State Correctional Facility," said the recording. "If you want to know the cost of this call press nine. If you want to accept this call press three…thank you for using…"

"Yo what up?" asked Mont-Mont.

"Ain't nothing big bro", answered Joseph. "I'm just chilling, waiting for you to touch down."

"Yo, who was that bitch that first picked up the phone?"

Joseph laughed and said, "That was my voice message."

"Its good thing I caught you at the crib."

"Nah, I'm not at the crib. I got that call forwarding on the phone. When you call the crib and I ain't there, it transfers to my cell phone."

"Word up?" asked Mont-Mont. Damn, he really been gone a long time, and needed to catch up with all this new shit coming out, he thought. "So, where you at?"

"I'm at this bitch crib," answered Joseph. "You wanna holla at one of her friends?"

"Nah, I'll see them bitches when I get out. You took care of those clothes for me?"

"Yeah, I sent them off already," answered Joseph. "You should have 'em this week. And we'll go shopping as soon as you get out. But you been gone too long, so you'll have to let me pick your shit out nigga", laughed Joseph.

"Did Light call?" asked Mont-Mont changing the subject.

"Oh yeah, he called. And I talked to your man, L. He said Light and Fats is driving him crazy, trying to keep them out of trouble on the Island."

Mont-Mont laughed, picturing L trying to talk sense into Light and Fats. Knowing his hands were definitely full!

"But yo, check this," continued Joseph. "The nigga they was upnorth for killing, got a little brother that's out here getting crazy money! We kinda cool. Anyway, he heard Light, Fats and L is on their way home, so he put a price on their heads as soon as they touch."

"What?!" Mont-Mont yelled into the phone. "Get me this nigga's name, all his information and make sure you get them guns I told you last week to get!"

"I already got them," answered Joseph. "And don't worry about the kid I was just telling you about. When you get out, I'll line him up for you. But I'll have that information on him, when you call back later."

Chapter 6

"You keep treating me this good, and I might have to cut off all of my other boyfriends," smiled Pam.

"Shit," laughed Big Lord. "Every nigga in the five boroughs knows this pussy belongs to me!"

"You know it's yours daddy," smiled Pam. "But I'm saying, what is up with the carats? You know; engagement, wedding, ring, marriage?"

"And babies?" smirked Big Lord.

"Oh, hell no! You can keep that! Once a nigga puts a baby in a bitch, he really becomes Scooby Doo. I'm talking straight up dog! What nigga you know, who don't thinks he has his baby mother locked down?"

"Come here girl," laughed Big Lord, "with your crazy ass."

"You know I love you to death, right?" he cuddled up with her. "And I been thinking about marriage for a while now, but when I propose to you, I want everything to be right. But if you keep doing what you was doing earlier, we might have the children before the wedding!"

Pam was Big Lord's one and only girl. He saw no need to cheat on her. Not only was she a handful, but she possessed everything he ever wanted in a woman. She was very beautiful, had a body that made men drool and women envious whenever she walked by. Pam was very humorous to the point had she wanted to be a professional comedian she could have easily pulled it off. She was also loyal, cooked her ass off, and her sex game was crazy!

Pam was Richard's wife Lisa's best friend. Actually, it was Pam, Lisa, Gina and Tonya that was close like sisters and grew up together. Richard met Big Lord, Divine and Moe-dog when he was on Rikers Island. Big Lord was Omar's people, and Moe-dog and Divine had came through Rikers Island at different times both becoming cool with Richard, but not meeting or getting the chance to know one another.

When Richard and Lisa moved downsouth to North Carolina, Gina started dating Moe-dog after the death of her baby father Divine, Tonya married a deacon in her church, and Pam became Big Lord's girlfriend. Although she was always fly from boosting and credit card scams, she knew she no longer had to do that because Big Lord was a millionaire, and whatever Pam wanted, he made sure she had it.

As they laid together in the big King sized bed, Pam got on top of Big Lord, looked into his eyes with a smile and said, " I have to go down to Fort Greene today and see my family, so I probably won't be back here until later on tonight."

"Okay, that's cool," said Big Lord. "Cause I gotta shoot out to Brooklyn, and meet up with Whitey. I owe him a little money."

Big Lord bought the big house out in Hempstead Long Island, but he still had his other house in Brooklyn. He only used the one in Brooklyn when he had business to take care of on that end, or if someone very cool with him needed a place to stay, or get paroled to. But the Hempstead house was where he and Pam lay their heads, so he made it a point not to let no one know where they lived.

Big Lord was born in Trinidad but at the age of ten, his parents had moved the family to America to take advantage of the many opportunities they had heard so much about. Big Lord had a brother, who later went to prison on a manslaughter conviction. The name "Lord" was given to him in 1987 when he was 16 and had joined a sect called the 'Nation of Gods and Earths', also known by many as the 'Five Percenters'. He was always big for his age, weighing in at 230 pounds and six foot tall earning him the name Big Lord. The name stuck even after he no longer practiced the lessons of the sect. He abandoned the "love, peace and happiness" teachings, and took something very different to the streets. And what he took to the streets was murder, mayhem, and more murder. After hearing about Big Lord's brand of terrorism, Omar quickly snatched him up and put him on his team. And under Omar's guidance, Big Lord learned all the rules of the game as well as how it was suppose to be played. Omar loved him more than any of his other soldiers because of his loyalty. Like the day the homicide detectives nearly beat Big Lord into a coma, and had threatened him with a hundred years if he didn't give them information concerning Omar. Big Lord did not utter a word. Or the time, when other notorious thugs from Brooklyn told him they would kill him and his family, if he didn't kill Omar or set him up to be killed. Big Lord agreed to their demands but instead told Omar everything. And after Big Lord's parent's was moved to a different area of the city by Omar, bodies dropped all over Brooklyn. Over the years they had become more like brothers than anything, and that's why when Omar left the drug game, he also left the drug spots and drugs he had left to Big Lord to do as he pleased.

Big Lord kissed Pam on the lips and then got out of bed. Only wearing his boxers, he began to do his every morning routine of one thousand push-ups.

Pam smiled, as she looked down at his big, broad, muscular back. She loved when a man took care of himself and stayed in shape. Too many ballas were letting themselves go, as soon as they've accumulated a little bit of money. But not Big Lord. He didn't drink or smoke either, and made it a habit to go to the gym or exercise at home whenever he had time to do so.

When Big Lord got to fifty on his second set of push-ups, Pam slipped out of bed wearing her panties and Big Lord's long button up Makavelli shirt.

Without stopping his push-ups, Big Lord felt her weight and breast press up against his back.

"See, that's why you're gonna get the baby before the ring!" said Big Lord losing his count.

Pam laughed, got off of his back and walked over to the stereo system in the big bedroom. She inserted a CD, and the sounds of a new hot R&B singer name Patricia Richardson came through the expensive speakers.

Pam smiled and began singing along with the song "I'm Always There." Even though the whole CD was banging, this was one of Pam's favorite songs on the CD. The singer was singing about standing by her man through all his struggles and when she mentioned the part about him being in jail, she looked at Big Lord working out and knew she would without a doubt do a bid with him if he ever happened to go to prison.

As soon as the song went off, Pam turned the stereo down and headed towards the night table to retrieve the dishes that sat there. Big Lord surprised her occasionally with breakfast in bed and this happened to be one of those mornings.

As Pam reached for dishes, the telephone also on the night table began to ring. She snatched it up on the third ring, wondering who could be calling this early in the morning.

"Hello, and who is this?" asked Pam.

"You got a heck of a way of answering your phone!" said Lisa on the other end.

"Bitch, what's up?" yelled Pam excitedly instantly recognizing Lisa's voice, and causing Big Lord to look up from doing his push-ups and lose count again.

"I ain't hear from your ass in about a year!" said Pam sitting down on the bed. "Every time I call down there, I get no answer."

"Gurrl," said Lisa. "Me, Richard and the baby stay on the go. We ain't never there!"

Pam laughed and said, "Listen to you, sounding all country and shit. Sounding like a female Chingy."

"Who?" asked Lisa confused.

"Girl, don't tell me that Richard got you in church so much, that you don't know who's who in Hip-Hop anymore."

"I ain't listen to that music in so long, I can't tell you anything about it at all."

"Word? Your brother Omar's artists stay on the radio and videos all day long! He's doing his thing."

"Oh yeah," Lisa said unenthused. "That's good. You know, I really thought I would hate living down-south when we first moved down here. But gurrl, after visiting New York last year, I know I can't live there anymore! I miss my family and all my old friends, but New York is too fast and too rude for me."

Pam laughed and wondered how her best friend could become so countrified so fast. She remembered going down to Atlanta years ago with her ex-boyfriend Big Gee, and she couldn't stand it down there. It was much too slow for her.

"Where's Richard?" she asked changing the subject.

"He's in the back yard playing with Dejanay," answered Lisa.

"And how is that cute little baby of yours?"

"Oh, she's fine. She's getting so tall and will talk your ears off! I don't know where she gets that from, because me and Richard is kind of quiet."

"Yeah right!" laughed Pam. "You always had a big mouth. But now bitch, you sound so…..different. Richard must still be laying the dick of Moses down on you!"

"I see you still got jokes," laughed Lisa. "With your filthy mouth, are you still with Big Lord?"

"Of course!" answered Pam. "That's my nigga. My very near future husband! He's right here working out."

"Tell him I said hello, and it was bad that he's like my brother, and didn't come to my wedding."

After Pam gave Big Lord her message he said, "Tell my lil' sis I love her, and I didn't think she would still be holding that against me. She knows if I wasn't outta town making moves, I would have been there. What's up with my boy Bishop?"

Pam gave Lisa his message, listened for a few seconds and then said to Big Lord, "She said she forgives you and loves you too. And she said Richard is fine and for the hundredth time, he does not go by the name of Bishop anymore."

Big Lord laughed and started on his tenth set of push-ups.

"What's going on with Gina and Tonya?" asked Lisa.

"Oh, I talked to both of them yesterday," answered Pam. "Gina's doing good. She just left Moe-dog, because she said he's back in the streets, and she do not want to go through what she went through with Divine all over again. And I don't blame her," said Pam as if Big Lord weren't out in the streets doing the same things as those she mentioned.

"Speaking of Divine," continued Pam. "Little Divine looks just like him, and bad as hell! And Tonya, she's not with that doofy looking deacon from church. She just got with some guy, she said she met, that just came home from jail."

"Tell Tonya and Gina I said hello," said Lisa.

"Me, Tonya and Big Lord didn't make it to your wedding," said Pam, "and that was because of different things that was going on I guess. But I'm telling you now, when me and Big Lord have our wedding, I want everybody there!"

"You know me, Richard and Dejannay will be there," smiled Lisa. "And don't tell Gina and Tonya, but we're coming to New York in a few weeks to visit. And I wanna surprise them!"

"Okay," said Pam. "You know I love you, right?"

"Yeah, yeah, yeah. I love you too," smiled Lisa knowing that she had three friends in New York City that loved her like a sister. And she felt the same way about them.

Chapter 7

"A yo John, tell them niggas I said when they finish, stay they ass out in Boston," said the young boy they called Nice, to his lieutenant "And tell Un I said get some more work out there to them niggas, before they run outta what they got."

Nice was only nineteen years old, but he been in the grind since he was ten! It was said that his body count was at least, half his age! He was getting money sending his young crew out of state to move drugs. Even though at times some of them came back in body bags, he continued to get that money. To Nice, the amount of money he was getting was worth the risk of maybe getting killed. But Boston was cool, because his cousins lived out there and held his New York soldiers down.

Nice was on a mission to become richer than Big Lord and Hook, that he had heard so much about. He knew he wasn't in their league as of yet, but it wouldn't be long before they was forced to recognize his climb to the top, he thought. He was very smart when it came to getting money. His only problem was he still lived in the Sutter Housing Projects in Brownsville. Of course it was out of choice. With all the money he made, he could have moved just about anywhere. But he had a street thug mentality and figured the best way to keep it real was to stay in the Sutter Houses where his soldiers lived and where he grew up. He took over the apartment when his mother moved to Tampa, Florida.

Nice had the projects locked down and flooded with drugs. His addictions were fast cars, fast money, and fast women. Not necessarily in that order. It wasn't a girl from his projects from old heads to the young heads that he could think of, that he didn't have sex with, at one time or another. In fact, he never had a problem getting girls no matter where they were from or located. The only real challenge he ever really faced, was the beautiful dark-skinned girl that presently sat next to him on the beige couch in his living room. He'd been trying to get with her for the last year or so, but she always refused his advances, no matter how much game he came at her with, or how much material things he flossed in her presence. He knew she was definitely wifey material, and still found it hard to believe she was finally sitting next to him in his well furnished apartment. He didn't know where her change of heart had come from, but he was glad to see that she finally recognized his stature. It was only last week, when he saw her Downtown Brooklyn shopping. She had four big bags of clothes in her hands, and it kind of threw him when he spoke to her and she excitedly responded, "Hey Nice! I was hoping I ran into you. I ain't seen you in so long, and it ain't like you come around my way too often these days."

Nice smiled and said, "See baby, if you would've gave me your number when I first asked for it, you would've seen me just about everyday."

"No doubt, no doubt," smiled the girl. "But I'm saying, what's up with you? I see you looking all good and everything."

"I try to make sure I'm always looking good," smiled Nice licking his bottom lip. "But the question is what's up with us?"

One of Nice's soldiers looked around the area to make sure there were no threats or enemies lurking.

"Stop playing hard to get," continued Nice, "and let a nigga show you what he can do for you."

The girl smiled and said, "Okay, I'll give you a chance. But I still say men are dogs!"

"Not me baby," smiled Nice. "I mean, what can I do to show you that I am not that?"

"For starters, you can walk me to my car."

With a grin, Nice motioned for his soldier to carry her bags as they walked to her red Honda Accord parked on Flatbush Avenue. Ever since that day, Nice had been enjoying her company. And for the past week, they spent every day together. They did not have sex as of yet, but the way the relationship was going, it would definitely be very soon.

Two of Nice's soldiers, sat opposite Nice and the dark-skinned cutie, as the sounds of R. Kelly's song "Step In The Name Of Love" played softly through the living room's stereo system. His lieutenant John, was in back room taking care of the business Nice had ordered him to do. The big screen television was on mute and Nice occasionally glanced at the basketball playoffs of the Los Angeles Lakers playing Phoenix Suns. He then gave the girl sitting next to him a deep passionate kiss.

"What do you wanna do today baby?" asked Nice.

She looked at her Angel watch with surrounding diamonds and with a smile said, "Today is special. So, I'm thinking about a movie, dinner and maybe bed, if you know what I mean."

"That's what I'm talking about!" said Nice with one of the biggest smiles, he probably had all year. Immediately, he thought about whether he was going to stay with the girl or not, after having sex with her. He figured being that it took him so long, he'd keep her for awhile.

"But what makes today so special?" asked Nice.

"Some days are just special," she answered before kissing him on his forehead.

Nice's lieutenant John, entered back into the living room and said, "I just got off the phone with Un. I gave him the message, and he said he'll jump right on that. And I told Rob and 'em to stay out there."

"That's cool," said Nice. "I got another area for a spot we can check out. It's out in Philly. I heard the whole area is a gold mine so we might have to bust some guns. We'll shoot out there tomorrow night, because me and my baby here, is gonna do it up today, and I don't want no distractions!"

The girl smiled, kissed Nice on his cheek and then looked at her watch again.

"Oh shoot! I have to pick up my mother from work. But first let me use your bathroom," she said getting up and walking away.

Nice smiled when he noticed all eyes were on her. She was definitely a keeper, he thought to himself. The short blue skirt showed off her heart shaped bottom. Nice continued smiling as she passed by an open mouth John, with her baby blue high heel Manolo Blahnik construction boots and holding onto a blue Louis Vuitton bag. She exited the living room, and it took all four men a minute to snap back to reality and resume their conversation about the drug area in Philadelphia.

Instead of going to the bathroom, the girl quickly and quietly walked to the front door and looked through the peephole.

With a smile, she opened the door for the three thugs holding the biggest guns she'd ever saw!

As soon as they entered the apartment, Light kissed the girl on the lips and said, "Kia, what room is they in?"

She pointed towards the living room, and then followed behind Light, Fats and L.

"So, what we can do is this," said Nice to his workers. "Yo John, you take these two dudes wit'chu. And me, Un and a few more of the peoples will meet y'all out there. Y'all take the guns and drugs, but don't try to open up shop until we get there. This is gonna be easy. Basically, all we gotta do is check the…"

"Put your fucking hands up!" interrupted Light walking into the living room aiming his gun at John, as Fats and L pointed theirs at Nice and two soldiers.

"Light, that's Nice right there," said Kia pointing.

L quickly searched all of them, taking the guns from the two soldiers. Nice and John both, was unarmed.

After Nice looked carefully at the three gunmen and realizing that he had no previous beef with them, he knew it had to be just a robbery. He also knew now, that he made the fatal mistake by keeping his safe in the same apartment where he rest his head. He looked at Kia with a gangster glare and knew before it was all said and done, he would definitely get her later on down the line. He was totally unprepared for this! He knew a lot of grimey girls in Brooklyn as well as other boroughs and states, but never figured Kia to be one of them. He then began to get a little nervous, realizing what Kia had called one of the gunmen. Hearing the name 'Light' must have registered with the two soldiers and John as well, because all three looked as if they had already shitted in their pants.

Looking at all three of them, it was no doubt in Nice's mind that this was the infamous Bulldog Crew he'd heard so much about over the years. But from what he heard, they were suppose to be in jail forever. Someone even mentioned to him that Kia use to talk to Light and had a daughter by him, but Nice chalked it up as just another thug nigga that had her before him. He always had girls who were in relationships with other killers at one time or another. But one thing was for sure, he knew it was only one way to get out of the situation he was in. He would have to talk like he had never talked before!

"Where's the money?' asked Light looking at Nice.

"It's in the safe," interrupted Kia, "in the bedroom. It's by combination and key."

"Listen Light", said Nice calmly. "I'm saying, y'all got me. I respect a robbery, and I ain't got no problem giving y'all whatever's in that safe. The key is under the mattress, and the number is eight left, two right, thirty left, four right, and seventeen left."

L took off to the bedroom with Kia following behind.

"I can take a loss," continued Nice. "And respect you, Light. Coming up, I looked up to you. Shit, I wouldn't mind being down wit' the Bulldog Crew myself."

Fats laughed and said, "Yeah, we put a lotta niggas down wit' us that we robbed!"

"Fuck Fats," laughed Light. "I'm feeling you kid. I always wanted to be a role model and shit. But what if I was to kill your little crew here?"

Without hesitation or blinking an eye, Nice answered. "They're workers," he said. "Which means they're expendable to me."

Fats and Light laughed, as John and the two soldiers glared at Nice not believing that he had sold them out.

"I don't believe you," Light said to Nice. "Yo Fats, let's see if he's fronting."

Fats took a homemade silencer out of his pocket and screwed it on the big gun he held. He then walked behind John.

Pap! Pap!

The two workers looked horrified, as Fats bust two shots into the back of John's head. He then walked over to the two soldiers. One of them covered his head with his arms, as if that would stop the bullets. Pap! Fats fired one time killing him instantly. The last soldier tried to run towards the front door, but Nice stuck his foot out tripping him.

Light laughed and said, "Yo, I like this guy!" as Fats shot the soldier in the head also killing him.

Throughout everything, Nice sat there calmly hoping they would spare his life. All he would have to do was continue to cooperate, he thought.

L and Kia, entered back into the living room carrying two big black duffel bags full of money and guns. Kia saw the three dead bodies sprawled out on the floor, and immediately began to feel nauseous. She heard a lot about what Light, Fats and L did, but seeing it in person was too much for her. L must have sensed it, because he immediately took the bag from Kia and pushed her softly towards the front door.

"So what's up?" asked Nice. "Can I roll or What?"

"Yeah come on," said Light grabbing one of the bags from L.

As soon as Nice stood up, Fats shot him with his last two shells hitting him in the face and head. Pieces of his head decorated the sofa.

"Why the fuck you do that?" asked Light. "I was feeling the dude. He looked up to me, and you know, I ain't never been a role model before."

"We'll just find someone else you can be a role model to," laughed Fats, "because that nigga there had no loyalty!"

Light laughed, as he followed Fats and L to the front door where Kia waited. They all left the apartment in good spirits except for Kia. She was more nervous than she had ever been.

$

The Brooklyn Homicide detectives, had already got the word from their sources that the Bulldog Crew were home, but who would expect the three dangerous gunmen to commit a massacre and robbery on their first day out of prison??!!

Chapter 8

Mont-Mont was glad to be home. His little brother Joseph had picked him up from the maximum security prison in a stretch white limousine. As soon as Mont-Mont got in the car, he couldn't believe his eyes. Two of the best looking Spanish girls he'd ever saw sat across from him with smiles on their faces as they sipped from their glasses of Don P. He couldn't believe it! Even the chauffer was a very pretty Spanish woman that looked incredible in her black and white uniform.

"Why you sitting next to me, big bro?" asked Joseph with a smile. "I know you been around dudes long enough! Both of them are for you. That's Wanda and that's her girlfriend, Nicola."

With smiles they both said in unison, "Hello!"

"You know I know your taste," smiled Joseph.

"That's what` I'm talking about!" laughed Mont-,Mont. "Let me get over here, and get to know these fine ladies better."

When he got up, the girls made room for him to sit in the middle of them. That's when Joseph pressed a button, and his seat turned to the front, giving his brother Mont-Mont some privacy. He pressed another button and a small television appeared from behind the partition. He took a sip of his rum and coke, and enjoyed the "Out Of Time" DVD starring Denzel Washington and Sanaa Lathan. Joseph was in love with the beautiful actress on the screen, and wished one day to meet her.

Mont-Mont was enjoying the conversation with the two pretty Latinas, and couldn't believe it when Wanda undid his pants and took him into her mouth. He hadn't been pleasured like this in over ten years! The most satisfaction he received during his incarceration, was jerking off to magazines with very beautiful women in them such as: Black Tail, Big Black Butt, Dark & Sweet, Black Video Illustrated, Fox and of course Buttman. He never did the homo thing, and it had never crossed his mind. Falling victim to that was for weak niggas, thought Mont-Mont. And he was far from being weak. It even upset him at times just thinking about how society viewed men in prison. Especially, considering that it was only a small number of men in the New York State prisons who actually had sex with other men. Those that did were looked upon as who they were, Homosexuals! Even gangsters that went that route who had props for getting busy, did not receive genuine respect from majority of the prisoners. After jerking off to so many magazines, Mont-Mont dreamed of the days when he would finally be able to have sex, that included anal, with the pretty Spanish mommies he knew he would one day have the pleasure of being with. But how could he even approach the sexual act with the perception that society had painted men in prison with?

Mont-Mont was cumming, and Wanda swallowed his unborn babies, as Nicola kissed him all over his face and whispered freaky words in Spanish into his ear.

The long ride back to New York, had put Joseph and Wanda to sleep, but Mont-Mont was wide awake as Nicola updated him on what had changed in the streets since he'd been gone. From what she told him, and from what he had heard over the years, he knew it was different faces in the game and also knew the rules of the streets was basically dead! It was more telling going on than ever before, and he was disgusted with it all. The only changes he enjoyed, was finally being out of prison, and seeing how his little brother Joseph had elevated in the drug game. He now had drugs in Maryland, Georgia, and two money making spots in Harlem. Though he had a lot of guns, he avoided unnecessary drug wars as much as possible. Joseph would simply close up shop and move to a different location before going to war. Mont-Mont knew how his little brother was, but as long as he was home, he dared anyone to even think about selling on the same block as his little brother, who had held him down throughout his incarceration. Like the Bulldog Crew, Mont-Mont did not know a thing about selling drugs. All the money he had ever made came from the barrel of his gun.

Before reaching their destination, their first stop was the shopping mall in upstate Middletown, New York. Mont-Mont didn't really know what was in style, so instead he let Joseph, Wanda and Nicola do all the shopping for him. Even the chauffer picked out a few things she thought he would look good in.

After loading the limousine trunk with bags, they were on their way to Harlem. To Mont-Mont, everything looked different, and everything was moving so fast. Especially the people! Even the apartment he grew up in looked smaller, but now it was well furnished, whereas when he was younger his aunt didn't really have any furniture.

"You don't have to stay here," said Joseph. "I got a mini-mansion out in New Jersey. I just took over auntie's crib, for whenever I'm in Harlem."

"Nah," said Mont-Mont sitting on the couch. "This is cool right here. I need to stay in Harlem, so I can always know what's going on in the streets."

"Oh shit!" said Joseph slapping his forehead. "I almost forgot. You got paroled to my homegirl's crib in Taft Houses."

"Don't worry about it," replied Mont-Mont kicking off his shoes and reclining back on the couch. "Call'er and tell'er I'm not coming. Fuck parole! That's like slavery as far as I am concerned, and I'ma nigga that runs from the slave ship, not to it!"

The girls laughed, as Joseph shook his head from side to side. He could see that his brother had not changed one bit.

"Anyway," said Joseph. "Everything you planned is set up for tonight. I'll come back through with the car, and we'll go get the fake driver's license and ID tomorrow morning."

"Don't forget to bring the guns with you."

"They're in your old bedroom already," said Joseph nodding towards the back room. He then took five thousand dollars from his pocket and placed it on the table in front of Mont-Mont.

"That's just a little pocket change," he said. "If you need more or anything else, give me a call. You got the number."

He then looked at the two girls as he headed towards the door and said, "Y'all two can stay here wit' my brother, and finish what y'all started. I'll be back later to pick y'all up."

As he got to the door, he turned around and caught eyes with the beautiful chauffer. "You too?" asked Joseph.

The chauffer smiled and tossed him the limousine keys. He shook his head with a smile. He didn't know what it was, that made Spanish girls love Mont-Mont so much, and vice versa.

Later that night, after sending the girls home with the chauffer, Mont-Mont, Joseph and Little Dee sat in the living room laughing, joking, and reminiscing.

"Me and your brother was mad cool," laughed Mont-Mont. "Yo, Disco was a funny motherfucker. Did you find out who killed him?"

"Yeah," said Little Dee putting his glass of Hennessy down on the glass table in front of him. "Three punk ass Brooklyn niggas! They call'em the Bulldog Crew, or some stupid shit like that."

"Word?" asked Mont-Mont standing up. "You know where 'dem nigga's at?"

Little Dee sucked his teeth and said, "If I did, they'll be dead already! I got ten thousand dollars on each of them nigga's heads as we speak."

"No doubt," said Mont-Mont walking over to the stereo and putting on the new rappers O-Fella's CD. "What's my name?/OH!'" came blasting through the speakers, as Mont-Mont turned it up even louder.

He then walked back over to Little Dee and began playfully throwing a flurry of open hand punches.

Little Dee laughed, got up from his seat and threw a few of his own. But when he threw the open right hand, he was not prepared for the hard right hook Mont-Mont threw to his head that landed squarely on the side of his temple that sent him reeling through the glass table.

Mony-Mont stomped him, until his face was a bloody mess. Every time Little Dee reached his hand out weakly, he was rewarded with another kick to his face.

"'I said what's my motherfucking name? OHHH!'" yelled the rapper through the speakers.

Mont-Mont reached down and grabbed Little Dee by the collar lifting him up from the floor. He then got behind him, grabbing him in the sleeper hold, and applied pressure to his neck as he'd gritted his teeth.

Little Dee's legs began shaking, as his eyes looked as if they were going to pop out of his forehead. Even with the music turned up loud, Mont-Mont could hear the snap Little Dee's neck made as he swung him from side to side with pressure. All those years in Attica lifting weights, had finally paid off.

He threw Little Dee to the floor, as Joseph watched in horror. He had never seen anything like this, and his glass of

Hennessy was spilling all over the floor due to how bad his hand was shaking.

Mont-Mont turned the stereo down, looked at his little brother Joseph and said, "I'll take care of the body, but get a mop and get that Hennessy off the floor. You know if auntie was here, she'd have a fit!"

Joseph could not believe what he was hearing. His brother had just punched a man through a glass table, and killed him with his bare hands, and he was more concerned with about what their auntie would say over a little spilled Hennessy on the floor had she been alive. He then knew for certain, that his older brother had truly lost his mind in prison.

$

Mont-Mont pulled up in front of the Cypress Housing Projects in the East New York section of Brooklyn. He got out the 600 black Mercedes Benz and greeted Light, Fats and L with pounds and hugs.

"Remember I told y'all about the little nigga from up my way, that wanted y'all dead?" asked Mont-Mont.

Yeah," answered Light. "When can we go get'em?"

"No need," smiled Mont-Mont. "I brought'em to you!"

He then walked to the trunk of his car, with Light, Fats and L following behind. When he opened the trunk, Little Dee laid dead, curled up in a fetal position.

Fats examined the dead boy's face with his hands and then asked, "What happened to his eyes?"

Mont-Mont reached into his pocket, and came out with two disgusting looking things that appeared to be eyeballs!

Fats snatched them out of his hand, shook them together in his hand, rolled them on the ground as if they were dice, and yelled out, "Snake eyes motherfucker!"

Light and Mont-Mont laughed uncontrollably, as L quickly shut the trunk of the car, and wondered why did he ever get with these fools in the first place!!!!!!

Chapter 9

"Let's get to work people!" said Omar loudly to his staff at Untouchable Records. He then entered his wife's office and after closing the door behind him, he said to his wife Gloria, "How is everything coming along?"

"Everything is good," she answered leafing through a very thick stack of papers in front of her.

"I just have to take care of a few recording budgets and a few other things," smiled Gloria as she reclined back in her chair. "This sure beats working as a home attendant! It was a good job, but the pay was basically nothing! And I had to put up with a lot of shit."

"Them days are long gone baby," smiled Omar sitting on the edge of her desk. "I try not to even think about my selling drug days. However, I'm reminded of it daily, because this music game has so much in common with the street game. Plus, all the thugs in this music shit, I know from the streets. But on a much brighter note, it's all roses from here baby."

He then leaned and kissed his wife on the lips, before picking up the telephone and telling the secretary to come into his wife's office.

A beautiful white woman that had a striking resemblance to the actress Denise Richards, entered the office with a pen and pad in hand. "Yes, Mr. Thompson?" she asked.

"Do you still have my friend Rondu's information?" asked Omar before blowing his nose with a hanky.

"Yes sir," answered the secretary with a smile. "How can I forget, as much as he calls, to see how I am doing?"

"You mean, to see how I'm doing," corrected Omar, as Gloria looked up from the papers in front of her.

The secretary blushed and said, "No, to see how I am doing. He claims, once I go Black, I'll never go back!"

Omar and Gloria laughed, and the secretary joined in their laughter. "This is what I need you to do," said Omar putting his hanky back into his back pocket. "Have some books sent to him for me. Street novels like, Coldest Winter Ever by Sister Souljah, My Brother's Keeper by Shaborn, and make sure you pick up The Death Of the Game by Akbar Pray. I definitely want my friend, Mr. Rondu Williams to read that!"

"I'll take care of it," said the secretary writing the names of the books down. Then as an afterthought she said, "He wanted me to come to Auburn Corrections to visit him, but I didn't think that would be professional or appropriate to mix business with pleasure."

Omar smiled and said, "It's none of my business what you do on your spare time."

"In that case," smiled the secretary, "I'll take those books up to him personally this coming weekend."

Before walking out of the door and closing it behind her, she turned around and said, "Just to inform him, that I've already went Black, and didn't go back as of yet!"

Omar and Gloria bust out laughing.

"She's something else," said Gloria shaking her head from side to side, as the secretary walked out of the office and closed the door behind her.

No one would have ever expected, Omar and Gloria to become an item. They were from two different worlds. Omar was from the streets, and Gloria knowing about the streets, never took part in any of the negative actions of that life. She had met Omar through Richard years ago. It was all behind the death of her son Kendu. He and Richard were best friends before he was killed by a thug name Rashien. It was then when Gloria met Richard at her son's funeral. She took a liking to the young boy, and when he later came home from Rikers Island after being acquitted in trial for murdering Rashien, she offered him a place to stay knowing that it would perhaps be too dangerous fore him to go back to the Fort Greene Projects. When Omar seen Gloria for the first time, it was love at first sight. The two of them had been together ever since, then marrying two years later. Besides having one of the hottest record labels in music, they also had a film company, a clothing line, and youth center dedicated to the memory of Kendu.

"I got a call from my baby sis today," smiled Omar.

"Oh yeah?" asked Gloria. "How is Lisa doing?"

"She's fine," answered Omar. "Her, Bishop, and the baby is coming up to New York soon."

"I can't wait to see them," smiled Gloria, "especially considering that its' been so long!"

"Yeah," said Omar. "I asked about Bishop, and she called herself correcting me. She said he doesn't go by the name Bishop anymore, it's either Pastor Brown or Richard."

"Fuck that!" laughed Gloria. "My son Kendu gave him the name Bishop, so I'll always call him that!"

Omar laughed, stood up from her desk and after looking at his watch said, "I have to go to my office and look over a few things. We're gonna drop OH's album in the fourth quarter, with the other big heads."

"Okay," replied Gloria. "So, is Moe-dog gone for good from the security post?" she asked changing the subject.

"Yeah he's outta here," answered Omar. 'Some guys just can't make the transition from the streets to the legal world. Just look at this music business for instance. When these rappers come into this music thing, they're bringing the streets with them, forgetting that it's only music."

"Yeah, you're right. I've never seen so many wanna-be thugs and gangsters in my life!"

"Now I hear Gina cut Moe-dog off, 'cause he's back in the streets with his partner in crime, Whitey."

"Oh boy!" said a wide eyed Gloria. "It's good to know Gina had enough sense to let him go. But I feel sorry for Moe-dog and Whitey, because they're headed into a world of trouble."

"No," replied Omar walking towards the door. But before walking out and closing it behind him he said, "It's not Moe-dog and Whitey that has to worry about trouble. They are the trouble! And it's those in the streets that are going to see trouble, like they have never seen it before!"

Gloria looked at the closed door her husband had just exited from, and thought what was the purpose of Kendu's Youth Center, if the older guys continued to set bad examples for these young Black and Latino kids? She knew there were a lot of poor and dangerous 'Whiteys', just as there were black boys who wanted to be like Moe-dog.

Gloria never wanted her son, Kendu's death to be in vain. Just thinking about him, had brought tears to her eyes. Kendu was a good person. He was not a gangster and never pretended to be. But he was no sucker either, and he was killed for displaying his heart, love and loyalty for his best friend, Richard.

Gloria wondered when would all the killings end, but just knowing that Moe-dog and Whitey were back together, snapped her out of the fantasy of how she wished the world could be. To make matters worse, Omar had told her the other day, that the Bulldog

Crew had made it home on a reversal of their case and was already causing havoc in the New York City streets.

Gloria also wondered what more could she do to help stop the children in the streets from going in a negative direction. She wanted to do more than the youth center. But the youth center was definitely a positive step that had changed many children's lives, and showing them the positive things they can achieve in life. Not having time to be into the bullshit one sees' when stationary in a ghetto environment every hour of the day, bound to be a product of the negative influences.

Gloria was no dummy to her history, and knew we; as Black people were great men and women; African Kings and Queens. But she just felt that we needed to act like Kings and Queens, and build us a nation within this nation. That was the only way for us as people to move forward, she thought. She didn't really pay too much attention to the Black Muslims or the other so-call Black leaders. In her mind, she felt neither was doing enough for the progression of our people. The Muslims were asking for reparations, and other black leaders said it was a waste of time and all they wanted was an apology. Gloria didn't see either as a waste of time if it included some kind of progress. But she was smart enough to know that the White people in power had proved historically and presently to be evil to the extent of not giving Black people anything! And she knew an apology meant nothing at all, if actions did not follow to change the present conditions of injustices that Black people encountered on a daily basis. So, she figured in order for Black people to make the progression in life, they would have to never forget what happened in the past, like the Jews, and at the same time open up businesses in the so-called ghetto areas of New York City and elsewheres. Also, unlike the many Black organizations and religious groups, you did not have to have a certain belief to be a part of what Omar and Gloria were trying to do.

"It would be so much easier, if these rich celebrities had opened up some businesses in the 'hood before they left it," said Gloria to herself, while putting the papers on her desk inside of an expensive looking bag. She then reached for the telephone and dialed Omar's office number.

"What's up baby?" smiled Omar knowing it was his wife on the other end of the phone.

"Don't forget," said Gloria, "we have reservations at the new restaurant you promised to take me to."

"I didn't forget baby. Are you done with the paperwork?"

"Yes, finally!" answered Gloria running her hand through her hair. "I think this new R&B group we signed is going to be a big hit! I'm loving their music."

"Of course," smiled Omar. "Anyway, I'm just about done here. Give me ten minutes. Okay?

Gloria sighed and said, "Yeah, okay?"

Omar knew something was bothering his wife by the way she talked, and he correctly figured that it was something she had been thinking about. He knew his wife.

"What's wrong baby?" asked Omar. "You don't sound good."

"No, I was just thinking," she said running her hand through her long hair.

"About what we talked about last night?" asked Omar.

"Yes," she answered. "I don't want our work to be for nothing."

"Our work can never be for nothing baby," comforted Omar. "Baby, the streets will always be the streets. But to keep the balance and to keep something positive, we just have to keep doing what we're doing. Trust me, I'm from the streets. And I understand that the drug dealers is not really the problem, because if the users stop using the drugs the drug dealers cannot survive. So, what happens is, people have many problems, whether its boredom, being in financial ruts, their wife or husband left them or whatever. That's the problem. The drug use is the effect of the problems. People use drugs to escape their problems. You get what I'm saying? Let's say I've been abused and couldn't handle the problem, and I turn to drugs and get strung out. So my family puts me in a drug program to get rid of what's basically is the effect. So, when I get out of rehab and if I still can't handle the problem of being abused, to escape it I'll most likely turn back to drugs. And these White people make tons of money with all of these programs to deal with your effects, not your problem. They don't even care about people's problems. But what you and I are doing, is dealing with people's problems by making them feel better about themselves and listening to their minds as an escape. Do you understand?"

"Yes!" smiled Gloria, feeling better already. "I understand you perfectly!"

"Good," smiled Omar. "Now let me get the rest of this work done, so I can get you to that restaurant I was telling you so much about."

"Okay," said Gloria hanging up the telephone.

She loved Omar with all of her heart. He was truly her everything, and he always made sense to her. He knew what to say to make her feel better, and most importantly, he listened to her at times without trying to solve what she spoke about, and she appreciated that. At times, she just needed an ear, and he understood that. She missed her son Kendu more than anything, and no one would ever be able to replace him. But Omar had come into her life, giving her a love she hadn't felt since the demise of her son, Kendu. Omar loved her, married her and gave her anything she wanted. They had a big beautiful mansion out in the Hamptons that possessed a tennis court, swimming pool, basketball court, sun porch, sky lights, walk-in closets, a modern kitchen, 14 rooms, and 'Omar's only' mini-theatre that boasted a big movie screen and stacks of porno DVDs. Omar called the room his 'Dirty Room.' When Gloria first moved into the mansion, she was so happy and excited she didn't know what to say. After all, she did come from the Lafayette Garden Housing Projects.

Gloria looked at her watch, and couldn't wait to get to the restaurant. Omar had made her so happy, and now she was going to make him feel the same way. Over dinner, she would give him the good news that she is pregnant! Ever since they've been together, all Omar talked about was how much he loved children.

Yes, he was definitely going to be happy, Gloria thought to herself with a smile as she walked out of her office for the day.

Chapter 10

"Now you ain't so tough anymore, are you?" Whitey asked the terrified Colombian drug boss.

"No, no, no," quickly responded the drug boss in a shaky voice with an accent. "I have no problem, you see?"

`"Put the duct tape over his mouth," ordered Moe-dog. "I'm tired of hearing this motherfucker talk. He's been talking since we snatched him!"

As Whitey followed the order, Moe-dog continued talking. "These stupid fucking Colombians! Give them a little drugs, and they all think they're Pablo Escobar! Do they actually think they can do whatever the fuck they wanna do!"

"Whitey didn't answer. He knew his friend was basically asking himself the question. He sat back in the chair opposite the drug boss, and smiled as he looked into the terrified eyes of the Colombian. He wondered how could a man kill people and put contracts on their lives, but be so afraid to die himself? Not wasting time to figure that out, Whitey decided to just sit back and enjoy the show of what Moe-dog had planned to do to the terrified Colombian. He knew his friend was thirsty to put in work. Even when they first captured the drug boss, Whitey saw the look in Moe-dog's eyes. The drug boss had never seen it coming. He and three of his top gunmen was leaving one of their drug locations in Spanish Harlem. The drug boss was highly upset when he saw the brand new black Honda Accord blocking his BMW from getting out of the parking space he practically owned. The hood of the Honda Accord was up, and when the drug boss and his goons approached the vehicle, he instantly thought about slamming the hood down on the short stocky Black man that worked on the engine but before he could reach for the hood, Moe-dog raised up from the engine with a smile. With a dumb smile he pointed at the drug boss's car and asked, "Is that your car?"

"You just move this piece of shit!" said the angry drug boss. "Before you and the car never been seen again!" he said in his accent.

It was the only thing he hated more than snitches and the police, and that was Blacks! Being he hated them so much, he enjoyed getting rich off of them and poisoning their communities at the same time. It was like killing two birds with one stone.

I'll be outta ya way in one minute boss," said Moe-dog wiping the engine's grease on his pants, as the three gunmen watched him closely just waiting for their boss to give the order to rid the Black man who had made him so angry. But before they could even think of doing anything, Whitey snuck up from behind them and fired two shots a piece from his nine millimeter into the back of the heads of the three gunmen killing them instantly. And like a small child, the drug boss fell to the ground and covered up into a fetal position, with his arms covering his face and head.

Moe-dog quickly slammed the hood shut and grabbed the Colombian drug boss by the collar lifting him up and dragging him to the Honda Accord. He shoved him into the back seat and climbed in behind him.

"Lay on the fucking floor!" barked Moe-dog to the drug boss, as Whitey started the car and pulled away.

They were glad that it was kind of dark outside and though there were a few people out on the block, no one got a clear look at their faces. Moe-dog had his gun to the Colombian's head and his foot on his back, as Whitey drove back to Brooklyn, in route to the Flatbush section. Once they reached Church Avenue, they parked the car and quickly rushed the Colombian drug boss to a near empty basement in a two family house. After tying the guy to a chair, Moe-dog took off his shirt and beat him senseless with his fist, drawing blood from his nose and mouth. "Please don't kill me!" cried the Colombian. "You take everything! I give you everything I have!"

Now that Moe-dog had the Colombian drug boss's mouth duct taped, all you could hear was a terrified humming sound, as he wore a wide eyed frightened expression on his face.

Moe- dog lit a cigarette, took three pulls and without hesitation, stuck it in the Colombian's eye.

"Mmmhhpppp!" sounded the drug boss through the duct tape as tears rolled down his face and urine soaked his pants.

Whitey laughed, and could see Moe-dog was enjoying himself. He could see that his friend was really missing Gina. Her absence had made Moe-dog bitter than he'd ever been. He had really come to love that girl, thought Whitey.

The dimly lit basement had plastic bags covering the floor, so the blood could easily be cleaned up whenever Moe-dog and Whitey had finished their victim.

"Scalpel," said Moe-dog to Whitey with his hand held out, as if he was actually performing a legal surgery.

"Mmmmhhppp!" came the loud muffled sound from the Colombian, as he shook his head violently from side to side with pleading and fearful eyes. He didn't know what Moe-dog had planned to do with the scalpel, but the thought alone caused him to pass out.

Whitey laughed and said, "Damn, the boy fainted!" He sat on the edge of a dusty desk, with an assortment of medical tools on top of it.

"He has to stay awake for this shit!" said an angry Moe-dog to Whitey. He then began slapping the Colombian until he came to. Without warning, he grabbed the drug boss by the hair and with his other hand, quickly slashed the Colombian's face in three different directions.

The Colombian's muffled screams went unanswered, as Moe-dog smiled and admired his work. Blood flowed and squirted all over the place. Whitey looked amused, and could see his participation in the torture was unneeded.

"Tweezers!" said Moe-dog to Whitey with his hand held out. When he received it, he began digging in the Colombian's face, trying to peel his skin off. The man tried to yell again before passing out for the second time. The rubber gloves Moe-dog wore were bloody, and blood splattered everywhere when he once again slapped the drug boss a few times to wake him. When the man came to, Moe- dog dropped the tweezers to the floor and angrily yelled at him. "What the fuck is your problem?! I'm trying to work here, and you keep falling asleep!"

From the tone of his voice, Whitey stopped smiling and wondered was his friend cracking up. He heard stories of men in the military who killed so many people they began to bug out! He knew Moe-dog killed a lot of people in his life time, and hoped his friend was not suffering from some sort of post war syndrome!

Getting tired of the Colombian drug boss, Moe-dog withdrew his nine millimeter from his waist and fired a shot to the back of the drug boss's head killing him instantly.

Whitey knew the Colombian was happy to be dead instead of enduring the torture Moe-dog had planned for him. Moe-dog tucked his gun back into his waist and walked out of the room. Whitey didn't know whether to wrap the body up or leave it tied to the chair. So he patiently waited for Moe-dog to return, and within minutes Moe-dog entered back into the room carrying an electric

Skilsaw. He plugged it in and began cutting off body parts with great determination.

Whitey wanted to make sure his friend was okay, so he tapped him on the shoulder and asked, 'Are you okay buddy?" Without waiting for an answer he continued, "Because I mean, he's not alive, so it's not like we're torturing him or anything. Plus, the hard work is gonna be cleaning up this mess. If my aunt finds a body part down here in this basement we are through!"

"Everything is cool," replied Moe-dog. "We'll clean up everything in no time. I just wanna send a little message to the rest of those Colombian bosses that we're not the ones to fuck with.

"Alright, that's cool. Let me go get some plastic bags," said Whitey making his exit upstairs, as Moe-dog continued cutting up the body with the skills of a butcher.

Whitey came back downstairs, and they put the body parts in four big black plastic bags. After scrubbing down the basement floor, they deposited the bags in three different sections of Brooklyn: Bay Ridge, Bensonhurst and Coney Island.

Whitey told Moe-dog, he had to make a quick stop in Queens as he drove through the New York City streets. He hadn't seen Tammy in days, and was missing her like crazy. He glanced over at Moe-dog and said, "For a minute I thought you was bugging out in the basement. Shit, I might still have you committed to the psycho ward when we get back!"

Normally, Moe-dog would have laughed at the comment or perhaps said something funny in response, but instead he looked out of the car's window with a far away look in his eyes.

"Yo what's up?" asked a concerned Whitey. "Is it Gina? If it is, we can shoot by there real quick before we go to Lefrak."

"Everything is cool," smirked Moe-dog. "I'll never let no bitch get me down."

As soon as those words left his mouth, he wished he could take them back. Because the truth of the matter, was that he was missing Gina and little Divine more than anything. He'd grown to love them so much over the years that he now felt kind of empty without them. But the legal world, and the family life bored and depressed him. He wished Gina would just accept him for who he was; a thug who loved her and her son. Didn't she accept Divine being a thug before he was killed?, he thought. Moe-dog knew he was addicted to the streets and like any other addiction, he would need rehabilitation. But the question was, did he want to be rehabilitated? Also, what the fuck was rehabilitation?, he thought to himself. He could not recall ever being 'habilitated', so how can he be re-habilitated? He shook his head from side to side in thought as he looked out of the car's window at all of the pretty girls walking by.

Whitey pulled over and parked the car. This was the first time Moe-dog had ever been to Lefrak Estates, and he hoped he wouldn't have to kill any of the wanna-be tough guys as he and Whitey walked pass building 97-07. The only guy they knew around here was a light-skinned thug named Shameek, but they didn't see him in the area as they walked into the building.

They took the stairs to the third floor, and before Whitey could put his key in the door, it was opened up by a beautiful light-skinned girl with almond shaped eyes. As they entered the apartment, she looked Moe-dog up and down with approval while licking her lips.

"Make your own introductions," said Whitey as he headed off to Tammy's bedroom. Moe-dog followed the girl into the living

room and after sitting down, the girl said with a smile, "What's up? You can call me Stefani, I'm Tammy's sister."
"Call me Moe-dog," smiled Moe-dog.
"I like that," smiled Stefani, "a man who finally admits he's a dog."
Moe-dog was not feeling her style at all. He didn't know what it was, but something about her turned him off. He pulled the nine millimeter from his waist, sat it on the table in front of him and leaned back on the couch with an unreadable expression on his face.

Stefani looked at the gun, and then up at Moe-dog. For some reason she began to get scared being in the same room with this guy that moments earlier she found to be so attractive. She got up from the couch, and quickly went to be around her sister Tammy and Whitey. She wanted no parts of Moe-dog.

Moe-dog then smiled when he realized that it wasn't Stefani at all that turned him off. He recognized that he was missing Gina and it would be hard for any woman to fill her shoes. But then he thought of someone he believed who would be able to take his mind completely off of Gina. All he had to do now was hope that he could find her.

Chapter 11

The house Kia's mother had left her in Jamaica Queens, was full of people today. Little children ran all around the house laughing and playing. Kia, her cousin Melyssa and her best friend Jenny laughed and talked in the kitchen as they cooked tonight's big dinner. Rice, beans, chicken, yams, Macaroni & Cheese and many other delicious dishes were being cooked along with various desserts to be served.

It was Light's birthday, and following his words of not having a big party, Kia cooked and invited only people she had considered to be family. She knew Light never liked the party scene and never went to any. She and Light had been together since they were children and she knew everything about him. She understood why he was so violent and his heart was heavy. She remembered everything as if it was only yesterday.

Kia's mother Mary, and Light's mother Carmen was the best of friends. They used to smoke weed together and everything else. At times, leaving Kia and Light alone to fend for themselves until they came back from doing whatever it was they did. Kia's father passed away from cancer when she was three years old, leaving her mother with money, memories and grief. From what she heard, her father was a good man and very successful in business. But things were hard for her pretended-to-be Auntie Carmen from Brooklyn and her son Maurice who everyone called Light because of his complexion. Carmen had taken beatings from Light's father David whenever he came home drunk or pissed off about something. And he must have been drunk or pissed off on a regular basis because every time Kia saw Auntie Carmen, she was wearing a new bruise or injury. She remember her mother crying and pleading with Carmen to leave David. Not only was he very abusive, but was also a neighborhood womanizer who made no attempts to hide it. However, Carmen stayed in the abusive relationship and little Kia never understood why. But she promised herself when she grew up, she would never allow a man to abuse her in any way. It was the day she came home from school, when she saw her mother and little Light crying and holding each other. From what she could gather through the crying, David came home that afternoon and accused Carmen of talking to one of his friends. Without even waiting to hear her side of the story, he beat her to death with a baseball bat in front of little Light. When the police and ambulance arrived on the scene, they found David crouched over Carmen, crying hysterically with her blood all over him and the bat still in his hands. After hearing the terrible news, Mary took Light to her house until she could decide what to do. She knew she could not take care of him because she barely had time for Kia, so instead of him being raised in a group home she was able to get the courts to grant custody to one of her closest friends. Mrs. Carol took custody of Light, and he was okay with it being that he clicked so well with her chubby son John, who everyone called Fats. But with no father figure in the home, the two became very rebellious as they grew in height, weight and age. They hit the streets like the majority of children raised in single parent households. But the two had money and murder on their minds. They just didn't have any guns, that's until they met Lamont who everyone called L for short. He had plenty of guns that he stole from his uncle down in South Carolina and brought back to New York City.

Light, Fats and L began to get money and put in work on many drug dealers in the streets, and their body count increased tremendously when they linked up with Big Dave, Tommy Guns and

Divine. Everyone in the five boroughs had learned, some of them the hard way, who the Bulldog crew were. Earning the name for carrying the .44 Bulldog handgun, they terrorized the streets with murders, robberies and extortion.

When Kia was old enough, she moved in with her cousin Melyssa, in the Sumner Housing Projects in the Bedford Stuyvesant section of Brooklyn, as her mother Mary moved from Brownsville out to a quiet section of Jamaica Queens. It was then that Kia and Light hooked up and became an item, and no one had ever understood or knew why their relationship was so strong.

Following the same illness that killed Kia's father, her mother Mary had also died of cancer leaving the big house in Queens and lots of money to Kia. Light and the daughter she had by Light was all she had, and basically that's all Light had.

"Is the chicken done?" Kia asked her friend Jenny as she stirred her bean sauce in a big black pot.

"Yeah, I'll take it out now," answered Jenny opening the oven all of the way.

"Me and my baby C-Allah, was suppose to go to Cancun last weekend but it didn't happen," said Kia's cousin Melyssa. "This nigga acts like he wants to spend more time with Light, Fats, L and Mont-Mont than he wants to spend with me! All the nigga talks about is Bulldog this and Bulldog that. Shit, he starting to look like a damn bulldog!"

Kia and Jenny busted out laughing, and when Kia was able to subdue her laughter she said, "I'm saying, don't tell me the nigga got you open already. You only been with him for about four weeks now."

Melyssa sucked her teeth and said, "Time don't mean shit! When that nigga stepped to me, it felt like I knew his ass for years.

And ya'll can't front, the nigga is super fine! But shit, I can't lie, when I first introduced him to Light he was so excited that they clicked, I thought the nigga was gay! But girl, that night in bed, he showed me otherwise," said Melyssa running her fingers through her hair, causing Kia and Jenny to laugh.

"Yall kids come in here and sit down," said Kia to she and Light's daughter, Melyssa's two daughters, and Jenny's son. "It's time to eat!"

"Let me check on this baby," said jenny referring to her eight month old daughter, as she got up and walked to the bedroom. "She might still be asleep."

"Light and them can eat after the kids get done eating," said Kia fixing the children's plates of food.

In the upstairs bedroom, Light, Fats, L, Mont-Mont and C-Allah sat around laughing, talking and smoking weed.

"C-Allah," said Mont-Mont laughing with tears in his eyes. "Yo, you're a funny nigga. What happened when you shot the dude? What he say?"

"Yo, that's my word," said C-Allah. "Every time I shot the nigga in the leg or stomach he yelled out, Ow, Jesus Mo-nelli boy, you're killing me!"

Everyone in the room laughed at the comedy way C-Allah told his war stories. He was a very funny and dangerous dude, and that's all it took for Light, Fats and Mont-Mont to like him. But for some reason, L did not care for him too much. To him, it seemed as if C-Allah was trying too hard to get down with the Bulldog Crew. When Light and Fats agreed to let him roll, L sucked his teeth and hoped the gangster comedian was more action than words. Because he had no intentions of putting his trust in anyone, that claimed to be one thing but proved to be another.

Everyone had always told C-Allah that he looked like the R&B singer known as Genuine. He had the braids and all, but C-Allah was thugged out as opposed to being smooth.

"Anyway," continued C-Allah, with Light, Fats and Mont-Mont hanging onto every word. "I didn't even shoot'em again. Every time I jerked the gun", he illustrated, "the nigga screamed 'ah, ah, ah."

Fats, Light and Mont-Mont were in tears. C-Allah stories was so funny, especially the way he relived it, even L had to laugh. 'He might even be a good dude', L thought to himself as C-Allah finished his story. L always had a problem accepting people, especially if they didn't immediately give him a good vibe. He wondered if he should maybe drop his guards with C-Allah and Mont- Mont a little, being they was now officially Bulldog crew members.

The television in the room was turned down low, and all five men in the room had just got finished watching the Dave Chappelle Show on Comedy Central. They all loved the show but complained about it being too short with too many commercials.

Light looked at his watch and wondered why Hook did not arrive as of yet. He said he was on his way two hours ago.

"I been putting in work for so long," continued C-Allah, "I can't remember whether I shot a nigga, or got pussy first. That's why I love y'all niggas, y'all put it down! Shit, y'all the reason I started reading the newspapers again. I got tired of reading my own shit."

Everyone laughed.

"Who put in that work on that Colombian nigga the pigs found chopped up and scattered all over the place?" asked C-Allah to no one in particular.

L put his glass of Hennessy on the floor, looked at C-Allah with his face screwed up and asked, "What's up nigga? You writing a fucking book or something?!"

The room got quiet, as L and C-Allah stared at one another for a full twenty seconds.

C-Allah then smiled and said, "Nah L, it's not like that homie. Pardon me if I offended anyone. I just felt that no one in this room is a snitch, so I thought it was okay to ask certain things. That's all. No hard feelings?" he asked looking at L with his hand outstretched.

L gave him a pound with a smile and said, "Everything is cool. And to answer your question, none of us did that to the Colombian. We heard about it on the news though."

"Well, fuck the nigga!" said C-Allah. "He just lucky I wasn't the one that did it, 'cause I would've been wearing the nigga's head on one of my platinum chains."

Everyone laughed, as Light smiled. He was glad to see the tension between his two friends disappeared. Because he really liked C-Allah, but L was his boy, and if things would have gotten ugly, Light would have shot C-Allah to the point of not being able to recognize him.

Just then, a slim brown-skinned guy entered the room wearing black alligator shoes and carrying a black bag. His crisp white button up shirt was tucked neatly into his black slacks.

Everyone in the room greeted Hook with pounds, hugs and much respect, as Light pulled up a chair for the Brownsville thug.

"Fuck took you so long?" asked Light. "I thought you wasn't coming for a minute."

"If I say I'm coming, then I'm coming," said Hook sitting down opposite L. "Kia said to tell y'all dinner is ready, but before we eat I got something for y'all."

He opened the black bag and pulled out four strange looking guns. They were definitely something the thugs did not see before in the New York City streets. They were, 296 Smith & Wesson .44 Specials. The Centennial hammerless gun was light and sure! The weight was 19.5 oz., and the Bulldog crew stared at the guns with their mouths open.

"This shit is crazy!" said Light excitedly, while turning the gun around in his hand, as Fats, L and Mont-Mont agreed and did the same.

"I heard you was now down with the team," Hook said to C-Allah. "But I got the news too late, before I got the guns. But I'll see if I can get another one, for you."

"That's cool," smiled C-Allah wishing he had one of the new guns that didn't touch the streets yet.

"Light!" yelled Kia from downstairs. "Dinner is ready!" Hook put the guns back into the bag, zipped it up and said, "Next time I'll charge y'all, but these here are on me. Now let's go eat, I'm hungry as a motherfucker! And oh yeah, Happy Birthday Light!"

Chapter 12

"Hey Gloria", said Denzel walking into her office. She looked up and could not believe her eyes. The man who stood in front of her desk with his shirt opened, was more than extremely gorgeous, she thought.

He closed the door behind him and hoped that they would not be disturbed. "You know," he said, "I've been waiting a very long time for this."

"Well, let's not wait another minute," said Gloria looking into his eyes.

Denzel sauntered over to her desk and brushed all of the papers on her desk to the floor, as Gloria walked around the desk to him. She stared at him as he removed his clothes. His body was nice and built, just the way she expected it to be.

Standing in front of him, she removed her clothes as well, and there they were naked and ready to fulfill their passionate desires and fantasies.

Gloria laid down on her back, on the long desk. She then parted her legs and waited for her lover to come to her.

When Denzel entered her, she could feel the heat from his body as he laid down on top of her. She squirmed with pleasure. It had been so long since she gave herself so completely to a man. Her body surrendered to Denzel's body as he gently kissed the side of her neck.

In and out he pumped, as she held on for dear life. His manhood filled her up completely with each stroke. She wrapped her legs around his muscular brown back and held on to his shoulders as he pumped. She could feel his steamy breath on the side of her neck. Every move he made caused her body to tremble with excitement.

Their bodies glistened with sweat as they made love, and she never wanted the pleasure to end.

As soon as her legs began to tremble and she was coming to a climax, Omar entered the office with two of the most dangerous looking thugs she had ever seen in her life! She pushed Denzel off of her and stammered with words she could not find.

"I'm ……..Please, Omar…..I ….um……"

"Gloria, Gloria, Gloria," said Omar shaking his head from side to side walking towards her as Denzel fearfully put back on his clothes in a rush."

"Gloria," said Omar as he brought his hand to her neck. She closed her eyes and prayed that her husband would not kill her for her adulterous ways with Denzel.

"Gloria baby," said Omar, and just when she thought he was about to apply pressure to her neck, her eyes shot open.

"Gloria baby," said Omar rubbing her neck gently. "It's time to get up, sleepy head, we got work to do."

Gloria looked around her big bedroom and was happy to see that her episode with Denzel was only a dream. The man she loved was no more than a foot away from her.

Omar knew something was wrong by the expression on her beautiful face. "What's wrong, baby?" he asked.

"Honey" she said with a concerned look on her face, "it was only a dream, so don't get upset. I would never cheat on you, but I had a dream you caught me making love to Denzel."

"Washington?!" asked Omar laughing.

"Yes", she answered. "But it was only a dream. I love you and would never, ever cheat on you."

Omar laughed so hard tears came from his eyes. When he was able to stop laughing, he said, 'Baby, that's nothing. It was only a dream, and I'm far from being insecure. Plus, do you know how many times I had dreams of me and Janet Jackson, Halle Berry and Lisa Raye putting it down?"

Gloria grabbed her pillow and hit Omar in the face and head with it. He laughed and jumped out of the bed as Gloria playfully threw the pillow at the man she loved.

She got out of bed and rolled her eyes at Omar as she walked to the bathroom with that sexy walk of hers.

Omar laughed and as he looked at his wife's perfect bottom disappear out of the bedroom, he knew he'd never saw or dreamed of a woman that could match the beauty of his wife. He then looked at the big picture of her decease son Kendu on the wall, and knew it was true about him being a playboy, because he definitely had his mother's good looks. 'Pretty Boy', thought Omar with a smile as he looked at the picture hanging on the bedroom's wall. He and Gloria had already found out through a sonogram from the doctor that they were having a baby girl, and Gloria cried tears of joy when Omar suggested they name the baby Kenya, in memory of her late son, Kendu.

Omar looked at his diamond infested Cartier watch, and then walked over to the telephone. All he had on was a blue pair of Askia Askari sweat pants. He sat on the bed and dialed the number that belonged to the Vice President of his record label.

When he got Daqual Longshore on the phone, he said, "I'm coming in today. I have a few things I wanna do…..yeah…..we can do that…..when?....okay, that's cool…. I also have to get in touch with J.Prince……yeah…..I don't give a fuck how many niggas is scared of him! Real recognize real……….No, I want his artist Yukmouth to get on Bone's album. Because the nigga is very under-rated, but he's official. Plus, I want that West Coast support. And you know Bone is completely off the hook, so I wanna get this thing popping......yeah, he's gonna have a few more guest appearance on his shit. Probably a couple of New York niggas and one of them niggas from the South. I'll let him decide on who.....yeah, yeah, for sure."

While he talked on the phone, Gloria entered back into the bedroom wearing only a tee shirt, and panties that looked too small for her nice round shapely ass.

"Damn!" said Omar watching her ass move from side to side as she walked. "Yeah, yeah, I'm here," he said into the phone.

He looked at his watch again and hated the fact that he did not have the time this morning to relieve his erection his wife had just caused.

When they caught eye contact, she smiled, showing her beautiful dimples making him frown. She knew what she was doing to him, and laughed as he proceeded to cut his telephone conversation short.

"I gotta go, I'll talk to you later. That's right Daqual, Untouchable Records only deliver hits! Okay, see you then," he said hanging up the phone.

He then walked to the bedroom door, and before exiting, he looked at his wife and playfully said, "I hate you, you're evil."

"Denzel didn't think so!" she laughed. And laughed even harder when she heard her husband respond, "Fuck Denzel!" as he descended down the hallway.

Gloria got dressed and joined her husband in the kitchen. As the maid poured coffee for her, Omar sat there reading the newspaper.

"This shit is ridiculous!" said Omar, as the maid placed a buttered bagel next to Gloria's cup of coffee before exiting the kitchen.

"I know its these stupid niggas," continued Omar to his wife as he read the newspaper. "They're still talking about the dead drug dealers in Brownsville, and the decapitated Colombian drug lord. Now seven more bodies been found, and we both know who's doing this shit. Because the crime rate just escalated crazily ever since Moe-Dog got back with Whitey and when them Bulldog Crew niggas came home. But I have no idea what they're doing it for. They all have money, except for Whitey, and that's only because I hear he spends it faster than he makes it, or should I say takes it! And the Bulldog Crew niggas is so stupid! It's common sense that every time the police finds a body with forty four shells in it, they're looking at the Bulldog Crew. Either these niggas is straight up stupid, or they just don't give a fuck! And all they go after is the craziest thugs or the richest drug dealers. But Moe-dog and Whitey ain't no better. Instead of just killing the person, they rip up the body parts!"

"But how do you know Moe-dog and Whitey did that?" asked Gloria while eating her bagel.

"Because when Moe-dog worked with my security team," answered Omar, "he would always tell me that's what he would do to one of the rappers if they ever disrespected him. And that's how I know who's doing what killings. The Bulldog Crew uses the .44 handguns and Moe-dog and Whitey do the torturing."

"But what about the body they found in Sumner Projects years ago, or the case the Bulldog Crew was convicted for?" asked Gloria before taking a sip of her coffee. "It sounds to me like they do torturing of their own."

"You got a point there," said Omar taking a sip of his coffee. "I'm just glad my boy Big Lord ain't doing that dumb shit. But I'm not surprised, he's a veteran that understands unnecessary killings fucks up your money. That's the difference between the old heads and these new jack niggas. That's why the game is fucked up now, these new niggas don't follow no rules of the game. But shit is getting very ugly, and maybe I see it more clearly now that I'm on the outside looking in. I don't know. And look at this here," said Omar pointing to another page in the newspaper. "The police shot another unarmed Black youth."

Gloria knew the newspaper had put her husband in a foul mood, but she also knew exactly what to say to lift his spirits. She took the newspaper from his hands, and with a smile said, "I talked to Lisa yesterday. She said they should be here this weekend."

"Word?!" Omar smiled excitedly. "My baby sis is coming this weekend? Yo, we gotta put something real phat together!"

"I hope not a concert!" laughed Gloria.

"Nah, nah, that's corny," he responded quickly. "And I know she's bringing my niece with her. Damn, I gotta find time to pick up some presents. I just have to decide what to get."

He then looked at his watch for the third time this morning since entering the kitchen.

"Oh man!" he said standing up knowing he was late for his meeting with one of his lawyers. "I'm late," he said kissing his wife on the lips. "I gotta run and take care of something. If you are not coming in today, call me at the office or hit me on the cell, because I also have to meet with a few people concerning Untouchable Wear."

He then dashed up the stairs to get dressed. He went into his walk-in closet, and grabbed a blue pair of pants and a white long sleeve button up shirt. Just because he was into Hip-Hop, did not mean he had to always wear jeans and sneakers, he thought as he grabbed a blue pair of alligator shoes.

After getting dressed, he was about to walk out when his telephone rung. He snatched it up before it could ring twice. After looking at the caller ID he said, “Good morning ma.”

“Hey baby,” said his mother Mrs. Alice cheerfully. “How are you doing? I called your house last night, but no one was home.”

“I’m okay. Me and Gloria had went out to dinner, but you could have called me on my cell phone. Is everything okay?”

“Yes, everything is fine,” she answered.

Omar looked at his watch and said, “Ma, I’m in a rush right now. But you can call my cell phone anytime, and Gloria may come into the office today so she’ll be here if you wanna talk to her.”

“Okay, said his mother.” “When you get a chance, call me. You know Lisa, Richard and the baby is coming to New York this coming weekend?”

”Yeah I heard,” smiled Omar. “I wanna put something real nice together, but I don’t know what yet.”

“Everyone is invited for dinner at your house,” said his mother telling him what the plans were, instead of asking him as she always did.

“Okay ma,” smiled Omar. “I gotta go. I’ll call you back later. I love you.”

“I love you too son, and I’m proud of you.”

“Thank you ma. Oh did Gloria tell you that you’re gonna be a grandma again?”

“What?!” she yelled excitedly into the phone. “She didn’t tell me, and you didn’t tell me nothi-“

“I gotta go ma,” smiled Omar cutting her off. “I’ll call later, but like I said Gloria is here.”

Omar went back downstairs and after kissing Gloria once again, he headed out of the house. He got into his money green SLR McLaren Mercedes Benz and drove away playing a CD by a newly signed artist to his label they called "Needles." He was feeling the rapper's flow and thought that he was maybe the best rapper to come out of Harlem since the late great rapper Big L.

Omar looked in his rear view mirror at his two body guards in the black Cadillac Escalade following closely behind him. Actually, he felt they weren't really body guards because they were guys he grew up with in the streets. So, he considered them more as his friends he looked out for who was willing to put in that dangerous work if he so desired them to. But he also kept a gun stashed in his car for protection as well. He just hoped he'd never have to use it again!!!!!!!"

Chapter 13

Whitey laughed with tears coming from his eyes, as he pointed his finger at the little Puerto Rican big head Midget sitting directly in front of him.

"Wait, wait, wait. Let me get this straight," said Whitey trying his best to subdue his laughter. "You're telling me and my partner here," he pointed at Moe-dog, "That if we don't get the job done and miss on this hit, we're dead as well?" He then bust out laughing again as Moe-dog looked on with a serious unreadable expression on his face.

They sat in a big well furnished living room. Three of the Midget's gunmen stood around listening to the exchange of words with their guns sticking out from their waist.

When Moe-dog and Whitey had first entered the money making Midget's home, he requested they'd be searched and unarmed before entering his "castle". However, they refused, explaining that they never did business unarmed, under any circumstances. The Midget then realizing that it actually didn't make any difference being that his gunmen were present, but he did show a bit of an attitude. He didn't like his rules to be broken for anyone, so he did not hide his displeasure at his rules not being obeyed. He told his gunmen in Spanish that if Moe-dog or Whitey's hands went anywhere near their waist, for them to open fire with no words spoken. He knew that's where they had their guns, because he could see the bulge protruding from the bottom of their shirts.

The Midget's name was Eddie, and he had drugs in different areas of the Bronx. But his biggest competitor happened to be his cousin, Julio. He knew if he could get Julio's lieutenant Pacheco murdered, then it would not be too hard to convince Julio to set up shop elsewhere. Because it was Pacheco that planted fear in people to not step on Julio's toes. But with Pacheco dead, the money making area would without a doubt fall in the hands and belong to Eddie.

Eddie came from a long line family of drug dealers and killers, and people still feared the family's reputation. In the early seventies his family had a hand in most of the heroin in the Bronx, and it was just a matter of time before Eddie took over his family's business in the illegal trade. Like his father in the early days, Eddie also had a few crooked police officers on his payroll. He also had a Napoleon complex, and because of it, he killed many people who he thought were trying to disrespect him because of his size. However, all of the people he killed, he was assisted by his gunmen, because Eddie was really a coward who became so power struck that he felt everyone should be afraid of him.

"Yes, I will have both of you killed if you fuck up this hit!" said Eddie with his face screwed up. "I want no shoot-outs! A nice, clean professional hit!"

"Okay, okay, okay," said Whitey wiping away the tears and finally being able to get his laughter under control. "I'm sure Big Lord told you we want twenty thousand dollars for this hit. But I'm curious to know, why you want us to do it, since you're such a big killer and all?"

He tried not to laugh again as Eddie explained the situation to he and Moe-dog.

"I can't have my men do it," said Eddie, "because they would know that it came from me if any of my boys are seen in the vincinity. And I don't want to go out there personally and terrorize the neighborhood once again."

"That's enough!" said Whitey doubled over in laughter as he tried to stand straight. "You're killing me!"

As he continued laughing, Moe-dog spoke for the first time since being inside of the house.

"Give us the information," said Moe-dog, "and the money and we'll handle the situation."

"No," stated Eddie. "I give you the information and half of the money. When you come back you get the other half!"

Moe-dog didn't say anything further. He just watched Midget Eddie go into his pocket and pull out a yellow envelope.

"Inside is ten thousand dollars and the information," said Eddie handing the envelope to Moe-dog. "I want it done quickly!"

Moe-dog took the envelope and asked , "what if your cousin Julio happens to show up?"

"He's harmless," answered Eddie waving his hand through the air. "Do not kill him. That's my first cousin for crying out loud."

"How will I know who he is, if he does happen to be there?" asked Moe-dog.

"Trust me," answered Eddie, "you will know!"

As Moe-dog and Whitey were escorted to the front door by two gunmen, Eddie yelled out, "Do not fuck up!"

Whitey continued laughing, as Moe-dog thought the Midget had definitely saw one gangster movie too many.

They got inside of the blue Honda Accord and drove to Hoe Avenue, and when they reached their destination, they sat in the car and observed the area. The car had dark tinted windows, so they weren't worried about being seen. Plus, no one in the area knew who they were, so they just waited to see how their plan would unfold.

Moe-dog took the yellow envelope from his pocket and examined the picture of Pacheco. He then read the small note, and just as Eddie had said, Pacheco pulled up on Hoe Avenue at exactly ten minutes after eight pm. He pulled up in a brand new Mercedes Benz with Salsa music blasting from the speakers.

"There goes our boy," Moe-dog informed Whitey. "But he has his kid in the car with him, so we'll wait until they get out."

Pacheco cut the engine and stepped out of the car with whom they assumed to be his son. Whitey was the first to laugh, when he noticed the kid was actually a big head Midget that looked just like Eddie!

"I can't believe this shit," said Moe-dog shaking his head as Whitey was bent over in laughter. "These niggas in the Bronx got Midgets running shit?!"

All the workers on the block paid homage to Pacheco and continued hustling, but when they saw Julio, they acted as if Jesus had finally returned!

"I don't know how we let Big lord talk us into this circus shit here," said Moe-dog as Whitey continued laughing. "Come on, let's get this shit over with."

They both exited the car and walked in separate directions. Whitey crossed the street, pulled a cigarette from out of his pocket and approached Pacheco.

"Excuse me sir," said Whitey with the cigarette dangling from his mouth. "Do you have a light?"

"No, I don't have no fucking light!" bellowed Pacheco.

"Calm down," said Julio to Pacheco. Then to Whitey he said with a smile, "here, I have a light" as he pulled a lighter from his jacket pocket.

Before Whitey could bend down to the Midget, a loud gunshot went off and Pacheco fell to the ground. Moe-dog had shot him in the back of his head blowing his brains out. He then turned and with his hat pulled down to his eyes, he fired three quick shots at the workers on the block making them run and scatter in all directions.

"Please, please don't kill me," pleaded Julio. He then fell to the ground and rolled under Pacheco's Mercedes Benz.

Moe-dog and Whitey made their getaway, and pulled away from the area to go and collect the other ten thousand dollars from Eddie. They were glad that no one saw their faces. Whitey wasn't sure if Julio gotten a good look at his face, but he wasn't really concerned about it. Because he would never allow himself to be taken to jail as long as he had his gun on him, and he always kept that near.

Just then, Whitey's cell phone began ringing. He flicked it open and said, "Hello?" After a pause he then said, "Yo Big Lord, what's the deal?....Yeah, we just took care of that.......What kind of circus shit you got us into up here?....Oh yeah......Another twenty thousand dollars?.....Yeah, I'll tell Moe-dog. He'll like that....You should've told us earlier and we would've took care of that. You put us in a fucked up situation."

Moe-dog quickly glanced at Whitey as he continued driving. But Whitey didn't even look at Moe-dog as he continued talking to Big Lord. "Oh, you just found out........Okay, don't sweat it......What about Julio? I think he saw my face ....Okay, that's cool," said Whitey ending the conversation.

Moe-dog looked at Whitey and asked, "What's up?"

"Well", began Whitey. "Big Lord just got a call from his homie G-man that got a lotta money up here in the Bronx, and he told Big Lord that Eddie is a certified informant. So, you know we gotta get rid of him."

"What about Julio?" asked Moe-dog briefly taking his eyes off of the road.

"He's already with G-Man's people," answered Whitey. "As soon as we left somebody snatched him off the streets. And Big Lord said, he's damn near dead already."

"Who's paying the other twenty grand?"

"Big Lord is gonna give it to us but it's coming outta G-man's pocket. It seems Pacheco was a thorn in everyone's side up here in the Bronx".

They then drove back to Eddie's house in silence, and upon reaching their destination, they were escorted back into the Midget's big living room by one of his gunmen. Eddie sat on the sofa with a big smile on his face and a yellow envelope in his hand.

"I already heard the news about Pacheco. Here is your money," he said handing the money to Moe-dog. "I hear my cousin was present and it shook him up pretty good. He just disappeared somewhere, so now I have to find him and comfort the bastard before I take over the area!" he laughed.

The three gunmen stood across from Moe-dog and Whitey, and kept their eyes glued to their waist as instructed.

Eddie looked down at Whitey's feet and said with a smile, "Don't trip white boy, your shoes are untied."

"Thank you," smiled Whitey waiting for this moment as he bend down to tie the long laces. And not even one of the gunmen, saw when he pulled the gun from his ankle holster as he pretended to tie his shoes. When they did notice what was taking place, it was all too late. Whitey came up firing hitting two of the gunmen in the chest and face, and before the third gunman could even clear his gun from his waist, Moe-dog shot him in the head two times killing him instantly.

"Enough!" yelled Eddie angrily jumping up and down. "That is enough already! What the fuck is going on!"

Normally this would have made Whitey laugh, but being he now knew Midget Eddie was a snitch, he found nothing funny or comical about the big head rat! He pointed his gun at Eddie and emptied every bullet out of his gun at the Midget.

Eddie fell to the floor and his little body slid under the coffee table as the bullets entered his face, chest and head.

"Come on, let's get outta here," Moe-dog said to Whitey. "Because this little snitch, might be wired straight to the motherfucking precinct! Plus, before you go and see Tammy, I got another job lined up!"

Chapter 14

"I don't know what's up with the nigga L," said Fats. "He suppose to be here by now. He knows where we're at."

"I know what's up with the nigga!" Light said angrily. "That lil'bitch he wit' got his nose wide open.!"

"Nar, nar, don't tell me that man," laughed Mont-Mont. "My boy ain't open off no bitch."

C-Allah sat there smiling, and then he spoke. "So, what's up? What y'all wanna do?"

"I heard them niggas on Willoughby and Troop is getting it," said Light. "Let's go over there and get our cut.'

"What they doing?" asked Mont-Mont.

"They moving that dope, and you know how good that dope money is," answered Light.

They all sat in Fat's girl Denise's apartment, located on Bedford Avenue, between Dekalb and Willoughby Avenues. So, if they made their move to Willoughby and Troop, they wouldn't have far to travel. Their soon to be victims were no further than a six block radius.

Denise entered into the livingroom and sat next to Fats as if she was part of their plan.

"Bitch!" bellowed Fat's to Denise. "Don't you see me and my dudes talking? Go lay your ass down somewhere. Stop being so fucking nosey! And you better not have that bitch in here while I'm gone, 'cause if I catch her in here, I'm a break her neck!'

Usually Fats didn't talk to Denise in this manner, but he was still upset at what he caught Denise and Tawanna doing two days after he came home from prison. Actually he didn't really care, but when Tawanna refused his participation, Fats had a fit! He had just came home two days prior and decided to surprise Denise, being that she didn't believe he was coming home. He pulled up in front of her house on Bedford Avenue and smiled when he noticed her young niece sitting on the stoop with her little face frowned up and looking bored. Fats remembered the little girl and noticed that she had gotten much bigger since he'd been gone, but her cute little dimples and long hair was still the same. He got out of the BMW he left with his mother while being in prison, and slowly approached the young girl.

When she saw Fats, her face lit up. Because she remembered when she was younger, the thug would always give her money and advice about boys that she never understood. Also, her aunt Denise always talked about Fats on a regular basis, even when he was in jail.

Fats smiled at the little girl and remembering her name said, "What's up Christina? Look at you, you done got all big and everything. You miss me?"

"Yeah," blushed the little girl. "You was in jail?"

"Yeah," answered Fats. "And never mess with boys that does things to go to jail. Okay?"

She smiled and nodded in agreement.

"Why are you outside, and where is your aunt?" asked Fats.

"She's upstairs with Tawanna," answered the little girl. "And she told me to go outside and don't come upstairs 'til she call me."

Fats wondered what was going on, as he pulled a stack of money out of his pocket. With a frown he asked the little girl, "Do you have a key to the door?"

"Yeah," smiled the little girl. "But she said don't come up there 'til she call me."

"Well look here," said Fats peeling a hundred dollar bill off of the big stack. He then changed his mind because he knew the corner stores would not have change or would try to beat the little girl out of her money. So, he gave her five twenties and said, "That's for you. Let me use your key and surprise your auntie. She doesn't know I'm home. Don't worry, you won't get in trouble. You have my word on that."

The little girl didn't care if giving him the key would get her in trouble with her aunt or not. She was just excited to get the hundred dollars and couldn't wait to get off of the stoop and go and spend it. So, she went in her pocket and came out with the key, giving it to Fats.

Fats smiled, and as the little girl ran off to the store with a big smile on her face, he yelled out to her, "Remember what I said about them little boys!"

He then walked up to the door and used the key to enter the house. When he got to the living room, he heard a lot of moaning and knew Denise had some guys in the house with her and Tawanna. Fats pulled out his .44 handgun and walked towards the bedroom. He couldn't believe his eyes when he slowly pushed the door open. Denise was shaking her head violently from side to side with her legs up in the air, her eyes closed and her mouth slightly open, as Tawanna ate her pussy as if it was the last supper! You could hear the licking and slurping going on, even with Denise moaning loudly on the verge of screaming.

When she was about to cum, her eyes opened and she could not believe it when she saw Fats standing in the doorway holding his gun. Her eyes were big as saucers, as Tawanna continued eating her out.

"Don't let me disturb the groove," smiled Fats. "I knew while I was gone, you had to fuck somebody. I ain't mad it's a bitch. Just make room for a nigga. I don't mind a little threesome."

Tawanna momentarily stunned from hearing his voice, jumped up out of the bed. But not thinking clearly, she looked at Fats with disgust and spoke her mind.

"Nigga, you ain't fucking me!" she said. "I don't know why your fat ass think you can even fuck me!"

"What ?!" asked Fats with his face screwed up. "Bitch, I will murder you!'

It was then that she knew she had made a terrible mistake. Her eyes had finally focused on the big gun he was holding and realizing that this was the infamous Fats! She stumbled for words, but none came to her mouth.

Fats took her silence as a form of disrespect as he walked over to her and slapped her in the back of her head with his gun.

Tawanna took off running with blood dripping from the back of her head, as she ran out of the house butt ass naked to get away from crazy ass Fats!

So, being that they didn't just go along with the program, Fats made Denise stay away from Tawanna and reminded her daily that she had betrayed him.

"That's how you check a bitch!" said Light smiling as Denise gave him the evil eye and sucking her teeth before exiting the livingroom.

"That's what I'm talking about my nigga," smiled Light to Fats. "I think you need to give L some lessons."

"Yo," said C-Allah standing up. "Let's make this move."

They all stood up and made their way for the door.

They then got inside of C-Allah's blue BMW, and when they hit Willoughby and Troop Avenues, it wasn't hard to tell who was who on the block. A long line of dope addicts stood around patiently waiting to get their early morning fix.

Five well dressed young boys made their sales in the open and barked orders to the fiends as if what they were doing was legal. Two other young boys sat in a brand new black Mercedes Benz, with the rapper Rick Ross's song "Everyday Hustling" bumping from the loud sound system. Both boys wore platinum chains, rings and watches flooded with diamonds.

The Bulldog Crew minus L, sat patiently watching the whole scene. One of the workers handed the two guys in the Mercedes Benz, a big brown paper bag, and received a re-up supply of drugs in return. The Mercedes Benz had then slowly pulled away from the curb.

"The bosses or the workers?" asked C-Allah.

"The bosses," answered Light. "We'll come back for them faggot ass workers!"

C-Allah pulled off following the Mercedes Benz closely, and told Light, Fats and Mont-Mont to duck down in their seats. When he was directly behind the Mercedes Benz, he rammed it from the back. When the two young boys realized what happened, they turned the music down in their car and looked out of the window behind them.

"Sorry about that duke!" C-Allah yelled out of his window with a stupid grin on his face infuriating the two young boys further. They noticed that he appeared to be in the car alone. So they both reached in the back seat of their car, and when they got out both of the young boys had baseball bats in their hands. They figured they would make this idiot pay for ramming the back of their car, as they approached the BMW.

C-Allah smiled, making the young boys even madder and when they got closer to his car, he gave the signal for his crew to act.

Light, Fats and Mont-Mont quickly opened their doors and stepped out of the car with their guns trained on the two very surprised young boys.

"Where's the money?" asked Fats.

One of the youth screwed up his face and said, "Y'all making a big fucking mistake! You know who my brother is?!

"I don't give a fuck who your fag ass brother is," said Fats. "You heard the stories, you know how the Bulldog Crew get down. Now, I'm a ask you one more time, where is the money?"

Hearing who these guys were, the two young boys faces showed fear. Because shorty even heard his so-called gangster brother, speak about the Bulldog Crew with admiration and fear.

"It's under the front seat," answered shorty, dropping his bat to the ground as his friend did the same.

Light looked at Mont-Mont, and he went to retrieve the money from the Mercedes Benz. C-Allah stood there with a smile on his face as he watched the scene go down.

"Now I'ma ask y'all one time," said Fats. "Is that all the money y'all got in the car? 'Cause if y'all tell me yeah, and I find more, I'm gonna set an example of why it's not a good thing to lie to me. Understand?"

The boys was clearly shook up, and shorty said, "There's more money in the trunk that we picked up from the other spots."

"Now we're getting somewhere," smiled Fats walking to the car to get the rest of the money.

The two young boys hated the fact that out of all mornings, no one was outside to see what was going on. The block seemed deserted on this particular morning. Most of the time, it was always someone hanging out on the block. But not today.

"Take off the jewelry!" ordered Light. "And empty out your pockets, and put everything on the ground."

They did as they were told and stood there in fear, as Light picked up the money and jewelry and C-Allah pointed his gun at the two boys with a smile on his face.

Fats and Mont-Mont came back to the BMW, both carrying two large paper bags full of money. Fats took the bag from Mont-Mont that he was carrying and said, "Y'all know what time it is, get right and let's get outta here."

Light bust off two shots, hitting both boys in the legs. They fell to the ground crying in pain and fear, and before Light and Fats got back inside of the car, Light looked at C-Allah and Mont-Mont with a smile and said, "I think y'all better kill'em. Y'all don't want them to tell his brother, whoever the fuck the bird is."

He got in the back seat with Fats and smiled, as he watched the scene before him.

Mont-Mont returned his smile, before shooting one of the youths in the head killing him. He then walked to the car laughing rejoining Fats and Light. The other young boy looked fearfully in C-Allah's eyes pleading for his life.

"Stay down little nigga," said C-Allah as he also shot his gun twice before walking back to his car with a smile.

When he got in the driver's seat he said, "Damn, I hate killing kids! Ah fuck it, he's still young," he said shrugging his shoulders, "I'll just look at it as an abortion."

The car was full of laughter as they drove away.

When they got a few blocks away and made a few turns, they were back on Willoughby and Troop Avenue.

"We killing these niggas too?" asked Mont-Mont smiling.

"Nah," answered Light. "It's too many people out here. Let's just get this money and bounce."

The five young boys was so much into their business serving the fiends, they didn't even see Light, Mont-Mont and C-Allah ease up on them. Fats stayed in the car with the money that they already had.

"Don't fucking move!" said Light with his gun pointed at them. The five young boys stood frozen with their mouths open. The fiends quickly scurried away rather being shot, than having to depart with their fix money.

After the five young boys was robbed of everything they had, Light and his crew got back inside of the BMW, and C-Allah was told to drive to Kia's house in Jamaica, Queens.

$

L sat in the living room watching television waiting for the girl in the kitchen to finish cooking. His mouth watered as he smelled the Oven Barbecued Citrus Chicken she prepared. He was really feeling her style. It wasn't often that he met a woman like her. She was very beautiful, church going, an excellent cook, hip to the streets even though she stayed far away from what went on in them, and most of all, she knew how to please him in the bedroom. He loved the fact that she allowed him to be him, never complaining and never asking about his personal business in the streets. He remembered the day he first met her. It was on a late night when he entered the McDonalds in Downtown Brooklyn. He was surprised that it was so crowded on such a late night. So he was about to turn around and leave, that is until he saw the beautiful dark-skinned girl standing two people ahead of him that forced him to change his mind. And it was just his luck when the people in front of him were no longer patient enough to endure the long line and left the restaurant with attitudes. L decided to be bold instead of using the gentleman approach. He leaned forward and kissed her softly on the side of her neck. She quickly spun around with her pretty face screwed up and said, "Negro, what is your problem?! Don't be putting your lips on me!"

L smiled and said, "I'm sorry, beautiful. Please don't take what I just did as any form of disrespect. I know I was a bit out of order but when I see something or someone I like, I go for it. Of course, we can't see what a person is about by looking at them only, but I confess, your physical beauty is what attracted me to you. Now I'm hoping your inner beauty is just as beautiful, and I would like the chance to see if that is the case. That's all."

The beautiful girl relaxed, and giggled.

"Now that is what I call game," she smiled, "that I've never heard before. And believe me, I've heard it all."

"I'm sure you have," replied L. "However, what I said was not game. I'm not in the habit of playing, and everything I say I mean."

L had the girl's full attention, and after exchanging names and finally ordering their food, they sat in the fast food restaurant laughing and talking. It was amazing how much they had in common.

"So, you're a church girl, huh?" L asked with a smile.

"I guess you can say that," the girl answered with a smile of her own. "But I wasn't always this way. I mean, I was never a hoe or anything, but trust me, I was 'bout it 'bout it," she laughed. "It was always the best for me. You would have never caught me eating in these kind of places."

To L, she had the most adorable laugh he'd ever heard, and he loved the sweet Jasmin smell of Creed's flower perfume she wore.

"What about you? What are you into?" she asked looking into his eyes as she ate her French firies. "And please, be honest with me."

"Well," began L. "I just came home from upnorth, in other words prison. I have a little paper, so I'm not pressed to do anything I don't wanna do. But I am in the process of thinking about what I wanna do with the rest of my life. I'm originally from Cypress Projects in East New York, but presently, I have a little apartment in Langston Hughs Projects in Brownsville that my sister left me being that she just got married and moved in with her husband. My moms and pops passed away in a car accident when I was six years old, so my sister took care of me 'til I was able to grind. But enough about me, do you have a boyfriend.

"Don't you mean a man?" she asked before eating another French fry. "I don't mess with boys!"

"Yeah," laughed L. "I meant a man."

"Well," began the girl, "I just got out of a marriage. I guess the only thing we really had in common was the love of God. He didn't understand me. I remember--"

"Enough about him," L cut her off with a smile. "Let's get up outta here."

He then took her hand in his, and walked her to her car and exchanged telephone numbers.

Just thinking about that night, caused L to smile as he reached for the television's remote and changed the channel on his big floor model television. He knew the Bulldog Crew was a bit upset with him because he was suppose to meet up with them, but when things didn't feel right, he always followed his instincts. Mont-Mont and C-Allah was cool, but to L, they could never replace Big Dave and Tommy Guns. He didn't feel that trust and closeness with them that he felt with his decease trouble shooters, and everyone knew in the streets, trust, closeness and loyalty was a must!

"Dinner is ready!" yelled the dark-skinned beauty from the kitchen, snapping him out of his thoughts.

L thought about asking her to move in with him, but then decided to take things slowly. He did not want to mess things up by rushing their relationship. He entered the kitchen and then sat down with a smile, as he looked at the beautiful Tonya.

Chapter 15

"Lord, we thank you for this food this evening," prayed Richard with his head bowed and his hands clasp together.

Lisa, her daughter Dejanay, Gloria, Omar, his mother Mrs. Alice and Richard's mother Mrs. Maria Brown sat at the dinner table with their heads bowed and eyes close, as Richard continued to give thanks.

"And thank you Lord, for watching over our family here. Through our struggles, temptations, sins, troubles, as well as good times, we continue to call on your name and worship you. It is only you who can make the impossible possible, and we thank you for allowing us all to be sitting at this table this evening. 'All good works for those who loves God,' Amen".

"Amen," said everyone at the table, raising their heads, opening their eyes, talking and passing the delicious food around the table.

Rice, different kinds of beans, collard greens, cornbread, chicken, fish, steak, ham, yams, macaroni & cheese, and many other delicious dishes sat on the table. But little Dejanay's eyes, could not leave the delicious desserts also on the big table: Sweet potato pie, banana pudding, and her favorite: peach cobbler sat in front of her. She licked her lips and stared at the dessert.

"Don't even think about it," said Lisa looking at her daughter as she began fixing her a plate. "You are going to eat some food first!"

Mrs. Maria smiled at her grandbaby, and then looking at Richard and Lisa, she said, "I hope you two are still leaving my grandbaby with me for the rest of the summer."

"Yes ma," smiled Richard. "But I already know when we get her back, she's going to be terrible, because you and Mrs. Alice is going to spoil that little girl to death!"

"That's right!" agreed Mrs. Alice smiling. "And when my other grandbaby gets here, I'm going to spoil that baby too!"

This was the first time everyone at the table had heard Gloria was pregnant. Those that didn't know, looked at her and Omar in surprise with their mouths open.

Gloria smiled so hard tears came to her eyes. Everyone congratulated she and Omar and talked about baby names, and then caught up with one another's lives, as they laughed and continued to eat dinner.

After everyone had finished eating, Omar and Richard excused themselves from the table, and Omar led the way to his 'Dirty Room.'

Upon entering, Richard sat in a very comfortable chair, picked up a magazine from the table, but after looking at the cover, he threw it back on the table as if it were a snake in his hands.

Omar laughed and said, "Oh, I forgot to tell you, this is the 'Dirty Room'. So Pastor Brown, don't touch anything."

He then smiled at Richard's attempt to not glance at the Black Tail magazine that sat on the table in front of him.

Omar produced a newspaper, handing it to Richard. As his brother-in-law Richard read the newspaper, Omar sat back and watched his reactions to what he was reading.

When he got half way through the story, he looked at Omar and asked, "Is this the Bulldog Crew, killing people and cutting them up?"

"It could be," answered Omar. "But I believe the killings you are reading belong to Moe-dog and Whitey."

"Moe-dog?" asked a surprised Richard. "What is he doing with Whitey? I thought he was with you."

"He was," responded Omar sitting across from Richard. "But he wasn't feeling being head of the security team. I guess it wasn't enough action happening being that no one violates my label or my artists. I should've known it though, because if I remember clearly, he was the one that bust that R&B singer in the head with a bottle in Club Dynamite and I had to pay to get the charges dropped because it got blamed somehow on my artist Bones. And Bones wasn't even in the area! But I want you to read on," said Omar nodding his head towards the newspaper in Richard's hand. "And when you finish, turn to page four."

Richard quickly read the rest of the article and couldn't believe how many dead bodies they talked about, and when he got to page four it was just as bad. "Bulldog Crew?" he asked as he continued reading.

"Yep!" answered Omar. "At least that's what I believe. I mean, I know they're doing the killings but they may be torturing these people too, so it's kind of hard to pin-point the Bulldog Crew's bodies as opposed to those belonging to Moe-dog and Whitey. But we both know when they talk about the .44 Bulldog handgun being used its no other than the Bulldog Crew."

"Yeah," said Richard closing the paper. "But it's only used if it's a simple hit or if they want someone to know they did it."

After a moment of silence, Richard asked, "So, what are you going to do about this?"

Omar laughed and said, "I ain't doing nothing! What am I suppose to do? Talk to these idiots, like they're actually going to change their ways because of what I say? Yeah, right! I mean, I'm from the streets so I do know and understand how this shit go, but to be real with you, I don't even know how to stop this thing. Ever since I got with this music thing and helping Gloria out at Kendu's Youth Center, I really became aware of the genocide of our Black youth, and there's no turning back from awareness. But again, what can I do? I was never a snitch, and I never will be. But I'm not in the streets anymore either, and I'm not going back to the streets blazing guns in a war with a bunch of psychotic idiots!"

"But man," he said sadly, "I love the kids at the youth center. And I know it won't be long before a few of them start idolizing these fools, or maybe even becoming victims to their guns! I get stressed out every time I read about these dudes, and even moreso now, being that me and Gloria's having a child of our own. To be real with you, I don't even wanna talk to Moe-dog or any of them niggas. Because you never know who's watching or talking, and the last thing I need is to come up in a Federal investigation. And you know how they get down. Look what they're trying to do to Suge, J.Prince and Irv Gotti! I don't need that shit. Did you know there's two new niggas down with the Bulldog Crew now? I guess they're filling in for Big Dave and Tommy Guns."

"This is crazy," said Richard. "But like you said, there's not a thing we can do. Everything is in God's hands, and I will pray on it. Now come on", replied Richard standing up, "Let's get out of this perverted room you have here."

Omar laughed as he stood up, and then said, "All the nudie magazines in here, gets sent to all my homies in prison. I never forget about them, the homies that is. And you see all these porn tapes?" he asked pointing to over 100 sex videos. "Believe it or not, but on every tape is a famous female rapper, R&B singer, or actress that some of my homies ran through. Even the joint with the singer/actress that was floating around California. Yeah, I have your favorite Oscar nominated actresses on tape having sex, putting it down!"

"I doubt it," said Richard. "None of my favorite anyway. Unless you have some Gospel singers."

"No, you got me there," laughed Omar as he followed Richard out of the 'Dirty Room', and into the big spacious living room where Lisa, Gloria, Mrs. Alice, Mrs. Maria, and little Dejanay sat around, looking at photo albums of old pictures.

"So, this is your son?" asked Mrs. Alice.

"Yes that's my baby," answered Gloria nodding her head.

"Oh yes, I remember him ," said Mrs. Maria. "Kenny was a very good boy. He had good manners and was very respectful. He and my son Richard, were like brothers."

"I thought you said his name was Kendu?" Mrs. Alice asked Gloria.

"No, his name is Kenny," explained Gloria. "But he loved the name Kendu, and it just stuck as his nickname."

"Oh I see," said Mrs. Alice still looking at the picture.

"Yes this boy was extremely handsome. I bet he had to fight the girls off of him!"

"Oh please!" said Lisa sarcastically in a joking manner. "He was a bonafide player! He didn't do too much fighting off. If anything, the girls was doing the fighting, after he mentally spinned them and sexed them."

Everyone laughed and the atmosphere was no longer sad.

"Kendu had so many girls," continued Lisa, "I'm surprised he didn't run into any of his cousins unknowingly."

"That's it!" said Gloria giving Lisa a playful stern look. "You better leave my baby alone. And plus, he told me you was almost one of his girls, before you met Bishop!"

"Gloria!" yelled Lisa with wide eyes as everyone laughed.

Richard and Omar sat down across from the women, and when Richard picked up one of the photo albums and looked through it, he saw a photo of Kendu and immediately got sad. He and Kendu was like brothers, and he loved him and missed him dearly. It was Kendu who looked passed his no-name brand clothes and befriended him when no one else would.

Looking at the photo, caused Richard to reminisce of the days they hung out together. Like the day when Kendu asked Richard to go with him to the Sumner Housing Projects to see a girl. Richard wasn't doing anything so he went along. When they got to Sumner Projects, Kendu knocked on a second floor apartment door, and the door was opened by an older woman with short hair.

"May I help you?" asked the lady.

Kendu threw her his boyish grin and asked, "Is Mattie here? I'm her cousin Melvin, and I've been looking all over for this girl. My aunt told me she might be here."

Richard knew Kendu was lying and wondered what his best friend was up to, as the two of them stood in front of the door.

"Yes, she's here," said the woman opening the door wider so they could enter. "Come on in."

When they stepped inside the small apartment, the woman looked Kendu in the eyes and with a flirtatious smile said, "Mattie's in Sharod's room putting the baby to sleep. Y'all can go back there. It's the second room on the left. The first one is my bedroom," she laughed.

"Thank you," smiled Kendu leading the way to Sharod's small ass bedroom.

Richard could tell from the way the older woman flirted and talked to Kendu, that if he really wanted to, he could have sex with the woman very easily. But Richard was not surprised, mainly because Kendu always had an effect on any women; young or old, he said a few words to. The women just loved him.

When Richard followed Kendu into the small bedroom, they both looked at Mattie's round ass as she put her baby girl into the crib. When she turned around, Richard noticed she was very beautiful. She was slim, brown-skinned, short hair and had the sexiest eyes Richard had ever saw. But the same beautiful eyes nearly popped out of her head when she saw Kendu standing there. Her mouth dropped open, and Kendu smiled and casually walked over to the small bed against the wall and sat down.

"You're crazy!" said Mattie as Kendu laughed. But she had to admit, she was totally turned on by his boldness.

She picked up the baby and said, "I'll be right back. Let me take my daughter in the livingroom with her grandmother." She then walked out of the bedroom carrying her daughter with a smile on her pretty face.

Before Richard could ask any questions, Kendu explained just about everything to him. "Mattie don't live here," said Kendu. "She's from Downing Place. When she comes back in the room, go chill in the livingroom. I'll be out in like ten minutes, fifteen minutes tops."

As soon as Mattie entered back into the bedroom, Richard brushed pass her and headed towards the livingroom as Kendu had suggested. The older woman sat on the couch trying to rock the baby to sleep, as Richard sat down across from her.

"This baby ain't hardly going to sleep," said the woman. "She's wide awake."

"That's your baby?" asked Richard knowing it wasn't. He just felt nervous sitting and was trying to make small conversation with the woman.

"No," smiled the woman. "I have no babies. I have one son and he's grown. His name is Sharod and this here," she said looking down at the baby in her arms, "is him and Mattie's baby. And they've been together for the longest."

Richard could not figure out what was going on as he wondered what in the hell was Kendu doing.

"I heard Sharod got locked up the other day for being in a stolen car," continued the woman. "I don't know what's wrong with these kids today. You would think they would learn something from the mistakes of others."

After a pause she said, "Now what did Mattie and her cousin had to talk about that was so important, that they had to kick you out of the room?"

"I have no idea," answered Richard looking at the small television she had on. But after three minutes he stood up from the chair he sat in and said, "Let me see what's taking him so long. They should be finish talking by now."

When he opened the bedroom door, he couldn't believe his eyes. Kendu had Mattie's legs up in the air, as he stroked deeply into her. Her moans were louder than the squeaking of the bed.

Richard quickly closed the door and headed back to the living room with a confused look on his face.

He sat back down, and when the woman looked at him he said, "They'll be out in a minute. I guess they're talking about some important family issues."

Three minutes passed and it was a hard knock at the front door. Someone was knocking with importance, and impatience!

"Who in the hell is knocking on my door like that?" the woman asked as she got up with the sleeping baby in her arms to go and answer the door.

Richard was not prepared for what happened next.

"I been going through all kinds of shit within the last four days!" said the short brown-skinned guy angrily as he walked towards the living room followed by his mother holding his baby. "The police caught me in a car I didn't know was stolen, and I lost my keys!"

He then noticed Richard and asked, "Who is this?"

"Oh," answered his mother. "That's Mattie's cousin friend. He's waiting for her and her cousin to come out of your room."

Without another word, Sharod walked towards his bedroom. Richard's heart pounded in his chest, and he silently prayed that Kendu was still not having sex with the girl.

"What the fuck!" yelled Sharod as he stepped into his bedroom. Richard and Sharod's mother rushed to the bedroom to see what all the commotion was about. When they got to the room, Richard was relieved to see Kendu finally dressed and sitting on the bed.

"What is he doing here?" asked Sharod repeatedly to no one in particular as if he were in shock.

"That's Mattie's cousin Melvin," answered his mother.

"No it ain't," said Sharod in shock. "That's Kendu!"

His mother threw her hand to her mouth and looking at Mattie said, "Oh my God!"

Kendu with his hand inside of his jacket pocket said to Sharod, "Yo, let me talk to you in the hallway."

"Nah," replied Sharod still in shock that Kendu was in his bedroom. "I don't believe this shit."

Kendu stood up, and everyone looked at the jacket pocket with his hand inserted inside of it. They moved out of his way as he slowly made his way towards the door.

When he and Richard made their way out of the apartment, they took off running down the stairs and out of the building.

As they headed back to Lafayette Gardens Housing Projects, Richard asked out of breath, "What was all that about?'

Kendu laughed and said, "Me and punk ass Sharod had beef for the longest! And because of that, his moms knows who I am, but only by name. And as you can see, I'm fucking the nigga's baby mother."

"Well, at least you had a gun on you, if things had gotten out of control in there," said Richard.

Kendu laughed even harder, as he pulled his hand out of his pocket along with the inside lining revealing nothing!

"I don't carry guns," smiled Kendu. "I carry game!"

Richard smiled, remembering that day. Just thinking about his deceased best friend, caused him to smile. He sat the photo book down he had in his hands, as everyone else continued to look through the photo albums laughing and talking.

Chapter 16

"All you bitches are crazy!' laughed Pam. "Starting with this bitch Lisa. When she was living in New York, she was one of the flyest bitches in Brooklyn. Now she moved down south, and come back looking and sounding like Laura from Little House on the motherfucking Prairie! And then we got my girl Tonya. Now this bitch, went from being money hungry, to a damn deacon's wife, to having a boyfriend that just came home from jail that no one knows anything about! With her secretive ass. And last but not least, we have Gina. Now this bitch is caked up with a lot of money, but can't find a man that's willing to kick back and stay outta the motherfucking streets."

Gina's baby father Divine, left her over two million dollars before he was killed in the streets by the police.

"What bitch would get a man named Moe-dog, and think he would be faithful?" continued Pam. "Didn't the name 'dog' give your dumb ass a hint?"

Lisa, Gina, and Tonya laughed so hard they were in tears.

"What about you?" asked Lisa.

"Oh no, I'm good!" answered Pam causing them to laugh even harder. They all sat in Gina's livingroom eating Vanilla ice cream out of big bowls. This was one of their over night and long overdue pajama parties they hadn't had in over five years.

All four women were very beautiful and they knew it. Lisa was light skinned, 5'1, bowlegged with long black hair. Pam was 5'5, natural long sandy reddish hair, slim and with a complexion that older people call high yellow. She was so funny that most people believed that she could have easily been a comedian. Tonya's complexion was jet-black, she had long silky looking hair, chinky eyes, 5'5, a nice body with beautiful lips. Gina was also 5'5, brown skinned, and like the rest, she had long hair. All four women had bodies that made men drool and women envious. They had known one another since the early days of childhood and were more like sisters than best friends.

"First of all," said Tonya rolling her eyes and holding her hand up to Pam. "The reason none of y'all met Lamont yet, is because I have to make sure he's for real first, and not just one of these ignorant negroes who's only a hard you know what for the month."

All the young women laughed and give one another high fives as Tonya continued talking. "But I'm saying though, so far he's living up to everything he says. I seriously believe he loves me, but after that terrible marriage I went through, I wanna give our relationship a little more time. So in a sense, I'm still finding out what he's about."

Then changing the subject, she asked Pam, "What's up with you and Big Lord?"

Pam tilted her head to the side with a fake attitude and said, "No bitch, it's lord to you! I'm the only bitch that can call him Big Lord."

"Damn!" said Gina. "You act like she called the nigga Daddy or something!"

Everyone laughed, as Pam continued to fake her attitude.

"That's why," she continued, "I'm not inviting none of you peasant little bitches to my wedding!"

"What?" said Tonya. "A wedding better not even happen if I'm not invited. It's bad enough I missed Lisa's."

"Come on," laughed Pam. "Y'all my girls for life! Nothing goes down if y'all not involved," she imitated Christopher Walken in the movie 'King of New York.' "No dope deals, no black jack, no nothing! If Big Lord fucks me in a park, to watch, y'all can come in!"

"You stupid!" laughed Gina along with Tonya and Lisa.

Lisa had on a very long white tee shirt, and just her panties underneath. She tucked her legs under her to get comfortable on the sofa.

"Damn!" said Pam. "I hope you got on drawls, sitting on my girl's couch like that!"

"Shut up!" said Lisa as everyone laughed.

They were all comfortable. Tonya and Gina both wore long night gowns, and Pam had on a white tee shirt and white thermal bottoms.

"Yo my wedding is going to be phat!" said Pam, flashing the diamond ring Big Lord gave her, when he proposed to her last weekend over dinner. "This is proper, but I like that shit Omar put on Gloria's finger. That rock is crazy!"

"Word," agreed Gina. "That shit is crazy. I know he spent a lot of money on that. When I asked about it, he told me it was a 5.05 GIA VVS Fancy pink very rare diamond. I think he mentioned a few million dollars."

"Yeah, that's crazy," replied Tonya.

"But you gotta understand," said Lisa. "Big Lord can't go out buying stuff like that, because the Feds would be all over him. My brother bought that ring, with legal money from the record label and all the other stuff he got."

"Damn," whined Gina changing the subject. "I miss my son! Everytime he spends the weekend with his grandmother and aunt, I miss that bad ass boy."

"I know what you mean," said Lisa. "Because this is the first time I don't have Dejanay with me, and I'm thinking about what she's doing. I know she's driving her daddy crazy."

She then pouted, and said, "Richard told Mama Maria, she can have her for the summer. But we're staying too, because I'll miss my baby too much if we was to leave without her."

"Momma Maria?" asked Pam with her lip turned up. "Where in the fuck did you get that from?! Damn, you country! I'm telling you, you better never have little Dejanay calling me god-momma Pam."

They all laughed and continued eating ice cream.

"Oh man!' said Tonya quickly jumping up and grabbing the television's remote. "The Gangster Larry show is on. Y'all got me missing my show!"

She then clicked it on the cable channel, and a trinidadian brown-skinned brother with braids and a gold tooth, stood on a stage with his face screwed up. Most of his guest were rappers and R&B singers. Sometimes he would have actors and actresses.

Gangster Larry was known for not biting his tongue when it came to his interviews, and the only rappers that appeared on his show, were those who felt they had some kind of street credibility. Gangster Larry was 36 years old, and it was rumored that he once did 15 years in prison for murder. Everyone loved the realism of the show.

Pam, Tonya, Lisa and Gina sat there eating their ice cream with their eyes glued to the television.

A brown skinned rapper from Harlem in New York City sat on Gangster Larry's green interview couch as the audience applauded the rapper's presence.

The rapper came out wearing a too tight leather jacket, jeans with a long chain attached to his front pocket to the back pocket, and diamond infested jewelry. He looked at the crowd and screamed out, "Ball---"

"Shut the fuck up with that shit!' said Gangster Larry cutting the rapper off. "Don't be coming on my show with that bullshit! It's bad enough you got my four year old niece saying that shit all day."

The rapper smiled reclining back on the couch. He then said, "Yo Gangster Lar, I'm feeling your whole vibe."

"You feeling my vibe, huh?"

"Yeah no doubt," said the rapper with a smile as he looked around the studio. "This is real gangsta!"

"Unlike you," responded Gangster Larry causing the audience to laugh. "From what I hear, your whole team is snitches. I hear you told on someone who's upstate. We all know your man had testified against two people. I mean, what the fuck is going on with your team? Y'all make Harlem look bad."

"Oh snap!" said Gina laughing. "That's right Gangster Larry, check those rat bastards!"

"Nah," said the rapper. "Anything we say, everybody already know about it."

"Even the police?" asked Gangster Larry.

The rapper smiled, looked at his diamond infested watch and said "Especially the police."

"Do you know what a corroborator is?"

"A corroborator?"

"Yeah, a motherfucking corroborator!" said Gangster Larry angrily."Damn, y'all rappers are stupid! Anyway, it means a snitch nigga who supports or confirm evidence. And it's just my opinion, but it sounds like that's exactly what you're doing when you say the reason this rapper ran down south because so and so got killed and so on. The police doesn't need to hear you say things like that. But moving along, what are you presently doing?"

"I'm doing it all," the rapper smiled looking down at his team's record label logo. "My team is doing big things, I'm making a lot of moves making seven dollars off of each record sold on a independent level. Yeah!!!!!"

"One thing I can say," said Gangster Larry. "Y'all got a lot of niggas thinking they're gangsters ' cause they got shot up like two of your mans did. But I'm a gangster and I always thought the gangster was the one doing the shooting, not the one describing hand signs done or testifying on niggas. In that case, I made a lot of motherfuckers gangsters, as many niggas I done shot and they told on me."

The audience and even the rapper laughed at what he said.

"Anyway," continued Gangster Larry standing up. "I'm not in the habit of talking to corroborators and snitches for long. Plus, that's our time. Tell the audience what to expect from you besides telling!"

The rapper glared at Gangster Larry and then told the audience, "My new album will be in stores very soon, and I'll also be starring in a DVD. I forgot the name of it but you'll hear about it soon. And I can never be a rat. Yeah!!!"

The audience clapped and yelled out the rapper's name with much love and respect.

"And that's our show," said Gangster Larry walking off stage as the credits rolled and the rapper's song played with the audience dancing in front of their seats.

Tonya, Lisa, Pam and Gina laughed so hard, tears were rolling down their faces. Tonya turned the television off and tried to talk through her laughter. "That man.....that man is crazy! And none of them so-called gangster rappers ever try to swing on him, or nothing."

"Hell no!" laughed Gina. "The nigga already did 15 years for a murder. And he look like he wouldn't hesitate to go back and do 15 more if he had to!"

"15 years?!" Pam asked wide eyed. "Damn, I know the first bitch he fucked when he got out of jail, he probably ruined her pussy! Left her shit looking like Tonya's shit!"

They all laughed as Tonya tried to come back at her.

"Don't even try it," she said. "You're the one who is always having sex with someone who names always start with big: Big Mike, Big Lou, Big Gee, Big Kendu, Big Lord. So, I know your vagina is big and all messed up!"

The girls laughed as they wiped the tears of laughter from their eyes. When Pam was able to stop laughing, she looked at Tonya and said, "You know what? You can suck my dick....the back part, bitch!"

Gina had to walk out of the livingroom, in order to stop laughing. She couldn't take it anymore.

"Y'all is too much," said Lisa through her laughter. "But I love y'all crazy people. I just don't love New York anymore. All of you, need to up and move down to North Carolina."

"You crazy?!" asked Pam twisting up her pretty lips. "I would never move down there. I love you and all, but it is way too slow down there for me. I couldn't take living around them county niggas with a mouthful of gold teeth."

"Not every guy down south wear gold teeth," said Tonya.

"That's right!" stated Lisa. Then changing the subject, she asked Tonya, "So, what does this guy Lamont do for a living?"

Tonya glanced around a bit nervously and then answered, "To be truthful, I'm still trying to find out. He said he does construction, and I guess that explains all the money he be having. But when I go to his house, I never see any dirty clothes or filthy construction boots them guys be wearing. And one time he went to the bathroom and I looked in his closet and saw a big bag of money and a lot of guns. I know drug dealer is written all over his face, but I'm telling you, he is a perfect gentleman. He never shows any signs of violence or anything. Maybe he just collects guns like a lot of these guys out here. I don't know, but I'm telling you, he's a sweetheart."

"Well, just be careful," said Lisa.

"Pam, Lisa, and Tonya!" yelled Gina from the kitchen. "Come here, I wanna show y'all something!"

Chapter 17

L pulled the trigger two times killing the drug dealer. The dead drug dealer's partner looked at L fearfully pleading for his life. "Please man, don't kill me! I got a wife and kids. Here, just take the money," he handed L a briefcase full of cash.

Light and Fats quickly walked back to their car, and before getting inside, Light said, "Yo L, kill that nigga and let's get the fuck outta here!"

This was a hit paid by a Coney Island drug dealer over territory. He paid the Bulldog Crew ten thousand dollars to get rid of his two enemies and competitors. With the supplied information, they caught the two men leaving a strip club they owned out in Hempstead, Long Island. The two big time drug dealers/businessmen were leaving the club for the night, and the tall one, J.J. knew something was not right the moment they stepped out into the parking lot. Nothing surrounded them but darkness and J.J. knew after this night, he would definitely have bright lights installed in the club's parking area. His partner Pharoah walked to the car as if he had not a care in the world. Especially being their two body guards walked very closely behind them.

Light, Fats, and L came out of the darkness each holding .44's with silencers attached. Any weapon they needed, Hook supplied them with it.

The two body guards didn't know what hit them, when Light and Fats fired bullets into their heads and chests. When Pharoah spun around, he was rewarded with two .44 bullets to his head from L's gun. That's when Light and Fats walked back to their car, and J.J. was now pleading with L for his life, or at least trying to find out who had put the hit out on him.

"I know you're going to kill me," cried J.J. "But please, tell me who put this hit out on me!"

"A nigga name Cadillac," answered L.

"I knew it!" cried J.J. "Yo man, I know you're taking the money anyway," he pointed to the briefcase. "But please, I beg you to take some of it from me as a hit back on Cadillac. It's forty thousand dollars in there! I'm telling you man, Cadillac is an untrustworthy motherfucker!"

L smiled and said, "Don't worry about him, I got that." He then pulled the trigger two times blowing away parts of J.J.'s chest. But when L looked down at the dead body, he could have swore he saw a smile on J.J.'s face.

He rushed to the car and when he jumped in the back seat, Light quickly pulled out of the dark parking lot.

"What the fuck was you conversating with the nigga for?!" asked Light as he expertly drove back to Brooklyn.

L laughed, lifted the briefcase of money and said, "Homie wanted this forty thousand to go on Cadillac's head, and I don't mind doing it!"

"Nigga are you crazy!" asked Light angrily causing Fats to bust out laughing. "That nigga was in no position to be putting no hits out. You was taking the money anyway!"

"This nigga's taking hits for a dead man," laughed Fats. L knew what to say to get them to side with his decision.

"I'm saying though," said L. "Hook said Cadillac wanted this done, but he also said he don't really know Cadillac like that! So, why start leaving witnesses now?"

"Word" agreed Fats as expected. "I ain't going back to jail. That's outta the question!"

"Fuck it," Light shrugged his shoulders. "Dead he is. I don't give a fuck, one way or the other."

Light drove out to Gravesend Projects in Coney Island, and when he pulled up, he saw Cadillac talking to four of his workers who was just standing around. He blew his horn and after Cadillac recognized who was in the car, he walked over and slid in the back seat with L.

"What's the deal?" Cadillac asked the dangerous thugs as Light pulled away from the curb.

"Yo," said L. "Everything is good. We took care of your little problem."

"That's what I'm talking about!" laughed Cadillac. "These punk ass niggas out here, was acting like them muh'fuckers was straight up un-motherfucking-touchable!"

As L filled Cadillac in on how they killed his enemies, Light pulled up and parked on the darkest street he can find.

Without turning the car off, he twist his body at an angle to look in the back seat at Cadillac and said, "We fixed your little problem, but I think we have another little problem."

"What's up?" asked Cadillac confused.

Without answering, Light got out of the car and stood on the sidewalk with his hands in his pockets.

"Go and talk to him," said L nudging Cadillac's elbow.

He slowly got out of the car and approached Light to see what this was all about.

"What's up?" he asked. "What's going on, Light?"

"Yo," said Light. "How many people you told we were doing this hit for you?"

"Nobody!" said Cadillac feeling insulted. "I don't get down like that. Hook can tell you that!"

"Okay, that's cool," said Light throwing him off point.

It was so dark on that block, Cadillac didn't even see the gun in Light's hand, and he couldn't believe it when he felt the first bullet to his stomach. He tried to run, but L stepped out of the car firing his gun hitting Cadillac two times in the back. He then walked over and fired two more shots to his face as he stood over him.

L jumped back in the car and Light pulled away, as Fats laughed out loud to himself.

"What the fuck is wrong with you?" L asked Fats. "Laughing to yourself and shit. I think you starting to crack the fuck up!"

"Nah nigga," laughed Fats. "I'm just feeling that little situation. You know, no loose ends! But that means, we also have to kill everyone we do a hit for!"

He started laughing again as if someone had just told the funniest joke he'd ever heard.

L shook his head and asked Light, "What's up with Mont-Mont and C-Allah?"

"My wife kia," answered Light, "met a nigga that's sweating her, who's getting major paper. So, I told C-Allah and Mont-Mont to handle that while I handle this. But if you been with the crew instead of chasing that little bitch, you would've known what was up, nigga!"

"I'm here now, ain't I?" smiled L rubbing Light softly on the back of his neck causing him to laugh and wiggle his head away, as he continued to drive back to he and Kia's house.

$

Kia was looking as beautiful as ever. She looked absolutely tempting in her lingerie inspired white and light orange dress, by Dolce & Gabbana with Giuseppe Zanotti sandals and Fendi bag. She sat in the passenger seat of the black Range Rover, as the rich Jamaican drug dealer name Steppa drove through the Brooklyn streets. He bobbed his head to the song "Dude" by Beanie Man featuring Ms. Thing. His gunman Ziggy sat in the back seat nodding his head to the song.

Steppa turned the volume down, looked over at Kia with a smile and said, "Me gwan treat 'chu good, seen? Me like you and me not like these bumbaclot boys," he said waving his hand through the air before taking a pull from his spliff. "I tell you one ting. Me love loyalty and money, stay right and me treat 'chu good, seen?"

Kia smiled as he continued talking, and before she knew it, they were pulling up in front of the apartment building on Dean Street in the Crown Heights section of Brooklyn.

Kia had been to this building with Steppa at least five times already. It was one of his stash spots where he kept a lot of his money, and now Kia just hoped that everything would go according to plan. She felt extremely nervous because lately, Ziggy had been giving her funny looks. At times it seemed as if he knew what time it was and what was being planned. He truly gave Kia the creeps. She even thought about telling Light to forget about this one, but now it was too late. She even once questioned Light on why he still wanted to kill guys and take their money, being that he had enough money of his own. But instead of answering, he just smiled and walked out of the room.

As Kia stepped out of the Range Rover she looked across the street at the blue BMW with tinted windows parked and knew Mont-Mont and C-Allah was sitting inside waiting for things to unfold. Ziggy also stepped out of the Range Rover with his hand under his shirt holding onto the nine millimeter he carried. His thick sandy red dreads, came down pass his ass and he looked up and down the street until his eyes settled on the blue BMW parked across the street.

Kia's heart began to beat rapidly and she hoped everything turned out okay. She had never been so scared in her life! As she tried to signal Mont-Mont and C-Allah to dismiss the plan without being noticed, Steppa took her hand in his and walked up the steps to the building, as Ziggy followed behind.

They walked up to the second floor and entered the plush apartment. As they headed towards the living room, Ziggy locked the front door. Kia had to find a way to let Mont-Mont and C-Allah into the apartment, but Ziggy was acting more paranoid today than usual.

They sat in the livingroom counting stacks of money out of a big green army bag, as Steppa smoked his weed and talked about the pleasurable things he wanted to do to Kia.

Finally the opportunity presented itself when Ziggy had announced that he needed to use the bathroom. Once he was gone, Kia kissed Steppa on the neck and said, "Daddy, I'm thirsty! Do you want something to drink?"

"No mon," answered Steppa. "Me cool."

Kia stood up and walked out of the living room as if she was going to the kitchen but instead she went and opened the front door for Mont-Mont and C-Allah.

"He's in the livingroom" she whispered as Mont-Mont and C-Allah stepped inside of the apartment with their guns in their hands. "And Ziggy went to the bathroom."

C-Allah headed towards the bathroom, as Mont-Mont followed Kia into the livingroom.

"Bumbaclod!" yelled Steppa standing up and reaching for his gun when he saw Mont-Mont with Kia. But he was much too slow. Mont-Mont slapped him in the back of his head with the .44

Bulldog handgun and disarmed Steppa for his nine millimeter when he fell to the couch.

C-Allah crept carefully toward the bathroom, but was caught off guard when Ziggy quickly swung the bathroom door open firing two shots. The first one missed, but the second one caught C-Allah squarely in his left shoulder.

As he fell backwards to the floor, he fired off his own gun. All four shots were professionally placed in Ziggy's face and chest. He was dead before he hit the floor.

C-Allah stood up, laughed and shot the already dead Ziggy again, in what was left of his chest.

"What kinda' business is dis?" asked Steppa in his Jamaican accent. "Wah' me say boy?"

Instead of answering, Mont-Mont looked at Kia and asked, "Is this all the money here?"

"Yeah," answered Kia. "It's more than halfa'million right there in front of you!"

Steppa sucked his teeth, looked at Kia and said, "Mutter skunt, ya' dead! You hear me, gal?"

"Not before you!" said Mont-Mont, as C-Allah came into the living room holding his left shoulder.

"Oh my God!" said Kia rushing over to him. "He's hit!"

"It's not that bad," smiled C-Allah. "Get the money and let's get outta here before the police show up, and we gotta shoot our way up out this bitch!"

He then pointed his gun at Steppa, as Mont-Mont and Kia quickly loaded the big green bag back up with the money.

After they were done, Mont-Mont slung the bag over his shoulder, looked at Steppa and said, "So I guess this is it, huh rude boy? Your show is over."

Steppa sucked his teeth again and said, “Bwoy, suck out ya’ mutter!”

Mont-Mont raised his gun and shot Steppa in the face two times with his .44 Bulldog handgun. It looked as if he had never had a head on his body.

Kia was on the verge of throwing up, as she ran to the front door to get out of the apartment and get some air. This was way too much for her, and she had no plans to ever get involved with this kind of business ever again, regardless of what Light said!

They made it outside and after getting in Mont-Mont’s BMW and pulling away from the scene, C-Allah looked at his wounded shoulder and said, “Drop me off at my car. I can make it to my aunt’s house from there. She’s a doctor. Take the money, and I’ll meet up with y’all later at Kia’s house. Okay?”

“We can go with you to your aunt’s house,” said Kia very concerned.

“No,” replied C-Allah. “If she see y’all, she’ll ask too many questions. And Kia, don’t tell Melyssa I got shot. There’s no need for her to be worrying.”

“I got chu,” said Kia, as Mont-Mont quickly drove through the Brooklyn streets to get C-Allah to his car.

Chapter 18

Pam paced her big bedroom wondering where the hell was Big Lord. She'd been waiting for him to come home for the last two hours. She hoped that this wasn't what it was going to be like after they got married. They were suppose to be going out to dinner, and it wasn't like Big Lord to be late when it came to taking her out. He even called and said he was going to be a little late, but two hours to Pam was straight up ridiculous! But what she didn't know was that Big Lord was presently at the car dealership buying her the new Mercedes Benz she had mentioned on more than one occasion. However, this was nothing new. He loved her more than anything, and had always surprised her with very expensive gifts. Like the morning, she woke up out of the bed to find a big diamond ring on her ring finger and Big Lord standing at the foot of the bed with his shirt off singing off-key to Jagged Edge's song "Let's Get Married."

Pam laughed with her hands covering her mouth with tears of joy flowing from her eyes. Big Lord had then gave her a funny exotic dance as he came out of his sweat pants. He removed the cover from the bed and crawled between her legs, kissing his way up her body. They occasionally slept in the nude, so there was no time wasted removing her panties and bra.

Big Lord's tongue was like magic as he expertly explored her love tunnel. He inserted two of his fingers in her and gave a "Come here" motion that drove her crazy! She closed her eyes and arched her back as she rubbed his curly hair. But what really drove her crazy, was when he left his two fingers in her, and inserted his wet ring finger in her anus and moved all fingers inserted, back and forth as he licked her clitoris very quickly.

"Oh, oh, oh," Pam moaned as her legs began to shake. She was in no control of her own body, and was cumming so hard she thought she would pass out from what her man was doing to her. No man had ever made her feel so loved and complete. She wanted this to go on forever, and just when she thought things can get no better, Big Lord entered her with the ten inches of his love muscle as he kissed, licked, sucked, nibbled and fondled her behind her ears as he stroked deeply into her. He then flipped her over and gave it to her from behind as he lightly pulled her hair, causing her to cum again, again, and again.

"You like that ?"asked Big Lord as he stroked into her.

"Yes, yes, yes!" moaned Pam.

"Then tell me whose pussy is this."

"It's yours daddy!" screamed out Pam. "This pussy belongs to Big Lord, baby! It's yours!"

Big lord turned her onto her back in the missionary position, and as he stroked into her, he put her toes into his mouth as he continued to stroke.

That was one hell of a morning, and he definitely left Pam's vagina sore and satisfied that morning! Big Lord had truly put it on her!

Pam looked at her ladies Vacheron Constantin watch Big Lord had surprised her with, and began to smile. Why didn't she think of it sooner, she thought as she sat down on her bed. Big Lord was only late to meet her, when it came to surprising her with a gift that she had always wanted. So, she relaxed, and patiently waited for him to show up. Now, Pam's mind was on what he had gotten her as a surprise.

Pam grabbed the stereo's remote and hit the button. The sound of Michael Baisden's voice on 98.7 Kiss FM came through the stereo's speakers.

"This is the bad boy Michael Baisden, on the hottest station in town! And today's topic is: Why do good girls love bad boys! Yeah that's right, I said it! The bad boy himself. We're going to go to the phones, but first let me dedicate this record to all you Bad Mamma Jammas out there!"

"Oh shit, that's my song!" yelled Pam standing up dancing, knowing damn well that record came out probably before she was born!

After dancing through two more hot songs, Michael Baisden came back on the air. "That's what I'm talking about! Why do good girls love bad boys?"

"Because they can fuck!" Pam said through her laughter. "Who the hell want some wimp ass nigga?"

She quickly reached for the phone and dialed into the station, but like always she was unsuccessful getting through.

"Damn!" she yelled at the busy phone with her pretty face screwed up in a frown, and just when she was about to push the re-dial button, someone was ringing her door bell.

"Now who the hell can that be?" she asked herself before turning down the stereo's volume and making her way downstairs to answer the front door. Maybe it was one of her neighbors. It had to be, she thought. Because she nor Big Lord, invited people to their home or ever mentioned where they lived. She knew what Big Lord did for a living, and accepting him for who he was, was also understanding that she would have to take precautionary measures when it came to being in a relationship with him.

Pam pulled the living room's curtain aside, and looked out of the big picture window at the light-skinned postal worker with a package in his hands and a clip board on top of it. At first she was a bit skeptical about opening the door, but then she thought about Big Lord, and knew immediately that the package was her surprise.

Pam opened the door with a smile that quickly turned into fear, because the postal guy pushed his way into the house dropping the package and clip board, and pulling a gun from the small of his back. She was frightened out of her mind and thought things could get no worse, until two more guys with guns wearing ski masks entered the house also, closing the door behind them.

"If you wanna live," said Light, "tell us where the fucking money is, and don't bullshit us!"

"Wha-wha-" stammered Pam. "What money?"

"Didn't he say don't bullshit us?!" asked Mont-Mont angrily with his face screwed up behind the mask. "Now we don't have time to fucking play with you! Where do Big Lord keep the money?"

L looked at the pretty girl and didn't really want her to die, but knew she would, if she didn't cooperate.

"The money is upstairs," said a very scared Pam. "It's in the safe, in the bedroom."

L smiled and asked, "Is anyone else in the house?"

"No," answered Pam in a shaky voice. "I'm here by myself."

"Lead us to the bedroom!" said Light grabbing the back of Pam's neck tightly.

They walked up the stairs cautiously, and when they got in front of the bedroom, Light pushed Pam through the open door before he and his team entered.

"Where's the safe?" asked Light through clenched teeth.

"It's-It's," stammered Pam. "It's in the closet."

Mont-Mont entered the big walk-in closet, and after finding the safe he yelled out, "Tell that bitch to give me some numbers to this motherfucker!"

Light looked at Pam and she began calling out the numbers. "15 left, 38 right, and 5 left," she yelled out to him, surprised that she even remembered the numbers as scared as she was.

Pam was from the notorious Fort Greene Projects in Brooklyn and growing up, she saw many bodies drop and knew many killers, but something about these three guys scared her to death! She could tell that they would not hesitate to kill her if she didn't cooperate with them.

"Yo," yelled Mont-Mont from the closet. "It's not too much cash in here, homie!"

Light quickly walked to the closet leaving Pam and L alone.

After a minute's time, he returned from the closet carrying stacks of money with Mont-Mont following closely behind him. He threw the stacks of money on the bed and after counting one of the stacks, he figured each stack came up to one thousand dollars a piece. He then looked at Mont-Mont and said, "This shit is only fifteen thousand dollars. I thought your little brother Joseph said the nigga Big Lord was a millionaire."

"Yo, if he said he's a millionaire, he's a millionaire," said Mont-Mont. "And he should know, because he re-up his drugs from the nigga. Just because we ain't find a million, doesn't mean the nigga don't got it!'

Light looked at Pam and asked, "Where is the rest of the money?"

"I don't know," answered Pam truthfully as she trembled with fear. "That's the only safe I know about. And he gave me the numbers , just in case I wanted to do any shopping."

"Yo, I hope you ain't lying ," said L with his gun pointed at her head.

"No, I'm not lying," she said with tears falling from her eyes. "I swear, I'm telling the truth!"

"Yo," said Light to Mont-Mont . "Let's look around the house and see if we can find another safe or something. Yo L, stay up here and keep your eyes on that bitch."

"He don't have to watch her," said Mont-Mont raising his nine millimeter.

"Blam!" the gun shot went off hitting Pam in the right side of her chest. She fell to the floor holding the gunshot wound with a horrified look on her face.

"Yo! What the fuck you do that for?!" L screamed in Mont-Mont's face. "What the fuck is your problem?! He told me to watch her! Stupid motherfucker!'

"Fuck it," said Light with a smirk. "Dead is dead! Just finish the bitch off," he said walking out of the room.

"Sorry man," said Mont-Mont apologetically. "I just got mad 'cause this shit makes my little brother look like a liar. Just let me finish the bitch off, so we can help Light find that safe that's up in this house somewhere."

"Nah," said L angrily. "I got this! Go downstairs, and when I'm done I'll be down there."

He looked at his watch and said, "We can't stay in this house too much longer anyway."

"Sorry homie," said Mont-Mont again, giving L a pound before walking out of the room.

Pam was breathing heavily with blood all over her hands, as she clutched the hole in her chest.

"Please......please," she tried to talk but couldn't get the words out. "Don't ....don't----"

L raised his gun and pointed it at her head. He was just about to pull the trigger when the telephone on the bedroom's night stand began ringing. He quickly looked at the phone and after the third ring, the answering machine came on and did it's job.

"Pam, pick up the phone!" yelled the female caller. "It's me, Tonya! When you get in, call me back. At the moment, I'm on my way to meet Gina, then we gonna pick up Lisa. Bishop is watching their baby, so us girls are going out. If you don't have plans with Big Lord, hit me on my cell phone, and I'll let you know where we are at, so you can meet up with us. Okay......bye big head! Love you"

L could not believe what he had just heard. He rocked back and forth on his heels, as if someone had just hit him with a sledge hammer. They had made a very big mistake, and he had to think quick! He was very glad they all wore gloves as he picked up the telephone and quickly dialed 911 while looking at Pam.

When the operator came on the line he said, "There's a woman here who is dying! Hurry up and get here! The address is -----"

After he hung up the phone and before running out of the bedroom, he looked back at Pam holding her chest and hoped that she would make it. He did not want her to die!

Chapter 19

"Oh my God!" cried Lisa hugging Gina and Tonya. Tears fell from their faces as they wondered who could possibly do something like this to their best friend, Pam.

Big Lord's mind was racing a mile a minute as he sat in the corner of the room with his head in both of his hands.

They all sat in the emergency's waiting area at the Nassau Hospital in Long Island. Pam's family were on their way to the hospital and of course, they blamed Big Lord for what happened to her. They had always hated the fact that she was involved in a relationship with a drug dealer, no matter how much material things he gave her. But Big Lord didn't care how they felt about him and Pam's relationship. In his eyes, she was a grown woman and they had no right to try and dictate her decisions she made in life. However, now as she sat in the hospital's waiting room, he knew Pam getting shot totally justified the way her family viewed their relationship and their decisions. But right now in Lord's mind, it still wasn't about them. It was about the unbearable pain he had in his heart, and the murder in his eyes beneath his tears for whoever done this to his fiancé.

The Nassau County police had asked him a whole lot of questions but only received a few answers, and none of them was what he did for a living or who he thought would do something like this.

When he came home that day from the car dealership, his heart beat so fast he thought he would have a heart attack when he saw the paramedics bring Pam out of the house on a stretcher and something white over her nose and mouth. After explaining to the police and paramedics who he was, they allowed him to ride in the back of the ambulance with Pam and two of the EMS workers, as the police followed closely behind.

After answering a few questions about Pam and himself, he called Omar in tears telling him what had occurred and what hospital they were at, and like a chain reaction, everyone received the bad news and were on their way.

When Lisa, Gina and Tonya showed, Big Lord was upset that he could not tell them anything more than the little bit that he knew.

He wondered who would Pam trust to open the door for, being the police said it appeared to be no forced entry. Why would someone shoot her for after emptying out the bedroom's safe? Who called the ambulance after she was shot? All of these unanswered questions were going through Big Lord's mind, until the presence of Omar and his wife Gloria quickly entered the waiting area.

Big Lord stood up out of his chair, looked at Omar with tears in his eyes and asked, "Why? Why Pam, man?"

"Relax. Have a seat," said Omar grabbing his friend's elbow to sit down as he sat next to him.

Gloria walked over to Lisa, Tonya and Gina, to give the two men space to talk as well as find out what she could from the three crying girls.

"I'm fucked up Omar," said Big Lord with teary blood shot eyes. "I don't know who would do this shit, but when I find out, any and everybody involved is dying!"

Omar had no doubt in his mind that what his friend had just stated would come to pass. And it disturbed him terribly, because he knew it would only be more senseless Black on Black crime. When will it all stop? he thought. The way things were going, he knew the Ku Klux Klan and other racist people was very happy at the rate

Blacks were killing one another. But he did understand how Big Lord felt as he looked across the room at his wife Gloria. It was no doubt in his mind that he would be thinking the same way had something like that happened to his wife. However, he still felt the need to talk Big Lord out of whatever he was thinking. Because he knew a lot of people would possibly get hurt and that included innocent people as well, and that was what he was trying to avoid happening. Also, things had changed so much for Omar, that he felt he could not go back to the streets even if he wanted to. He was now a legitimate citizen that a lot of people depended on, and he could not just throw it all away because Pam had got shot. Of course he felt extremely saddened, because Pam was also like a sister to him, but he felt he would be letting a lot of people down for the sake of revenge. He was now a very powerful CEO of various businesses that did a lot of positive things in the Black communities, but he was also loyal to Big Lord. So, it bothered him that he could not be in the streets seeking revenge with his friend. He was torn between sticking to the advice he frequently gave the children at Kendu's Youth Center, and hitting the streets and getting busy with his comrade who was more like a brother to him than a friend.

Omar looked at Big Lord and letting it be known where he stood said, "Yo, I feel your pain and you know I do. But you just can't go out there killing everybody. And you know I can't get with that. I love you, but you know things changed."

"Yo Omar man, you my nigga for life!" Big Lord said sincerely knowing Omar's position in all of this. "I know you changed your life, and I can even appreciate what you're doing with the kids and shit. And as a real nigga, I would never pull you back into something you've worked so hard to get away from. Trust me homie, I got this!"

"So, when all of this is over, then what?" asked Omar. "Are you getting out of the game? Man, you see what this shit brings. We cannot keep putting our families and loved ones in the mix like this! I know Pam's your fiancé man, but shit also affects other people as well," he said nodding his head in the direction of his little sister Lisa, Gina and Tonya.

Big Lord then looked over at Lisa, Gina and Tonya crying uncontrollably, while Gloria tried to console them to no avail.

"You see that there?" Big Lord asked Omar without taking his eyes from the small group of women. "There's going to be a whole lot more of that, but it'll be for whoever's responsible for my fiancé being shot! I appreciate the speech Omar, but you can save that for the kids at Kendu's Youth Center! Because my mind is made up and the only thing that can stop me is my own demise, homeboy!"

Just then, Pam's parents rushed into the emergency's waiting area. Mr. Callabrass looked as if he was going to kill somebody as his wife clutched his arm tightly with tears falling from her eyes. They was just about to go to dinner when they received the phone call from Lisa telling them that Pam had been shot by someone who entered her home. The whole Callabrass family had become hysterical and upset upon hearing the bad news. Pam's brother had vowed to kill Big Lord or anyone who had anything to do with his sister being shot. But of course her brother Aaron wasn't even in Big Lord's league and he knew it. He was just talking more out of anger than anything else. Although he did have a gun, he'd never shot anyone in his life.

Lisa approached Mr. and Mrs. Callabrass, and after hugging them both, she told them everything she knew which wasn't much.

Just as they were about to sit down, a white clean shaven doctor came from the back area drying his hands with a paper towel.

Mr. and Mrs. Callabrass , Omar, Gloria, Lisa, Tonya and Gina had approached the doctor hoping to hear some good news.

When Big Lord was able to snap out of his thoughts, he also approached the doctor. He didn't even notice the presence of Pam's parents until now, and he could tell they were blaming him, from the way her mother was giving him the evil eye.

"I'm Mr. Callabrass," said Pam's father nervously shaking the doctor's hand. "How is my daughter?"

"Hi, I'm Doctor Willis Snyder. Uh, your daughter is breathing, but she is in critical condition. She had lost a lot of blood, so there's no telling how things can turn out. I'm doing everything I can to save your daughter, but it is still too early to be certain about things being that she was shot so close to the heart. But we have a very good medical staff here, so things should turn out okay for your daughter, sir."

"Thank you doctor," said Mr. Callabrass. "And please keep me informed on everything concerning my daughter."

"I will," said the doctor. "If you're up to it, you can follow me and I'll take you to see your daughter."

With that said, Mr. and Mrs. Callabrass followed the doctor to the intensive care unit where Pam was being treated.

"Did any of y'all get to go back there?" asked Omar to no one in particular.

"Yeah," answered Big Lord sadly. "Me and the girls went back there already. Man, they got tubes everywhere in her!"

They all sat back down and talked amongst themselves as to who might have done something like this, and who knew where Big Lord and Pam lived.

"It has to be someone who lives out here in Long Island that seen me and Pam come and go," said Big Lord to Omar. "Or probably somebody followed one of us to the house. Damn! I should have been down low, and kept her down low as well. Shit, we were doing too much motherfucking flossing!!!!"

"Don't start blaming yourself," said Gloria. "Right now, the most we can do is pray that she'll be okay."

"Excuse me," said Lisa standing up. "I'll be right back. I have to go and call Richard and let him know I'll be there soon, and let him know what's going on."

She walked away looking for a payphone and when she did, Gloria, Omar, Big Lord, Gina and Tonya pulled out their cell phones and quietly laughed. It felt good to laugh for that brief second at such a sad time.

"Damn, that girl is countrified!" said Gina.

Mr. and Mrs. Callabrass came back from seeing Pam and Mrs. Callabrass was crying as if she'd already lost her daughter, while her husband held onto her in a supportive embrace.

Mr. Callabrass had then let go of his wife and approached Big Lord. He pointed his finger into his chest and angrily said, "Nigger, if my daughter dies, I'm going to kill you myself!!!!!"

Before Big Lord could respond, Omar and Gloria stepped in front of Mr. Callabrass as Omar said angrily to him, "Listen Mr. Callabrass, I know that's your daughter and you love her. We all do! Especially Big Lord! Everything right now, is about Pam. It's not the time for no petty dislikes. Pam is family to every last one of us, and that's why we're all here, shedding tears and praying she comes out of this thing! This incident was probably just a break in, with nothing to do with Big Lord. Everything right now is about Pam, Mr.

Callabrass. Trust me, I do feel your pain. Pam is like a little sister to me. I watched her grow up with my little sister, and you know that."

Mr. Callabrass's face softened up as he stared at Omar. He then grabbed his wife's hand and walked out of the hospital without saying another word.

Lisa came back from the pay phone with a confused look on her face as she watched the Callabrass's departure.

"What happened?" she asked no one in particular.

Before anyone could answer her question, Big Lord's cell phone began ringing. "Hello?" he answered angrily.

"Yo Big Lord, this is Dakim from the Polo Grounds up in Harlem, baby."

"What's up?" asked Big Lord. He then said, "Listen little nigga, I'm not doing any business right now. Go see one of them faggots from Broadway."

"This ain't about business. Well, at least not that kind of business," said Dakim. "It's about your girl. I heard about her getting shot. Actually, I heard about it minutes after she got shot, and who did it."

"What?!" yelled Big Lord into the cell phone causing everyone in the emergency's waiting room to look at him.

"Yeah man," continued Dakim. "A nigga name Joseph from Harlem that's caking a little bit, had something to do with it. I know you know'em, 'cause he copped from you a few times. Anyway Big Lord, he got a crazy ass brother name Mont-Mont that came home from jail not long ago. He runs with them crazy ass Bulldog Crew niggas from outta Brooklyn! And I was wit' that punk ass nigga Joseph when he gave his brother information about where you rest your head. The nigga said he was driving through Hempstead and by happenstance, he happened to notice your car in the driveway, and you know your car is so tight, everybody knows your ride!"

Big Lord listened to the young boy on the other end of the phone point out one of his biggest mistakes he made in the game.

'Yo," continued Dakim. "I'ma call you back so we can make a deal. Just make sure no one knows or finds----"

Big Lord hung up the phone before he could finish talking. He then rushed out of the hospital without saying anything to anyone.

Lisa, Gina, Tonya and Gloria looked on wondering what the phone call was all about to make him run out of the hospital the way that he did. But Omar knew Big Lord had just gotten some information concerning who shot Pam, and he also knew a lot of bodies were going to drop before it was all said and done!!!

Chapter 20

L had a lot on his mind. He layed in his bed all morning just thinking about everything that had occurred. Had he known Pam was Tonya's friend, and Big lord was cool with Omar and Richard, he would have made sure the incident had never taken place. But it was all too late now. So he couldn't do anything at the moment but ride the situation out, and hope Tonya would not find out that he was involved. But the streets were talking, and the name "Bulldog Crew" was on everyone's tongue.

L knew putting Mont-Mont down with them was a big mistake. Mainly because he was too trigger happy like Light and Fats. Now thinking about it, he was glad that Fats wasn't there, because had he been, Pam would have sure enough been dead. Because no matter who objected to what, Fats rarely left the scene of a crime without putting a bullet or two in the head of his victims. So L was glad that Fat's wasn't there and was with C-Allah at the time scoping the whereabouts of a rich Queens drug dealer they had planned to rob and kill.

L didn't really have anything against Mont-Mont, he just wished he was a little more level headed like Tommy Guns, Big Dave and himself. Instead of being like Light and Fats. Already, Mont-Mont had killed two big time drug dealers from Harlem, one from Brooklyn and two from out of Queens. Every time he killed someone, you could see bitterness coming out of him, and with smiles, Light and Fats had no problem assisting and feeding him more victims. As far as C-Allah was concerned, L had no real problem with him either, but he didn't care for his funny acting ways. He figured it was some kind of 'Pretty Boy Syndrome' and he hated niggas acting like that. But unlike a lot of pretty boys, he knew C-

Allah wouldn't hesitate to get dirty and kill niggas. He heard about what he and Mont-Mont did to the two young boys over on Willoughby Avenue. But to L, it seemed as though C-Allah had two different personalities, and because of that, L was in no rush to do anything with the pretty boy thug.

L wondered what he should do today as he looked over at Tonya sleeping peacefully. He did not want to wake her, because she hadn't slept in nearly three days worrying about her best friend Pam. When she tearfully told L what occurred, he knew then that he could not tell her that he had any involvement in what went down. He had never felt for any woman the way he felt for Tonya. L was definitely in love. She was everything he'd always wanted in a woman. Also, she had a good job as a registered nurse, and loved him for who he was and not for what he could do for her like the many other girls he once was in relationships with. But had he known Tonya in her earlier days before she became a Christian, he would have never got the chance to be with her without spending some big money. Because five years ago, Tonya was very money hungry and almost every big time drug dealer in Brooklyn had tried to land her in their bed. But she was far from a hoe. In fact, she didn't even have sex with the majority of the guys she was involved with. Because she knew the art of seduction of getting men to spend their money without even having sex. She figured correctly most of the time, that all she had to do was look beautiful sitting beside them while feeding their egos and agreeing with everything they had thought to be right, leaving the stupid bastards believing that they had so much in common. And of course, it worked! The proof of it, was that Tonya was one of the most tricked on girls in Brooklyn! The guys would always try to make her wifey, and some of them even took care of her better than they took care of themselves! But all of that changed after she was raped by the thug Shameek and three of his soldiers who felt they couldn't get her otherwise. The rape, plus the beating they had later administered to her that landed her in the hospital for months, had changed her outlook on life. She had totally changed her ways, became a Christian, and married the deacon in her church. However, the marriage was short lived, because she and her husband were more like brother and sister than husband and wife. Tonya loved him but she was not in love with him. Now L was something totally different. She loved everything she knew about him and was deeply in love with him.

L leaned over and kissed Tonya on her forehead before getting out of bed. He walked into the living room and before he could turn on the television, the telephone began ringing. He snatched it up on the second ring hoping it did not wake Tonya. He knew she desperately needed the rest.

"Hello?" asked L sitting down on the couch.

"What's up baby boy? This is Fats."

"Oh, what up homie? What's good?"

"Ain't shit. You coming through today? Everybody is here. We're all at Kia's crib."

L looked at his watch and asked, "Why, what's up? What's popping today?"

"A whole lot," answered Fats. He then asked, "What's up wit' homegirl? You still wit'er?"

"Yeah, yeah," answered L without telling him that she was in the bedroom sleeping. "I'm not telling her I was there when her friend got popped though."

"You ain't suppose to. Yo, hold up….. Light wanna holla at you real quick."

L waited a few seconds before Light came on the line.

"What's up nigga?" asked Light.

"Ain't nothing," answered L. "I'm about to get dress, and I should be at Kia's in about an hour and a half."

"Nah, nah," said Light. "We about to roll out. Fats gotta go and change his clothes, so we shooting out to the Pink Houses real quick. Then we gotta go pick up his bitch, so we can pick you up before we go pick up Denise."

"Okay," said L. "That's cool. I'll be out in front of my building waiting on y'all."

"Yo, guess who I talked to for a brief minute."

"Who?" asked L curious to know.

"The nigga Bishop!" laughed Light. "He's suppose to come by Kia's crib later today."

"Word?!" asked L excitedly. "I ain't seen that nigga in mad years!"

"He said he wanted to talk to us," said Light, "but you know I don't play that phone shit!"

"You know what it's about, right?"

"Yeah, yeah," answered Light.

"Yo kid, I'm out!" he said changing the subject. "We'll see you in a minute!"

"Aiight cool," said L hanging up the phone. He then smiled to himself, because he knew it would definitely be church today. Whenever Richard wanted to talk, you could expect to hear some bible scriptures or a long lecture about being saved.

After getting dressed and kissing Tonya, L grabbed one of his guns and headed out of the apartment to meet up with the infamous Bulldog Crew. They picked him up and made their way to Bedford and Dekalb Avenues.

When they pulled up in front of Denise's house, young boys and girls on the block wondered who was getting out of the two black Mercedes Benzes, and when they stepped out all eyes were on them. Those who knew who they were quickly got out of the area wondering what they were up to.

Instead of going straight to Denise's apartment, they first headed towards the grocery store on the corner owned by some Arabs. No one in the neighborhood had ever violated the Arabs, because they were known to have an assortment of weapons in their store and would not hesitate to kill anyone who posed a threat to them or their establishment. But when Light, L, Fats, Mont-Mont and C-Allah entered the store, the owner Abib Mustafah Ali's face turned pale as though he had saw a ghost! His young friend Suliman Muhammad looked on, wondering why his boss and father figure looked so terrified at the sight of the five young Black men that entered the store. He stood near the freezer with his hand near his waist just in case he had to reach for the gun he carried. He was eager to kill a Black person that posed a threat to his people, especially his boss and mentor Abib Mustafah Ali.

The Bulldog Crew purchased their sodas, potato chips, and cigarettes and walked out of the store.

Suliman Muhammad relaxed, looked at his boss and wondered why his hands were shaking. He knew Abib to be the toughest one out of their whole Arab crew, and had even served in the Iraqi Army at one time. So he could not understand why his boss was showing signs of fear of the five young Black niggers!

"Abib, what is the problem? What is wrong?" asked Suliman.

Abib looked at his young comrade and with a shaky voice said, "Suliman, you know who I am and I fear no man but Allah. But

I am no fool either. I am a very wise man and that is why I have lived this long. But you saw them five black men?"

Suliman nodded his head "Yes".

"The eyes are the windows to the soul," continued Abib. "And who you have just saw come into the store, was the Katibat Al Mawt!"

Suliman's mouth dropped open, because his boss had just told him that they were in the presence of the "Squad of Death!"

After picking up Denise, the Bulldog Crew were in route back to Jamaica Queens to Kia's house.

When they reached their destination, they noticed a rented blue Ford Taurus parked next to Kia's car. Pulling out their guns, they entered the house after Light used his key. Walking into the kitchen, they relaxed and put away their guns when they saw Richard had already arrived.

Richard sat at the kitchen table preaching the word to Kia, Melyssa and Jenny, as they looked on with smiles on their faces at the handsome Pastor.

"When a man finds a wife," said Richard, "he finds a good thing. The two shall come together and bec—"

"Hold up!" interrupted Light causing Richard and the three girls to look in his direction, as he, the Bulldog Crew and Denise entered the kitchen.

"Man, you ain't been here a hot minute yet," smiled Light, "and already you're try'na get niggas married and shit! That 's why I ain't write your ass back, when you was writing me when I was up north!"

Everyone laughed as Richard got up and hugged Light, Fats, and L. "It's good to see all of you." Smiled Richard. "Especially you, L. Considering you are the only one, that responded to any of my letters."

L laughed and really felt good seeing his friend Richard after all these years. He always saw Richard as family.

Richard then looked at the new Bulldog members and shaking their hands said, "You two must be Mont-Mont and C-Allah."

Everyone looked surprised that he would know their names.

"Don't be surprised ," smiled Richard. "Information even comes to those in the church about the streets."

"So," smiled Light. "How long are you in New York?"

"Not long," answered Richard. "But you know I had to come and talk to y'all."

"And we already know what's about!" laughed Fats.

"Let's talk in private," said Light leading the way upstairs until Richard touched his arm.

"No disrespect," said Richard. "I know Mont-Mont and the good brother C-Allah here is okay, but I would like to speak to you, L and Fats."

"That's cool," said Mont-Mont sitting down at the kitchen table. "I'm hungry anyway. Kia, hook a nigga up!"

"Boy," said Kia. "You better call one of them Spanish lil' bitches to serve you nigga!"

"See," responded Mont-Mont. "That's why I fucks with the Spanish mommies. They don't give you all this yadda, yadda, yadda when it's time to make a nigga comfortable."

"Yeah, my nigga!" said Kia causing everyone to laugh.

Denise introduced herself to Kia, Melyssa and Jenny.

C-Allah kissed Melyssa on the side of her neck as Mont-Mont raided the refrigerator taking bites out of everything he saw.

Light, Fats, L and Richard sat in the upstairs bedroom having a very heated discussion.

"Why did y'all shoot Pam?" asked Richard. "That's family!"

"We didn't know," said Light shrugging his shoulders. "If we would've knew, the bitch wouldn't had got shot."

"Don't look at me!" laughed Fats. "I wasn't even there, or know what the broad look like!'

"Fuck you want us to say?" asked Light shrugging his shoulders again. "We didn't know who the bitch was and she got shot. Shit happens!"

Light was making Richard very upset with his 'I don't care' attitude and he did not hesitate to let it be known when he pointed his finger at Light's chest and said, "See, that's why you need to stop doing what you're doing! Innocent people are getting hurt and y'all don't know who's who!'

Fed up with the whole conversation, Light angrily said, "Yo Bishop, you know what? I don't give a fuck! Fuck Pam, Fuck Big lord and fuck whoever else that want it! Shit, you can get it too, nigga!"

"Whoa!" said L speaking up for the first time. "Light, chill out man. That's Bishop! We can't start flipping on each other!"

"Nigga I don't give a fuck!" replied Light with his face screwed up. "Matterfact, I don't wanna hear no more of this shit!" he said walking out of the room.

Fats laughed and walked out behind him.

"Yo Bishop," said L. "You have to believe me man. We didn't know. I was the one to find out after she was shot. And she would have been dead if Tonya didn't call."

"Tonya?" asked Richard confused.

"Yeah," explained L. "Tonya's my girl, but she doesn't know I was there or what I really do for a living. But when I heard her voice on the answering machine mentioning you and Lisa's name, I knew a very big mistake was made. I'm the one who called the ambulance."

It all made sense now. L was the one who Lisa said, no one got a chance to meet Tonya's boyfriend as of yet.

Richard looked at L, gave him a firm handshake and said "I understand. But you know if Divine was still alive he would agree with me on this one, right?"

"Yeah, I know man," answered L. "I know."

Chapter 21

Hook and two of his soldiers stepped out of the restaurant in Manhattan, and was greeted by New York's evening chilly weather.

Hook smiled while buttoning up the light jacket he wore, but changed his mind when he saw four young boys coming his way with angry looks on their faces.

"Yo, watch them niggas!" Hook told his two soldiers.

The four young boys still at quite a distance wasted no time at all as they pulled for their guns and began firing at Hook recklessly. None of the bullets hit their target, giving Hook and his two soldiers a chance to pull for their guns and fire back as well.

Both of Hook's soldiers was gunned down by the four youths, but Hook could not see himself going out like that. He let off six shots from the .50 Caliber handgun he held in his hand, as he ran towards his black Mercedes Benz.

Blam! Blam! Blam! Blam! Blam!

He knew he hit three out of the four young boys coming for him as he reached his car and jumped into the driver's seat and quickly drove away from the area. He also knew the police would probably be on the scene before he could even get to the FDR Drive to get back to Brooklyn.

He turned his car's stereo volume up to five, pushed the cigarette lighter in and turned on his windshield wipers. All three things made the dashboard on the passenger's side drop open. After placing the gun into the built-in stash spot, he pushed the dashboard back into place and made the necessary adjustments to keep it locked. He wasn't worried about the police getting his license plate number, because when the dashboard dropped, his license plate raised up into the trunk leaving nothing to be seen.

Hook wondered who the hell was gunning for him! He knew it couldn't be a robbery, unless the young boys were accustomed to robbing their victims after killing them! This was definitely an attempt on his life, and he was ready to kill whoever put the hit out on him. It was a good thing the four young boys were amateurs, he thought. Because had they not been, Hook would've been left back there dead with his two soldiers!!!!

$

"I don't give a fuck!" yelled Big Lord. "You came in here, telling me Little Petey, Mike, and Preme got killed like I'm suppose to get fucking teary eyed?! When the bitch called me, and said the nigga Hook was in the restaurant, all y'all niggas had to do was walk up to the nigga when he was leaving the place and give it to the punk motherfucker! I don't care about his two soldiers dying! It's that nigga I wanted!"

The young boy sat on the sofa in the livingroom of Big Lord's apartment in Brooklyn on Jefferson Street. He was scared to death, as he sat across from Big Lord, Moe-dog and Whitey!

The sounds of Oh-Boy's new song "Break Bread Wit' Me" came blasting through the livingroom's expensive stereo.

Whitey stood up, pulling out his nine millimeter and with no emotions or words, shot the young boy one time in the head. He then walked over to the stereo and after turning it down asked Big Lord, "So, what do you wanna do?"

"You know what I wanna do!" answered Big Lord angrily. "I want the Bulldog Crew, Hook, and whoever's close to them dead! I don't care how much money y'all want! And listen to me, I want y'all to be more ruthless than y'all ever been! You hear me?!"

"Do you have any information on these niggas?" asked Moe-dog.

"Yeah," answered Big Lord with a frown. "I found out where one of their bitches lives, and I know where one of their little brothers is at. Matterfact, that's the little cock sucker that crossed me! I want 'em dead! I want everybody dead, and like I said, I don't give a flying fuck how much it cost me to get the shit done!"

"The first job is getting this piece of shit out of your livingroom," said Moe-dog pointing at the dead young boy slumped over on the sofa with blood pouring out of his head!

$

"I didn't know who the fuck them young niggas was!" Hook said angrily over the phone. "Now I'm hearing them niggas was down with Big Lord! I ain't never have beef with that nigga, but you can bet your ass, the shit is on now!"

Light laughed and said, "It seems we got the same enemy. I hear the nigga Big Lord want me and my team dead as well."

"But what the boy want wit' me?" complained Hook.

"My man Mont-Mont shot his bitch," laughed Light. "He probably think you da' one that had it done."

"Man, y'all boys got me in all kinda shit. But look here, the boy wanna get busy? Then we can tear the whole Brooklyn up! 'Cause ain't nobody doing shit to Hook!"

Light laughed again and said, "And I hear the dude got Moe-dog and Whitey moving with him now."

"What?!" Hook screamed into the phone realizing how serious the beef really was. "Fuck it, the shit is on! If y'all need money, guns or whatever, I got it! Get in touch with the rest of the Bulldog Crew and meet me at my crib in the 'Ville. I got a little information on one of them boys!"

"Bet!" laughed Light as if the whole situation was a joke. "Yo Hook, we'll get up with you in an hour!"

$

"Where's your brother?" Moe-dog asked the tortured Joseph.

"I don't know," cried Joseph telling the truth with no teeth left in his mouth.

He knew his friend Dakim had set him up. Dakim had always wanted to be the man in Harlem. So when Big Lord called him back and said he had three free kilos of cocaine for him and to get it, all he had to do was set Joseph up, he was more than eager to take advantage of the opportunity. He was already familiar with Joseph's drug spots and workers, so all he would have to do now was wait until the very dangerous Mont-Mont met his demise and he would be free. But he had no idea how ruthless and dangerous the men he was playing with were. So he called his friend Joseph up and said, "Yo, what's up? I'm down on the block and I got something major we can get into."

"Word?" asked Joseph. "What's up yo?"

"Yo, you know we can't talk on these mouth pieces about business," said Dakim. "The pigs run the farm, baby. I got my cousin's van. Meet me on the block."

"Give me an hour," said Joseph hanging up the phone.

It took him 45 minutes to get to 145th Street and Edgecomb, and when he saw Dakim leaning against a beige van with tinted windows, he double parked his car, got out and approached him.

"Yo, what's good?" Joseph asked giving him a pound.

"Check," said Dakim. "My cousin from outta Brooklyn gave me a gold mine! I just ain't got the work to supply the muh'fucker! That's where you come in."

"Nah, I ain't fucking wit'Brooklyn!' said Joseph.

"I said my cousin's from Brooklyn, not the spot! The spot is in the Bronx, and I wanna show it to you."

"Aiight bet," said Joseph. "I'll follow you in my car."

"Nah," stated Dakim opening the van's door, "let's ride together. Park your whip."

Before Joseph could respond, Dakim jumped in the van, turned the ignition and turning on the radio. The sounds of Beyonce's song, "Me, Myself and I" came blasting through the speakers, as Dakim bobbed his head to the music.

After Joseph parked his car, he jumped in the stolen van's passenger's seat. And before Dakim could even put the van in drive, someone in the back of the van grabbed Joseph by the neck trying to choke life out of him.

Big Lord applied pressure as Dakim quickly jumped out of the van and walked away. Whitey jumped in the driver's seat, put the van in drive and pulled away from the area, as Big Lord and Moe-dog dragged Joseph to the back of the van. They took turns beating him with the brass knuckles on their hands. They would repeatedly knock him out only to wake him up again.

"I'ma ask you again," said Moe-dog. "Where's your faggot ass brother at?"

Joseph knew he would not escape this situation alive no matter what he said, so he made up his mind to die with some kind of honor. He looked at Moe-dog and Big Lord through bloody eyes that were swollen and said, "Fuck y'all! My brova' gone kill all y'all muh'fuckers!"

Tears mixed in with his blood, as Big Lord pulled his gun out and shot Joseph in the head two times.

"Why the fuck you ain't let me finish torturing him?" asked Moe-dog in a state of confusion.

"Because I got tired, of looking at his punk ass alive," answered Big Lord. "Plus, we got other things to do."

He then opened the van's side door and threw Joseph's dead body out of the moving van!!!

$

"Shut the fuck up!" said Mont-Mont with a two foot metal pipe in his hands. He then hit Tammy in the head with it knocking her out cold.

"Yo Light," said an angry Mont-Mont. "Wake this stupid bitch up for me. And when I catch her man Whitey, it's wrap! I'll teach this dumb bitch what happens when she fucks with them dirty cracker dogs!"

Light laughed and threw the pitcher of cold water he had in his hands in Tammy's face. She was beaten beyond recognition. They had her gagged, stripped down naked and tied down to her bed. Her sister Stefani lay dead in the living room with two bullets to the back of her head.

When Tammy came to, Mont-Mont asked Light to grab her legs.

Laughingly he did so, and Mont-Mont shoved the long pipe in her vagina causing her to pass out for the final time as the blood ran down her legs. He then pulled out his nine millimeter with the silencer attached and shot Tammy one time in the forehead. She laid there on the bed with the bullet to the head and the pipe stuck in her vagina. They left the pipe in her, being they both wore gloves. They were both hip to forensic science the police used to track down killers. Being in Attica for all those years had given them the opportunity to run into all kinds of convicted killers and learn as much as possible from the mistakes they'd made. Maybe if the prisons still had college and other beneficial programs the Governor had taken away, the inmates would have had positive things to occupy their minds, instead of learning from the everyday war stories that only led to producing some new ones.

"They think this shit is a fucking game?!" asked Mont-Mont with his face screwed up. "You don't kill my brother and think you're getting away with it!"

Getting into Tammy's house was easier than they thought it would be. When they first knocked on the door, Stefani looked through the peep-hole and after seeing how handsome Light was to her, not only did she wonder who he was, but also what he was knocking on their door for. Her sister was holding out on her, she thought as she opened the door with her sexiest smile. But before she can even ask who he wanted to speak to, she was pushed to the floor as Light and Mont-Mont barged into the apartment with their guns in their hands.

Before Stefani could scream or say anything, Light shot her two times in the back of the head with his silencer attached .44 Bulldog handgun.

Tammy didn't hear anything from the bedroom as she layed there in bed sleeping, and as they walked towards the bedroom, Mont-Mont pulled the pipe from the black bag he carried.

When Tammy felt the pain shoot up from her legs to her head, she woke up immediately. Mont-Mont smacked her in the head with the metal pipe knocking her out cold.

When she came to, she was bound and gagged, with two madmen standing over her with one of them smiling and the other holding onto a metal pipe.

Now all because of her relationship with Whitey, Tammy and her sister was murdered at an early age!

"So, who do you think set your brother up?" asked Light.

"Not who I think," answered Mont-Mont. "It's who I know! All of a sudden his main man Dakim just up and disappears. But guess what? I know where the hamster is hiding!"

"That's what I'm talking about!" smiled Light. "Let's get outta here kiddo!"

Chapter 22

"The war is on," said Omar shaking his head sadly as he read the newspaper. "This shit doesn't make any sense. I'm surprised the police don't know who's doing all these killings. Especially nowadays, with so many snitches in the streets!"

"Maybe the police wants to sit back and watch the two groups kill one another," suggested Richard.

"No, that can't be it," said Omar shaking his head. "Too many innocent people are getting killed. You know, I was at this youth center the other day and we had a discussion about what we would like to see more of in the 'hood. And believe it or not, after jobs, almost everyone said they would like to see peace."

"That's a good thing," smiled Richard, "Now we just have to work at achieving it."

"I believe we can," said Omar in deep thought. "But in order to do it, we need to open more youth centers, create more jobs for our people, and police our own neighborhoods. I mean, I know we always gonna have the Moe-dog's, Whitey's, Bulldog Crews and so on, but these racist trigger happy policemen who's coming in our neighborhoods killing our children are no better. They're killing us at an alarming rate. And fuck what these politicians are saying, shit is getting worse. I remember when I was young, the police would chase you through alleys, across roof tops and all through projects to catch you. But if you got away, you got away. Because nine times outta ten, what they chasing you for would be for bullshit anyway. But nowadays, if you try to run they wouldn't waste time chasing you, they'll just zero in on your back and shoot to kill. Them lazy bastards. Even sneaking on the subway now, can get you killed. And if you're fortunate enough to have never been arrested, then you'll have the benefit of having one of these negro Reverends to put a march together to protest your death for a day or two. Man, fuck marching! Excuse my language, but these people don't have no problem letting us walk off our anger. We have to come up with a different tactic. We need peace in our neighborhoods, and the key to achieving that is changing society so shit like this doesn't happen!"

"We went from talking about the Bulldog Crew to police officers," laughed Richard. "I guess there is no difference, huh? But seriously, from what I've read, the Black police officers couldn't even police our neighborhoods. Because they don't get respect in their own precincts, so them policing where we live may be an illusion. Those in control doesn't want a reality of that."

"Fuck what they want," said Omar annoyed. "It's about what we want! You don't see any Black officers gunning down people in the streets. Why is that? Either Black officers are more compassionate or White officers are exercising their racist side in our communities. Come on, what do you think would happen if Black police officers were in an all white neighborhood, and shot an innocent white man 41 times? Or killed little Johnny taking a short cut home across a roof top? Shit, not only would the Black police officers responsible be convicted in court, but every black police officer in that department will be relocated elsewhere to assure that it would never happen again. But back to what you were saying; I agree that Black police officers don't get respect in the police departments, and it's just as much racism in there. But I do think that would change, if the Black officers in these precincts were from these same neighborhoods and were allowed to police them to make sure citizens were safe. I remember reading an article in a magazine, a Black officer said every time he arrested a white youth in the white area where he worked, he would get upset, because his superior officer would know the suspect's family, and after contacting the parents the youth would be sent home from the precinct sometimes without even any kind of warning! Mind you, these white youths would sometimes be over the age of 18! Also, he said when he was called to respond to a situation, once he arrived at the home he was told by white people from the area that they did not want him and would only file their complaint with the white officer, so he would have to leave and a white officer would be brought in to handle the situation. Their situation! Imagine that! Shit, we should do the same thing, and tell white officers to get lost, because we'll handle our own problems or request a black police only!"

Richard laughed, but he could see Omar's logic. It did make sense to a degree, he had to admit.

"What I wanna do," continued Omar, "is create more jobs for our people in these poor areas. Those ghettos! And niggas coming out of prison. I just opened up three hair salons in Brooklyn, and two supermarkets in Queens, and all of the people that works for me lives inside of those areas. Imagine if every Black celebrity opened a business in the areas they grew up in. Shit most of them could fix up the whole neighborhood where they come from with all the money they got!"

"Are you two going to sit in this living room all day long?" asked Gloria walking into the room looking like a young version of Phylisha Rashad from the Cosby Show.

"The party is in the backyard!" she announced with her hand on her hip looking at Omar and Richard.

"We're coming now," replied Omar as he and Richard stood up from the sofa and made their way to the backyard.

They entered the big backyard area and the sounds of Jay-Z's song "Justify My Thug" blared through the speakers, as Lisa,

Gina and Tonya sat pool-side with their feet in the water as they talked. They were trying to enjoy themselves, but things were not the same without their best friend Pam.

"Here," smiled Gloria handing Omar and Richard two aprons. "It's time for you two to work the grill again. We need more hot dogs and hamburgers. Let's get to work," she walked away smiling.

Omar and Richard put the aprons on and proceeded to get busy as they continued conversing about what they talked about inside the house.

Little Dejanay and little Divine sat together on a beach chair playing with toys, wearing their cute little bathing suits.

"My baby is open!" smiled Gina as she looked at her son and Lisa's daughter. "That boy is bad! But whenever he's around Dejanay, he's on his best behavior. Displaying manners and all."

"He must get it from his father" laughed Tonya. "Because you sure ain't got no manners."

The three girls laughed.

"Lisa," said Gina, "this bitch definitely didn't get a chance to meet big Divine, right? Because if she did, she would not had said that. Divine didn't give a fuck! I mean, he treated me like a queen and all, but all that mannerism shit you can forget that!"

She then added, "So, my baby does gets his excellent mannerisms from me, heifer!"

They all laughed, and Lisa thought about how close Divine and her husband Richard was. They were so close he even laid his life down for his friend. He loved him like a brother and had never showed any signs of betrayal towards his comrade.

"So, what's up with Lamont?" Gina asked Tonya. "Why didn't you invite him to the cook-out?"

Tonya paused before answering.

"Huh?" she stuttered. "Oh, I did ask him, but he had other things to do," she lied.

The truth of the matter was, she found out what L really did for a living, and hated the fact that she allowed herself to fall in love with him. She also heard from an old friend in Fort Greene Projects, that L was part of the infamous Bulldog Crew and had also played a role in Pam getting shot. The streets knew everything! Tonya was surprised to find all this out, and to hear that a war was going on and whoever got in either side's way was getting murdered! A few people had even saw Moe-dog and Whitey with Big Lord and knew that the Bulldog Crew had finally met their match.

When Tonya had first heard the rumors, she went straight to L's apartment in Brownsville and confronted him.

"Why didn't you tell me that you're part of this Bulldog Crew?" she asked angrily. "I'm walking around like you're the sweetest angel and don't even know my life is in danger for just being with you! No wonder these guys around here is scared to speak to me! L, you're a killer!!! I don't believe this."

When she first entered the apartment, L was doing push ups in his living room as the O.G's new CD played through the stereo. He had no idea what he could tell Tonya as she stared angrily at him waiting to hear his response. He didn't know how much she knew, so he decided to just tell the truth and hoped she would understand.

L grabbed his white tank top off the couch and after putting it on, he turned down the stereo. He then sat down grabbing Tonya's hand directing her to sit down as well, as he tried explaining everything he could without exposing too much.

"It's a long story baby," began L. "Basically, yes I've been running with a few of my homies since we were kids. You know, doing stick ups and other kinds of stuff. Before we knew it, we were known as the infamous Bulldog Crew that had beef with the world!"

"So, you're working construction is a lie?" asked Tonya very quietly.

"Yes," answered L in a tone just as low.

He figured he'd might as well come clean.

"When I first met you," he continued, "I couldn't tell you what I did for a living. I knew it would've only scared you away. Tonya, before you, I have never met a beautiful, intelligent, caring, humorous woman who loved me for me, and not just what I can do for her. You mean everything to me, and I don't want to lose you. Ever! I'll make sure nothing happens to you, even if I have to put myself in danger. Since we've been together, I even thought about leaving this life alone on many occasions. But I've accumulated so many enemies, that quitting now can possibly mean straight up getting killed."

"Bishop did it!" said Tonya trying to understand.

"Bishop's problems, died with Diving. My situation is much deeper than that."

"It doesn't make any sense. If you have so many enemies, why would you create more?"

L got up and paced the living room floor, running his hand over his corn-row braids.

"Well, besides the money?" he asked himself before giving her an answer. "Once you're accustomed to putting in work, and you create so many enemies nothing really matters anymore. It's like playing a game of survival. And the winner is the one who outlives his enemies, or stay in a position where niggas is scared to come against you. In a sense, it's very hard to explain."

Tonya couldn't believe the words coming out of L's mouth. She had never in her life been with a man that was considered to be so ruthless to others, and at the same time so caring and loving to her. It was as if, he had two different personalities, and she wanted to know who the real L was being that she loved him so much. Tears came to her eyes as she asked her next most difficult question. L knew sooner or later it would come.

"So, why you shoot Pam?!" she asked painfully.

L sighed, sat down next to her and said, "Baby, please believe me. I did not shoot Pam. I can't really go into details," he said, knowing to do so would put Light and Mont-Mont out there and that was something he would never do!

"I'm the one who called the ambulance," he continued. 'I heard your voice on the answering machine and couldn't believe the mistake that was made."

Tonya buried her face in her hands and cried. She then stood up from the sofa sniffling and walked to the door.

L quickly followed behind her and when they reached the door, he spun her around to face him and looked into her tear streaked face. He kissed her gently as he wiped her tears away with his thumb.

Tonya looked back into his eyes as she continued to sniffle and cry. She then said, "I need to be alone for a while."

"I understand," said L giving her a hug and a kiss on her cheek. He really hoped this wasn't the end of their relationship.

Tonya pulled away from him with a little smile, letting him know that she loved him and that everything would be okay in time. But actually, she wasn't sure if it would be.

"I would like to meet Lamont," said Gina standing up and tying a big yellow towel around her waist. "He seems nice."

"You already met him," responded Lisa causing Tonya to look at her like she lost her damn mind or something!

"What?" asked Gina confused and sitting back down. "When did I meet him?"

Lisa and Tonya looked at one another without answering. The sounds of Janet Jackson's song "I Want You" played through the speakers as Gloria helped Omar and Richard put the food on the table.

After a ten second pause, Lisa sighed and said, "I have a big mouth. I should've never said anything. But we're all like sisters and we never hid anything from one another. So, I just felt that I should tell—"

"You met him at Lisa and Richard's wedding," interrupted Tonya getting it over with.

"At their wedding?" asked Gina trying to remember and wondering who Lamont was.

"Yeah," answered Lisa refreshing her memory. "He was down with your Divine. He was one of the Bulldog Crew Divine had there."

"Oh, you're talking about L!" said Gina excitedly. "All this time I'm hearing the name Lamont and it's L. Damn girl, you went and got you a gangster!" she laughed.

Lisa and Tonya didn't.

"Them niggas stay in the newspapers," continued Gina. "Them boys is crazy. Matter of fact, they came to my house not too long ago to check on me and little Divine. And they got two new niggas running with them now. I'm talking two cuties!' she smiled.

Lisa and Tonya both had their heads down as Gina talked. Lisa then looked up sadly and said, "They are the ones that shot Pam."

"What?!" yelled Gina causing Omar, Gloria and Richard to look in their direction.

"I know you didn't just say what the fuck I thought you said," continued Gina with her face drawn tight. "Didn't they know that's our fucking sister?!!" she yelled angrily.

Chapter 23

Light, Fats and Mont-Mont were out trying to find Dakim, the young boy who had little Joseph set up and killed. They had just left Kia's house no more than an hour ago. They put their plan together and figured they would have no problems snatching up Dakim once they located him. They tried to get in touch with L, but his cell phone just kept ringing. Light was getting tired of not being able to contact him when he needed to. He had plans to sit down with his comrade and find out what in the world was going on with him. To be sure L was alright, Light sent C-Allah out to look for him to make sure he was okay. Of course C-Allah wanted to go with them to handle their business instead, but Light felt that it was more important for him to hit the streets and try to make contact with L. After hanging up the phone, C-Allah was pissed off as he went out into the streets looking for L.

When the Bulldog Crew left Kia's house, the only ones left in the house was Kia, her and Light's daughter Drea, Melyssa, her two daughters, and Jenny along with her two children. They had just got done eating breakfast when someone rung the door bell.

"I got it," said Melyssa getting up from the table. "It's probably C-Allah or L," she said walking to the door to answer it. She hoped it was C-Allah. She had a bad feeling when she had spoken to him this morning. She was in love with him, and she did not understand why he felt he had to be in the streets with the Bulldog Crew causing unnecessary Havoc and mayhem. She felt he was too sweet of a person to be doing the things he were doing. She made a mental note to sit down with him and talk about it the next time she saw him.

"Ding-dong, Ding-dong!" the front door bell rung again.

"I'm coming!" yelled out Melyssa to whoever was ringing the door bell, as she walked to the door and looked through the peephole. A white guy stood on the other side of the door wearing a suit and tie, with a briefcase in his hand.

"What do you want?" asked Melyssa through the door.

"Hello ma'am," said the white man with a friendly smile. "I do not mean to disturb you, but my name is Michael Spitzer and I would like to show you some discounts we have on Home Furnishings ma'am," he said holding up his briefcase so she could see it." I promise you, it would only take a minute of your time."

"What, what would a minute hurt?" thought Melyssa as she opened the door. She was about to give the white man a friendly smile, but was surprised and caught off guard when Whitey quickly grabbed her by the neck applying pressure, as he stepped into the house followed by Moe-dog and Big Lord.

Melyssa tried to fight and yell but it was useless, because the pressure Whitey applied to her neck silenced every attempt she made. He then pulled out his nine millimeter with the silencer attached and shot her in the head two times causing blood to splatter all over the living room's coffee table. He then quickly and quietly closed the front door.

Whitey was the only one out of the three men to have a silencer on his gun. All three of them was about to go upstairs, but heard voices coming from the kitchen.

"Melyssa!" yelled Kia clearing the kitchen table. "Who's at the front door?"

When she got no answer she looked at Jenny and said, "That must be C-Allah."

"Yep!" responded Jenny getting up and helping Kia clear the table as the children sat there.

"Don't fucking move or say anything!" ordered Big Lord through clenched teeth as he entered the kitchen followed by Moe-dog and Whitey. All three had their guns out.

Kia dropped a plate to the floor causing it to break in small pieces, as she and Jenny stared at the three gunmen horrified with their mouths open.

"Who else is in the house?' Moe-dog directed his question at Kia.

"No-no-nobody," stuttered Kia frightened out of her mind.

"Who's upstairs?" asked Whitey.

"Just my 8 month old daughter," answered a very frightened Jenny.

The four children sat at the table looking from their mothers to the three mean looking men holding guns.

"Take her upstairs!" Big Lord ordered Moe-dog pointing at Jenny. Moe-dog grabbed Jenny roughly and half dragged her up the stairs as the children began crying and Kia pleaded for all their lives.

Once upstairs, Moe-dog placed a pillow against Jenny's head and shot her four times at point blank range. Kia was dragged up the stairs next.

"Why did the Bulldog Crew fuck with my fiancé?" Big Lord repeatedly asked himself over and over again.

Using a jacket to muffle the sound of gunfire, he forced Kia into a closet and shot her two times in the head. Jenny's 12 year old son became the next victim. Moe-dog dragged the boy into the same bedroom where Kia had been killed

"I'm sorry," pleaded the boy. "Please don't kill me."

"Alright,' said Moe-dog before pumping two bullets into the little boy's skull killing him instantly.

Moe-dog and Whitey then killed the other three young girls, leaving their little bodies twisted on the floor on top of one another. The room was a massacre!

Big Lord walked into the next room, finding Jenny's 8 month old infant sleeping through the commotion. He gently picked the baby up and walked into the bathroom. After running the water in the tub until it was half full, he was about to drown the baby but was stopped by Moe-dog and Whitey.

"Don't do it Big Lord," said Moe-dog walking towards him. "Give me the baby. The baby is too young to identify us."

Big Lord looked down into the face of the sleeping infant and handed the baby to Moe-dog who took the baby back in the room and placed her into the bassinet. It didn't surprise Moe-dog that Big lord was about to kill a baby, it surprised him to see that Big Lord was just as ruthless as he and Whitey!

They were just about to leave when they heard someone ring the front door bell. They made their way downstairs with their guns drawn hoping it was a member or even all of the members of the Bulldog Crew at the door.

Denise hoped it would be okay to visit Kia without being accompanied by Fats. She and Kia hit it off the moment they met one another and like she promised, she made it her business to visit Kia again, not knowing that it was definitely the wrong time to do so.

"Ding-Dong, Ding-dong," the bell rung again.

Big Lord looked through the peep-hole and then opened the door for the young lady.

"Is Kia home?" asked Denise with a smile.

"Yeah," answered Big Lord. "Come on in."

When Denise stepped into the house, she was startled by Moe-dog and Whitey standing off to the side with guns drawn. When she looked around and saw Melyssa lying dead on the floor she screamed.

Whitey slapped her in the face with his gun and dragged her upstairs, as she tried to fight him off to no avail.

When Denise was dragged into the bedroom, she threw up everything in her stomach when she saw the three young girls dead on the floor lying on top of one another.

Whitey quickly and quietly placed the gun to her head and pulled the trigger two times. He then re-joined Big lord and Moe-dog, and then all left quickly from the house.

$

"Nigga, you better get your dick hard and do what the fuck I said!" screamed Mont-Mont with his face screwed up.

Dakim was terrified, and now he truly understood the big mistake of crossing Mont-Mont and the rest of the Bulldog Crew. To make matters worse, he had the misfortune of being in the same room with three of the craziest members:" Light, Fats and Mont-Mont.

"I can't do it!" cried Dakim over and over as he stood there naked. He looked down at the skinny dark-skinned woman tied spread eagled to the bed butt naked with tears falling from her eyes and he knew he'd rather die than do what Mont-Mont had ordered him to do.

Mont-Mont pointed the gun at his head and was about to pull the trigger, when the woman yelled out, "No! Please don't kill him! He'll do whatever you say!"

She then looked sadly at Dakim and said, "Don't worry about it baby, just do what they say."

Dakim thought for a moment, and then reluctantly climbed on top of his mother! He pumped in and out as the tears fell from his eyes.

"Oh shit!" laughed Fats as he watched the horrendous scene. "And don't stop until you cum, nigga!"

Light laughed and watched with amusement. He sat down and crossed his legs when he noticed that he was getting an erection. He couldn't wait to get home to Kia, he thought as he openly massaged himself.

Mont-Mont stood in the middle of the floor with his face screwed up and ordered Dakim to stand up.

"He did what you said!" screamed Dakim's mother. "Now let us go!" she cried "Please let us go!"

Dakim openly cried and could not even look into his mother's face after committing such a horrific act. And when Fats walked over and shot his mother in the head two times, he lost his mind.

"Ahhhggg!!!" screamed Dakim as he rushed Fats knocking him over the bed. The gun fell from Fat's hand as he wrestled with the naked Dakim on the floor.

Light was doubled over in laughter, before walking over and shooting Dakim once in the head killing him instantly.

"You stupid muh'fucker!" laughed Fats getting off of the floor. "Why the fuck you let'em rush me for?"

Light continued laughing instead of answering. But Mont-Mont was all business, as he pulled a straight razor from his pocket and with two swift motions cut Dakim's dick off. He then shoved the decapitated bloody penis into Dakim's mouth.

Light and Fats continued laughing as Mont-Mont handled his business. After he was done they headed out of the house that was located in Yonkers, New York.

Light looked at Mont-Mont like he was crazy and asked, "Yo, you ain't gonna wash your hands nigga?! Don't touch me, you nasty muh'fucker! Hands smelling like straight up dick!"

Fats laughed before closing the door behind them as they headed back to Kia's house.

Chapter 24

"What the fuck is wrong with Big Lord?! screamed Omar very angrily. "He must've lost his fucking mind!"

He had just finished reading the newspaper and the story of Kia, Melyssa, Jenny and the children being slaughtered sickened him to his stomach. He knew even if Gloria had gotten shot, he would have never committed such a heinous and cowardly act towards women and children. And when Omar read the story about Dakim and his mother, he completely lost his appetite.

"Baby, please try to calm down," Gloria pleaded with her husband.

"She's right Omar," said Richard sadly.

It was 8:00 am on a Saturday morning as they all sat in Omar and Gloria's kitchen. Lisa and Dejanay were upstairs still sleeping.

"I believe God is going to punish all of them," continued Richard referring to Whitey, Moe-dog, Big Lord and of course the entire Bulldog Crew.

"He said 'Vengence is mine'" continued Richard. "So we just have to put it in God's hands and pray that this nonsense ends."

Ignoring what Richard was saying, Omar grabbed his cell phone off of the table and quickly dialed a number hoping to catch the party he was calling.

"Yo, who dis?" asked Big Lord answering the phone.

"Big Lord, who the fuck do you think it is? Tell me! Who else would be calling your dumb ass after seeing what I saw?"

"Oh what's up Omar?" said Big Lord knowing his friend was upset over what he probably read in the newspaper or saw on the TV news.

"What the fuck you mean 'what's up?" yelled Omar through the phone. Then calming down a bit he said, "Listen, I know it's a tragedy that Pam got shot, but y'all taking this shit way too fucking far! And you know what I'm talking about! I don't have to spit the shit over the phone. The shit wasn't even all that serious. Pam is going to be alright."

"What the fuck you mean it's not that serious?" asked Big Lord angrily. This was the first time he had talked to Omar in this tone of voice.

"Them punk muh'fuckers shot my fiancé," continued Big Lord, "and you're telling me it's not all that serious? Getting out of the game, must've caused you to lose your muh'fucking mind! And unlike you, I still know the meaning of loyalty to those I love nigga."

"What the fuck you mean by that nigga?" Omar asked angrily. Without waiting for Big Lord to answer the question, Omar continued talking,"If I didn't know the meaning of loyalty, I would of never put your ass in the game in the first place! And maybe I shouldn't have, because you already forgot the rules that goes with the fucking game!"

"What rules nigga?" asked Big Lord.

"See, you done forgot already, because you can't control your anger, so now you're just like the rest of these niggas out here in the streets playing a game and not following the rules! And the number one rule the old timers enforced was 'Do not fuck with people that ain't got shit to do with the game', they're off limits to the shit we do. Especially women and children, idiot!'

"Fuck the old timers! I guess it's okay to shoot my wifey, huh, answer that nigga!"

"Just because they violated the rules of the game, doesn't mean you have to do the same thing! If a nigga snitch on me, should I snitch back? Come on man, you sound ridiculous!"

"I don't wanna hear that shit nigga! If that was your bitch Gloria," said Big Lord causing Omar to really get upset at what he called his wife, "you wouldn't be talking this bullshit! You act like I violated the game by snitching on a nigga or something muh'fucker!"

"Nigga what you did is just as bad," said Omar angrily before hanging up the phone on Big Lord.

The conversation he just had with Big Lord pained him terribly, because he knew his long time friendship with his comrade who was more like a brother than anything, had come to an end. He knew things could never be the same with the two of them ever again. Of course he loved Big lord, but he developed a stronger love for positive Black people in the ghettos that truly wanted to do something with their lives. Especially children! And like he always said, "There was no turning back from awareness."

"Baby," said Gloria rubbing her husband's face. "I know how close you and Big lord are, and I know this thing gets you down. We just have to continue doing the things that we are trying to do. Remember Russ, I want that Kimora money!" she joked causing her husband to smirk. It was a joke the staff at Untouchable Records would say about Omar and Gloria, comparing the two to Mr. Russel Simmons and his beautiful wife Kimora Lee Simmons.

"I heard the two of them are divorcing or separating," said Omar about the celebrity couple. "But you know how rumors are."

"I hope it's not true," said Gloria. "They make a good couple and I love them both."

"You know," said Omar in deep thought about he and Big lord's friendship. He couldn't get the phone call out of his mind.

"When I think about my friendship with Big lord, I think it's strictly based on the past when we both was out there in the streets thugging it out. But now it's like, I grew apart from him or something."

"You simply changed," said Gloria.

"Maybe," said Omar. "But then the streets definitely changed also, and for the worse. Niggas nowadays getting in beef with each other and when they can't get you they get your mother or your girlfriend. That's some real coward shit, and the real rules of the game never tolerated that sucker shit. Sometimes I really think these dudes out here---"

"Good morning," interrupted Lisa walking into the kitchen wearing a pink bathrobe followed by cute little Dejanay wearing a miniature identical bathrobe.

"Good morning daddy," Dejanay gave Richard a kiss.

"Hey princess," responded Richard. He instantly thought about what Moe-dog and Whitey and Big Lord had done to those women and children and knew in his heart that had it been Lisa and Dejaneay, he would've been out for blood! He was a man of God, but he was also a man that would not hesitate to protect his family. Matter of fact, that was the cause of him going to jail many years ago. He killed the crazy thug Rashien from Fort Green projects, who threatened to kill his parents. That's why when the whole crazy beef was over, Richard moved his wife and his little daughter out of New York City to get away from it all. Because even though he left the streets alone, he knew too many people was familiar with his name and reputation, and he did not want to repeat a similar beef with an up and coming thug who wanted to get a reputation off of his name. So, he felt that it would just be better to leave the state as well as the game behind him.

"What's up Pumpkin?" smiled Omar to Dejanay with his arms open wide.

"Good morning Uncle Omar," she said wiping the sleep from her eyes. Before allowing her uncle to pick her up, she looked up at her father Richard. He gave her a reassuring smile and only then, did she allow herself to sit on her uncle's lap.

Omar did not take offense to what had just taken place. In fact, he appreciated what his brother-in-law and sister taught his niece. When he and Gloria have their child, he would teach him or her the same thing. Especially having a girl! Omar knew at least eighty percent of the women in the world was raped or molested at one point in their lives, either when they were children or when they became adults. And most of the time, these terrible acts were committed by someone they knew or trusted: Father, uncle, brother, boyfriend, friend, teacher, preacher and can't forget the family friend. But also he heard the stories of men doing the same to young boys. Just look at the Catholic church, he thought. He knew he lived in a very sick world. He also knew for a fact that women and girls raped and molested young boys as well. Because he happened to be a victim of that when he was a child. His mother would let her sister; his aunt Sarah baby sit him when he was only 7 years old and not even an hour after his mother left, everything would go as routine. Aunt Sarah would stick her tongue down young Omar's mouth or either have his young face buried in her private area. She would tell him to just pretend that he was eating an ice-cream cone. One day while between her legs, Aunt Sarah had an orgasm so intense, she pulled his face into her private area so hard his nose started bleeding as she damn near suffocated the young boy. The sex went on until he was 15 years old and she had always told him that if he told anyone he would be punished severely. So, it became their dirty little secret.

But after getting older and getting tired of his aunt, Omar no longer gave into her demands and had even grown to hate her. Also, it later came out that she had a secret crush on his father and maybe being that Omar was the spitting image of his father, she played out her fantasy with him.

That's why over the years growing up, Omar was so over-protective of his little sister Lisa, and when he first found out that she got raped by her ex-boyfriend Shameek when he and Gloria had come back from Jamaica, he went nuts! He would've killed Shameek if Divine hadn't already done the job. But secretly Omar still blamed himself for not being in New York when his baby sister needed him most.

"Where's the maid?" asked Lisa after kissing Richard and sitting down at the table.

"I told her to relax," answered Gloria while pouring Omar and Richard another cup of herbal tea and taking Omar's newspaper off of the table. She then got up and walked over to the oven pulling out two huge bowls with her cooking gloves.

After making everyone a plate of pancakes, eggs and chicken sausages, she sat back down at the table and prepared to eat breakfast with her family. Before eating, everyone bowed their heads in prayer as Richard gave thanks.

"Lord, we thank you for this food you've place before us. We thank you for allowing us to rise this morning, and protecting us and keeping us in your good graces. We would like to thank---"

The telephone in the kitchen began ringing, interrupting Richard in mid-prayer, but no one got up to answer it. They all kept their heads bowed until Richard was done giving thanks to God.

"God, continue to bless us and show us your way. Amen."

They all raised their heads and being that the phone was still ringing, Gloria got up to answer it.

"Hello?" she said. "Hold up, stop yelling in my ear. I can not hear you, say that again. What? That's good news!" Gloria said, causing everyone at the table to wonder who was she talking to and what she was talking about.

"That's great!" she continued. "Oh yeah? ....Well, that's to be expected. Maybe he needs to get them, or they just might be able to change things for guys like him..... Well, you know how fickle Hip-Hop can be at times. It's the only music that has an age limit no matter how good you are coming into the game. Or maybe he can just lie about his age like the other rappers and there.....Like who?....Oh God! He looks every day of fifty! And he claims he's twenty-one," she laughed. "And those are the ones always talking about keeping it real......Okay, hold on."

Gloria then passed the phone to Omar and with a smile said, "It's Daqual on the phone. He said the new O.G.'s album had moved up the charts, and everybody is calling for guest appearances, asking for interviews and everything else. And they're damn near on every radio station. Also, he said the new artist Terror we signed, album is crazy hot, but he's thirty-six years old, so we might have to put him with the O.G's in this crazy game."

Omar smiled and after taking the telephone, he stood up and walked out of the kitchen with the cordless phone to discuss the future of the O.G's and Terror on 'Untouchable Records.'

"Are you going to the hospital today to see Pam?" Gloria asked Lisa.

"Yes," answered Lisa putting down her fork. "I figured I'd go around 2:00 this afternoon. First, I have to take Dejanay out shopping. Gina is coming with me, she has to buy a few things for little Divine. If you want, you can come with us."

"I wish I could!" sighed Gloria. "But I have to go down to the office today, and make sure everyone is dong what they're suppose to be doing. And sometimes, that can take hours!"

But she knew she didn't have to go to work today, or ever for that matter. Gloria just enjoyed her job in the music industry and could not stay away from the business aspect of it.

"Gloria," said Richard. "Have you ever heard of a gospel singer name Juanita Bynaum?"

"No," answered Gloria. "I never heard of her."

"Really?" asked Lisa excitedly. "Richard, you have to let her hear the CD!"

"I already had plans to," smiled Richard pulling the CD out of his bathrobe pocket. He then stood up and walked to the next room to put the CD in the livingroom's sound system.

"Richard!" yelled Gloria with a smile, "I'm not in the mood for no Kirk Franklin! Put on some Jay-Z, Oh-Boy, or the O.G.'s!"

Lisa laughed and said, "It won't be no Hip-Hop music being played in this house today! Not with DJ Bishop Bish on the sound system, with his big bag of gospel CDs' he brought with him!"

"Oh God!" said Gloria slapping her forehead as Lisa and little Dejanay laughed.

"Do that again Auntie," said Dejanay laughing.

Gloria slapped her forehead again with a smile causing the little girl to laugh uncontrollably.

The sounds of Juanita Bynaum's song "Shake Me Again" played loudly through the livingroom's sound system, and Gloria was surprised to find herself really enjoying the CD.

"I like that," smiled Gloria. "See, I can listen to that."

"Told you!" smiled Lisa.

Little Dejanay ignored her pancakes and sung along to every word of the song, as Gloria looked at her with a smile. Even Omar entered back into the kitchen with a smile, looked at Lisa and Gloria and said, "That's hot, I'm feeling that! Whoever that is, will be perfect on 'Untouchable Records'!

"Yeah, right!" said Lisa causing everyone to laugh.

Chapter 25

For the last two weeks, L had really been going through it with Tonya. One minute she would be lovey dovey with him, and the next she would act as if she couldn't stand to be close to him as if he was her enemy. He knew it was all because of what happened to Pam, and after finding out everything that had taken place, she was in a state of confusion about things. But he knew she loved him, so he figured she would maybe get over it within her own time and that he could not rush things. He understood wounds took time to heal.

L also had a lot on his mind concerning the Bulldog Crew. He talked to Light yesterday, and of course Light was ready to kill the world!

When Light, Fats and Mont-Mont entered Kia's house the day she was brutally murdered, they could not believe their eyes. The first person they saw was Melyssa lying dead on the livingroom's floor. When they ran upstairs with their guns drawn and saw the massacre, they already knew who committed the gruesome killings.

Light, Fats and Mont-Mont was ready to kill Big Lord, Moe-dog, Whitey and anyone who resembled them!

Fats was hurting more for Light over what happened to Kia and their daughter, than he was over the death of Denise. He did love his girlfriend, but he was more curious as to why she had visited Kia without his permission. He hated when she did things without his knowledge, and presently he was more upset about her not telling him she was going to Kia's house than he was over her death!

Mont-Mont also felt his comrade's pain. He was more than ready to kill or lay down his life for his friends if necessary. He just waited for Light to say when!

"So, what you wanna do?" Fats asked Light.

"First lets get out of here," answered a very angry Light. "Grab that baby. We'll drop her off at Jenny sister's house. And we'll call C-Allah on the way to L's crib."

They all left Kia's house and piled into Mont-Mont's car. After dropping the baby off to Jenny's hysterical and crying sister, they got to L's apartment and sat in his livingroom. Light ranted and raved.

"This shit don't make no fucking sense!"yelled Light. "Yo, here it is we got crazy beef in the streets with these punk ass niggas, and I can't even get in touch with you when I fucking need you! At least C-Allah----"

"See that's the problem right there!" interrupted L. He was tired of pretending, and now was the time to get it all out in the open. "You so caught up in killing niggas," continued L, "that you can't even see I ain't feeling that nigga C-Allah!"

"Look Light," he said calming down. "I'm sorry to hear about Kia, your daughter and the rest of them. That's my family too. And you know I love you, man. But I don't feel comfortable around the nigga C-Allah, and you know I don't do shit with no one I'm not comfortable with. I just get funny feelings about duke, even though I know all three of y'all is feeling 'em. The nigga moods just change too much for me."

L figured he might as well get everything out in the open now so he looked at Mont-Mont and said, "Even though this nigga do a lot of dumb shit and I barely wanna fuck with him, at least I can say unlike C-Allah, the nigga Mont-Mont is the same way all the fucking time."

"L, C-Allah is a good dude," said Fats as Mont-Mont agreed with him as usual.

"I don't give a flying fuck!" yelled Light. "This is not the fucking time to be like little girls talking about who we like and who we don't like! Them faggot ass niggas killed my motherfucking family, and it's time to get busy! If you ain't feeling the nigga C-Allah, then so the fuck what! Don't do nothing wit the nigga! But when I call you to get busy nigga, then its fucking time to roll! You hear me?!"

"That's cool," answered L getting tired of the whole conversation. Of course, he also felt Light's pain of losing his family, but he wanted to continue moving off of intelligence and not succumb to emotions. That's when people made mistakes, he concluded to himself.

"So what's up?" asked L. "What we gonna do?"

"I just talked to Hook on the phone on the way over here," answered Light. "And he said he got some information for us, but he couldn't talk about it over the phone. He was in Virginia and said he'll be back in the morning so we'll talk to him then. But for now, let's shoot over to Jefferson Street in the 'sty. I heard the nigga Big Lord be in the area on the regular!"

That was only yesterday, and now L looked at his watch, grabbed his blue New York Yankees baseball cap and headed out the door.

He jumped in his silver 2002 CL 55 AMG Mercedes Benz and pulled away from the curb, as he listened to Hot 97 radio station and the sounds of Kanye West's song "Jesus Walks" blasted through the system as he drove through the Brooklyn streets. He thought about Tonya all morning and wondered where she was. He called her house, her cell phone, and even her job said she didn't come into work today. With all the killings in this war going on, he hoped she was okay. He hadn't talked to her in two days now and he definitely missed her presence.

L pulled up in front of one of Hook's apartment buildings on Lincoln place in the Crown Heights section of Brooklyn. It was a hot day and expensive cars and SUVs lined the curb.

Hook, Light and Fats stood on the sidewalk when L pulled up. Before L could get out of the car, Light was already walking to his vehicle to greet him. When L stepped out of the car, Light gave him a pound and said, "What's up my nigga?"

"Ain't nothing baby boy," answered L. "What's going on?"

"The nigga Hook just gave me some information," said Light. "So we gotta get ready to get out of here," he said looking at his diamond infested Cartier watch. "I know you ain't feeling C-Allah and Mont-Mont, so I told 'dem niggas I'll get up with them a little later. I'm saying, you're my nigga!"

They gave each other another pound, and it felt good to the both of them to finally be back on the same page once again.

"Yo, y'all gotta hurry up," said Hook before walking over and greeting L, with Fats walking behind him. They then were on their way to handle their business.

L drove his own car, and Light rode with Fats. After exiting the FDR Drive at 23rd Street in Manhattan, they saw what they were looking for.

A platinum color 2003 four door S-Type-R-Jaguar was parked in front of the Italian Deli. The deli fronted as a restaurant, but in the back room the purest heroin and cocaine was being sold at top dollar to only certain drug dealers, businessmen, certain celebrities, etc.

L got out of his car and jumped into the back seat of Fats car. He waited on his instructions from Light.

"As soon as he come out it's on!" said Light pulling out a .50 Caliber handgun he got from Hook. He also reached underneath his seat and grabbed his .44 Bulldog! Fats and L followed by pulling their guns from the waist line of their pants.

"We gotta stay in the car until he comes out," continued Light. "Hook was definitely right about the area."

People quickly walked by, bumping one another as if they all were in a rush to get to an important business meeting or something.

When Big lord exited the deli, Light, Fats and L pulled their baseball caps down to their eyes, but not enough to block their vision. But Big Lord was not alone. Two big Italian guys walked closely beside him and Moe-dog and Whitey trailed closely behind. From the bulges that appeared with every step they took, it confirmed the fact that all of them possessed guns on their body.

"More of them than we expected, but fuck it let's go!" said Light opening his door and stepping out of the car. Fats and L followed his lead with their guns out in full view.

Whitey was the first one to see the trio approaching them with their guns being raised. "Look out!" he yelled as he ducked and pulled for his gun.

The two Italians didn't know what was going on, they were only following their boss's procedure to make sure the customers made it to their cars safely without being robbed.

Light's first bullet entered into the head of one of the Italians, blowing his brains out all over the sidewalk.

It was chaos in Manhattan! People heard the shot and ran in every direction screaming, crying and trying to get out of the area. It was as if the World Trade Center was falling down all over again, the way people were trying to get out of the way.

The other Italian pulled for his gun, but was rewarded by a .44 slug to his face from L's gun. L fired again hitting him in the chest, but he was already dead from the face shot.

Big Lord, Moe-dog and Whitey fired shots from their guns as well, as they tried to get away from out of the area. But the Bulldog Crew did not let up. Especially Light and Fats! They fired their guns at the same time, quickly walking towards Big Lord, Moe-dog and Whitey as if returned fire wasn't even coming back in their direction.

Whitey fired two shots as he made his get away but caught a bullet to his back from Fats's gun that caused him to stumble and fall to the concrete.

Big Lord made it to the car and quickly turned the ignition causing the engine to come to life.Moe-dog let off three shots missing his targets before jumping in the passenger's seat of Big lord's car. He wanted to go back and help Whitey, but to do so would definitely cost him his life. Plus, he knew the police was already in the area. He could hear the sounds of sirens as Big lord pulled away from the curb burning rubber as he made his get away.

When the police pulled up on the scene with their sirens blaring, L had also already made it to his car and pulled away from the scene.

"Come on!" Light yelled at Fats. "We gotta get outta here!" But Fats acted as if he didn't hear him as he quickly walked behind a crawling Whitey and fired two shots to the back of his head damn near blowing it completely off!

"Freeze!!!!" yelled one of the two officers first to arrive on the scene as he pointed his gun at Fats. The officer's back up unit did not arrive to the scene as of yet, but the sirens could be heard in the distance.

The officer and his partner aimed their guns at Fats but did not see Light walking up behind them, and when Fats spinned around with his gun raised above his head, one of the officers opened fire hitting him in the face and head killing him.

But with blind rage and anger, Light emptied his .50 Caliber on both officers blowing away flesh, brains and body parts! He then ran to his car dragging an already dead Fats.

Miraculously, Light made his getaway before the area was blocked off by police re-enforcements!

As Light drove back to Brooklyn, tears fell from his eyes as he glanced over at Fats who had always been more like his biological brother than anything. Now Light definitely felt as if he had nothing at all to live for. Kia, his daughter, and now Fats were dead, leaving him all alone in this world. He felt more bitter than he'd ever felt in his life. It was a pain that was unexplainable, and his bitterness blinded him to the point of blaming everyone, even those down with him, because of Fats being killed. That included L as well, for escaping the area before the police arrived on the scene. Never mind the fact that L told Light and Fats, that it was time to move out!

After glancing at Fats once again, Light made up his mind that he would make everyone pay after first locating Big lord and Moe-dog!!!!!

Chapter 26

"So, what's up my nigga? Just let me know what you wanna do and you know I'm down!" said Mont-Mont over the telephone. He was hurting bad inside over the death of Fats. All day long, the local news stations had been talking about the big shoot out in lower Manhattan that left five dead, including two New York City police officers.

The police commissioner stated that five individuals were being sorted for questioning and anyone with information was to call the police and tell what they know. The mayor of the city stated that whoever did these killings would be captured and convicted. All of the witnesses that was on the scene had stated that it was so much gunfire going on, no one had the balls or heart to risk their lives to see who was doing the shooting. The police department was being criticized for letting the gunmen escape the area, instead of blocking it off. The families of the slain officers, were mourning and asking for justice.

"I don't know what I wanna do yet," answered Light, "except getting that nigga Big Lord and Moe-dog!"

"I talked to L yesterday," said Mont-Mont. "He said some shit about he tried to call you, but couldn't get in contact. He also said the homie Bishop wants to talk to you."

"Fuck he wanna talk to me for?!" Light yelled into the phone. "The nigga better pray he don't catch one in the fucking face as well! I ain't got time to talk to that nigga! He better mind his motherfucking business!"

"I hear you man," said Mont-Mont shaking his head from side to side. "Anyway, I'm with you on whatever you wanna do!"

After a brief pause, Mont-Mont said, "I know the homie L don't feel me and C-Allah much, but we should've been there at that shoot out man. Maybe Fats would still be alive if we were."

"Yeah I know," said Light agreeing. All night, Hook was telling him the same thing. He sat in Hook's house last night and watch Hook pace the living room's floor not understanding how things with the Bulldog Crew had gotten so out of control. At first Light had tried to defend his friend's L's honor because he still had a lot of love for his childhood comrade, but Hook had made a lot of sense.

"What is wrong with the boy L?" asked Hook totally not understanding. "He know Mont-Mont and C-Allah was suppose to be there! Who cares if he don't like them?" he asked throwing his hands in the air.

"I don't know man," said Light, not mentioning the fact that it was he that told Mont-Mont and C-Allah not to come along . And Hook not knowing that, continued to curse L all night long.

"Listen," Light told Mont-Mont. "Call me back later today. We can meet up in Vanderveer Projects, I gotta go through there a little later. Where's C-Allah?"

Mont-Mont looked over at C-Allah sitting on the couch in deep thought and said, "He's here wit' me. You know he's fucked up over what happened to Melyssa."

"Yeah I know," said Light. "And I know we can't bring any of them back, but tell'em we gonna make it right! I'm gonna behead these niggas when I catch them!"

C-Allah sat in Mont-Mont's livingroom at his 143rd and Bradhurst apartment. He leaned back on the couch and stared up at the ceiling thinking about his next move. He never expected things to go this far. Too many innocent people had gotten killed. He thought about Melyssa and it pained him terribly. He had grown very attached to her and her two daughters. But he also knew that their relationship would not had lasted had she still been alive, because he knew she would've never understood what he did for a living. But one thing was for sure, he definitely wanted to get his hands on those who killed her and her children.

"A yo," said Light, "Hook got me thinking about a lot of shit. But now ain't the time to get into it. We really have to sit down and talk. Matterfact, we can kick it after we leave Vanderveer."

"What's the Vanderveer move about?" asked Mont-Mont.

"I don't wanna talk about it over the phone," answered Light. "But make sure you're strapped up right."

"No doubt!" responded Mont-Mont.

"Oh shit!" yelled C-Allah looking at his watch causing Mont-Mont to look in his direction. "We gotta get outta here!"

"What's up?" asked Light hearing C-Allah in the background cursing.

"Nah, everything is okay," explained Mont-Mont. "He just want me to roll wit'em to the Bronx to pick up something from his aunt's crib. And he said we gotta be there by a certain time before she leaves."

"Oh," said Light. "Well, when you meet me in the 'Veer, you can bring him with you."

"Aight, I'll tell 'em later."

"Bulldog love," said Light hanging up the telephone.

Mont-Mont hung up the phone and said to C-Allah, "Hold up, let me get right."

He then walked into his bedroom, removed the nine from his waist, and opened his closet. An assortment of guns lined the closet shelf. He placed his nine millimeter on the shelf and grabbed his .44 Bulldog handgun and a chrome plated .357 automatic handgun. He tucked both guns into the waist of his pants and walked towards the livingroom where C-Allah waited.

"You ready?" asked C-Allah opening the front door.

They made their way down the stairs and all the guys standing in front of the apartment building dispersed when they saw Mont-Mont coming down the steps. They were terrified of him, and did not care who knew it as they got out of his way. They knew his body count was crazy but what really shook them, was the story the streets told of what he did to Dakim and his moms.

As soon as Mont-Mont and C-Allah got to Mont-Mont's car, at least twelve homicide detectives came from nowhere with their guns pointed at Mont-Mont. C-Allah took off running as two of the detectives chased him down the street. Three gun shots went off and Mont-Mont knew it was from C-Allah's gun. He thought about pulling for his gun as well but he knew he had no chance of getting his gun out.

"Put your fucking hands in the air!!!" yelled a detective with his gun cocked back and pointed at the back of Mont-Mont's head.

Mont-Mont put his hands in the air as ordered and five cops rushed him to the ground cuffing his hands behind his back and taking the guns from his waist.

"Lamont Hall," said one of the tough looking detectives, "you are under arrest for multiple counts of murder and weapons possessions! You have the right to remain silent and all the rest of that shit!" he said as he led Mont-Mont to the brown un-marked detective's van parked across the street. "Anything you say, will be held against you motherfucker! You have the right to cou---"

Despite Mont-Mont's current situation, he smiled to himself because he knew the detectives had no witnesses against him. He left no one alive on his killings, so he knew this was just a scare tactic the police was forced to try to use because of the pressure from the Mayor and the general public that wanted the infamous Bulldog Crew arrested.

Before they threw Mont-Mont in the police van, he saw the two detectives return back to the scene minus C-Allah, and he felt good to see his comrade was fortunate enough to escape the police. It was a sure sign that the Bulldog Crew could not be stopped!!!

"The bastard got away!' fumed one of the detectives. "But I'll get his black ass next time!"

"Fuck him!" said his partner. "We got the one that really matters."

All the guys on Mont-Mont's block stood around watching the police take him away. They all looked as if they were angry but actually they were happy and relieved to see him get locked back up. They just could not show their joy because it was no telling if Mont-Mont would be fortunate enough to slip through the system on a technicality, and no one wanted to face that or the possibility of having to see the remaining free Bulldog Crew. They just saw one of them get away!

Mont-Mont was driven to the 79th precinct and before he was even locked in the pen the interrogation began.

"Where is your boy Light? Give us some information on L! Who was the guy that just shot at the police officers and got away? Was that C-Allah? Give us some information on some of these killings and we swear to you, we'll let you go. You have our word on that." The questions were coming so fast and sounded so ridiculous to

Mont-Mont, he had to laugh despite the serious situation he was presently in.

"Please save yourselves the trouble of playing good cop/bad cop," laughed Mont-Mont. "Y'all know I've been through all this corny shit before. Just let me make my one phone call so I can call my lawyer."

He figured he'd call Hook to obtain a lawyer to come down to the precinct to make sure he'd get a fair line-up. Also, a good lawyer should be able to get the weapons charges thrown out and all he would have to do is two years or less for violating parole, being that he had never reported to a parole office. He wasn't worried about the murder charges because he had never left witnesses around to tell on him.

The officers locked Mont-Mont in the pen and as he waited to make his one phone call, he looked at his watch and he knew Light was already in the Vanderveer Projects waiting on his call.

However, that was one appointment Mont-Mont knew he could not keep so he laid back and tried to get comfortable on the hard bench in the smelly pen. It would definitely be a long night.

Chapter 27

Light waited at the Vanderveer Housing Projects in Brooklyn wondering why Mont-Mont hadn't given him a call yet. He sat in his Mercedes Benz parked on New York avenue and waited for his target. He was just waiting for the guy to appear.

Light's car had tinted windows dark enough not to be seen, so he knew he would have the element of surprise on his side. He tried calling Mont-Mont several times but received no answer. As he sat in his car, he wondered what happened to the Bulldog Crew. Nothing with them was going right. He felt that L was too caught up with Tonya, C-Allah was acting strange as usual and Mont-Mont was not answering his calls. Maybe he'd do as Hook suggested and move solo, he thought to himself. It seemed to him anyway as if everyone had already crossed him. Just as he was about to turn on his radio, he saw the person he was waiting for.

Moe-dog walked quickly towards his car parked on New York Avenue. Something did not seem right to him. He just had a funny feeling that something terrible was about to go down. He thought about going back to Karen's apartment in building 1368 but changed his mind as he re-adjusted the gun on his waist and kept stepping. Something told him to follow his first instinct, but he ignored it.

Like a hawk, Light watched his every move from inside his car. He knew Moe-dog was very dangerous but he had the element of surprise on his side. He just had to wait for the perfect opportunity to present itself.

Moe-dog had been in a relationship with Karen ever since he and Gina had officially broken up. Actually, it was through Gina that he met Karen. She and Gina went to school together but they weren't the best of friends. In fact, they hated one another. One day when Moe-dog and Gina was at the Eastern Parkway Caribbean Day Parade in Brooklyn, Gina felt someone staring at her. She turned around and was not surprised to see Karen standing there with her homegirl. Also with her and her friend, was her man at the time, Smooth and his right hand man Rob-Lo. Smooth and Rob-Lo were conversing and paid no attention to the two young women evil eyeing one another.

Moe-dog acknowledged what was going on and watched Gina and Karen with a smile. He knew Gina was very pretty, but he was surprised to see that Karen was just as equally beautiful. He pulled his baseball cap down to his eyes as he noticed the two guys with Karen. Not that he was worried about them or anything. He had his .45 automatic on him and plus he knew who the two guys were. They got busy in the streets but was nowhere in Moe-dog's league and he knew it. And so did they!

"What the fuck you looking at?" asked Gina with her lip turned up as she eyed the two girls.

"What?" yelled Karen angrily hoping to get Smooth and Rob-Lo's attention. She wanted to let Gina know that she and her man were outnumbered. But that didn't stop Gina.

"You heard what the fuck I said!" fumed Gina.

"What's up?" Smooth asked Karen realizing that it was a problem between the two girls.

"This bitch here frontin'," glared Karen.

"I'ma smack the shit out of this bitch!" said Gina walking towards Karen with Moe-dog trailing closely behind.

"Yo, hold up!" said Smooth stepping in the middle of the two girls with his face screwed up.

"Get out their way," replied Moe-dog.

"What?!" barked Smooth about to reach for his gun as his man Rob-Lo stood next to him.

Moe-dog took off his baseball cap, and Smooth and Rob-Lo looked as if they had saw a ghost. Their faces quickly softened up.

"Oh shit," said Smooth. "Moe-dog, what's up?"

"It's a girl's thing," replied Moe-dog. "Let them handle that."

"No doubt," said Smooth as he and Rob-Lo moved out of the way.

Karen couldn't believe it! She thought Smooth and Rob-Lo were the ultimate thug niggas and now she saw they were actually scared of the short dark-skinned guy who stood directly in front of them. Karen knew she had no wins with Gina in a one on one fight, so she quickly walked away with her friend Nicole trailing behind her. And from that day on, her relationship with Smooth was over! But for weeks afterwards, all she did was think about Moe-dog and she was delighted when she had finally ran into him in the streets and was told that Gina was history!

Moe-dog had just finished arguing with Karen inside of her apartment. She was crying about him not spending enough time with her. He tried to explain to her over and over again, that he had money to make and enemies to get rid of, but she was not trying to hear it. She told him the relationship was over and she did not want to see him again, so without another word he walked out of her apartment with a smile. Because he knew the relationship was far from over. He knew for certain that Karen was in love with him and just upset at the moment. But what he did not know was that Karen's little brother Donald use to sell drugs for Divine when he was alive and had always looked up to Light and Fats. After hearing in the streets that Moe-dog had beef with the Bulldog Crew, it was the perfect opportunity for Donald to become a member of the dangerous crew of thugs he always wanted to be a part of. Never mind the fact that Donald had never killed or hurt anyone in his life! And although Moe-dog was his sister's new boyfriend, he and the quiet gangster had never really took the time to get to know one another.

When Light had first come home from jail, he saw Donald Downtown Brooklyn and recognized him as on e of the young boys that used to work for Divine. When Donald saw Light looking at him, he couldn't believe his eyes! He quickly let go of his girlfriend's hand and approached Light with a Kool-Aid smile.

"Yo Light, what's up?!" asked Donald excitedly. "When did you get out? Is the rest of the Bulldog Crew out?"

Light smiled at the young guy and said, "I just recently got out and yeah, the rest of my homies are home too."

"I'm saying," said Donald. "I know you're doing your thing. When you gonna put me down with the Bulldog Crew?"

Light laughed at the boy before answering.

"Little nigga," said Light, "this game ain't no joke. You think you're ready to wipe out a whole family if you had to?"

"No doubt!' answered Donald knowing damn well he wasn't ready for the league the Bulldog Crew played in.

"What's up with that pretty sister of yours?" asked Light changing the subject. "I hear every nigga in Brooklyn is try'na holla at her. Is that true shorty?"

"Yeah," answered Donald. "But she only fuck wit'niggas that's getting major paper, or thug niggas."

Light smiled and said, "Yeah, I hear niggas is taking penitentiary chances just to be with her. But tell'er the king of thugs is home! Take my number, and tell 'er to use it when she's ready for some real thug loving."

He gave Donald his number and thought nothing of it, that is until he got a call from the youngster early this morning. When he recognized the young boy's voice, he frowned because he was in no mood to talk to him or his gold digging, thug wanting ass sister.

"Yo, what's up!' barked Light into the phone.

"What's up Light?" said Donald excitedly hoping that what he was about to tell Light would put him down with the Bulldog Crew. "I got some important information for you."

"Talk about it!" said Light.

"Yo," began Donald. "I heard you got beef wit' Moe-dog and Big Lord. My sister fucks with the nigga Moe-dog. He always comes to the crib. I don't really know the nigga and I don't fuck wit'em. He act like he all dat and shit!"

Light listened to the dumb little young boy who mistakenly confused gangsterism for conceitedness.

"Is the nigga at your crib now?" asked Light getting to the point. He had no time to be playing with punk ass Donald.

"Nah" answered Donald. "But he'll be over today. I heard him tell my sister over the phone that he'll be over at 4 o'clock, later on today. He always park his car on New York Avenue between Newkirk and Foster where you come out of the projects. My sister never walks wit 'em to his car, so that's where you can get the nigga at."

"Good Looking!" said Light.

"So when you gonna put me down wit '---"

Light hung up on Donald before he could even finish his sentence. He got the information he needed and that's all that mattered!

Moe-dog was three cars away from his own, when Light's opportunity presented itself. Moe-dog stopped walking and spunned around to see who was calling him. He smiled when he saw the very beautiful Karen running towards him with a smile on her face to apologize and tell him that she loved him. Light had already slipped out of his car to make his move.

Karen's smiled turned into a look of horror when she was three feet away from Moe-dog and saw Light standing directly behind him with a gun pointed at the back of his head. She was in a moment of shock. She didn't even see or hear her brother Donald running at top speed towards her screaming out her name and in tears. He never thought his sister would follow Moe-dog to his car. When his sister's friend Diane told him Karen went to catch up to Moe-dog to apologize, he could not believe his bad luck as he sprinted after her.

Moe-dog noticed Donald running towards him crying, and he noticed also the horrified look on Karen's face. He felt it coming but it was too late to respond. But he spinned around anyway.

The first bullet from Light's gun tore into Moe-dog's forehead blowing away parts of his brain. He was dead before he fell to the ground, but Light fired two more shots to his body anyway. He then aimed his gun at Karen and fired two shots into her skull, as Donald continued to run in his direction screaming with tears falling from his eyes. It was a hot day outside, so a lot of people witnessed the double homicide as they ran to safety.

Light calmly walked back to his car and drove away, as the young boy Donald cried over the body of his sister and swore to get revenge.

Light knew he left a lot of witnesses at the scene and the police would definitely come looking for him, but he didn't care. As far as he was concerned, he died with Kia, his daughter Drea and Fats. He felt it was nothing for him now to live for. Except one thing. Finding and killing Big Lord!!!!

Chapter 28

"You talked to Light?" Mont-Mont asked C-Allah over the telephone.

"Nah," answered C-Allah. "I tried to call' em, but he's not answering his cell phone and I don't even know where he's staying at. I need to find 'em, so if you hear where he's at, get at me. I even went to Hook's crib, but he didn't hear from him. It's like he vanished from the earth! And you know the police is looking for him for killing Moe-dog. It seems he did it in broad day light and left a lot of witnesses."

"Damn!' said Mont-Mont angrily. "I was suppose to be wit'em when that shit went down. And if I would've been there, I would have killed everybody on that block to make sure they ain't see my nigga's face!"

He then sighed and said, "All of this because them punk ass cops killed the homie Fats. But if you talk to Light, tell 'em I said a branch fell but the tree won't fall!!!"

"No doubt," said C-Allah. "If I talk to'em, I'll tell'em. But the nigga is real low-key, wherever he is."

Then changing the subject he asked, "So what's up? Are you aiight? You need something? If so, I can do it today."

"Nah I'm good," answered Mont-Mont. "A coupla' bitches my lil brother had transporting for him, stepped up to the plate for a nigga. One of them even wanna marry a nigga if I was to blow trial and shit."

"Nigga, you better get married now!"

"What the fuck you talking about getting married now?!" barked Mont-Mont. "I'ma beat these punk ass cases they got me on! I'm saying, they ain't got no witnesses!'

C-Allah laughed and said, "Calm down nigga, I'm fucking with you. You're gonna be aiight."

"If it's somebody telling, just make sure they don't get to testify nigga!"

"Come on man, that's without saying!" sighed C-Allah. "I got that. I'm just trying to catch up to this nigga Light! If you get in touch with him or find out where he at, let me know so I can holla at him."

"Yeah I got you," said Mont-Mont. Then changing the subject he asked, "Did you talk to L?"

Sucking his teeth C-Allah answered, "I'm not wasting my time with L. I know the nigga don't like me. Plus, he don't tell me shit! I don't even know all the niggas we got beef with out here in these streets. I see shit in the newspapers and ask 'em about it, and the nigga start looking nervous like I'ma fucking Fed or something! Like the nigga Hook said, the dude L act like he don't wanna fuck wit'us or something."

"I don't know why the nigga Hook is talking like that!" said Mon-Mont angrily. "He's way outta line! He's not Bulldog Crew. We are! And if we got a problem amongst each other, we deal with it! Man, I hope he ain't shit on L's name to Light."

"Yeah he did," said C-Allah.

"Damn!" said Mont-Mont angrily. "Yo, I'll talk to you later today. I gotta ask this CO bitch that just came in something," he said looking at the pretty light-skinned female CO making her rounds around the cell block.

"And I'm going to call L right after I call you back," said Mont-Mont hanging up the phone.

Before Mont-Mont could approach the CO, two inmates stepped to her and started talking to her, about nothing!

CO Valerie Walker was used to the chitter-chatter, but never showed no real interest in the inmates. She would only laugh and talk with them, because it made her eight hour shift go by a lot quicker. Most of the inmates would tell her all of their personal business, from what they were in jail for, all the way to their family problems and failed relationships.

Mont-Mont hated guys like that. He felt it made real niggas in prison look bad. And when he got closer to the CO and the two inmates, just as he expected, one of the inmates, a tall light-skinned guy with braids was telling the CO about his family problems.

"My sister was suppose to come up today," said the guy, "but she couldn't make it. I hate when she put dumb shit before me. She work at a strip club off Jamaica Avenue and—"

"When you're done with your psychiatric counseling," Mont-Mont rudely interrupted the guy but speaking to the CO as he continued stepping to his cell, "make sure you come and see me."

The two inmates and the CO looked at his back as he walked into his cell as if he owned the world.

"Who the fuck that nigga thinks he is?" barked one of the inmates to impress the CO, but she paid him no mind. She was more curious as to who the guy was and she wondered what in the hell did he want to talk to her about.

"Y'all know him?" she asked the two inmates standing in front of her.

"Nah," answered the dark-skinned inmate happy to beat his friend to answer her question. "He just came in yesterday. I hear he's suppose to be somebody, but fuck that nigga! My name is P-Banger!"

CO Walker wanted to laugh in his face, because the guy was near fifty years old, walked with a limp, most of his teeth were gone, and he still was running around like a kid joining gangs and spitting out razors. The most bizarre sight in the world were men who were stuck in their second childhood, thought CO Walker. She wanted a real man, and none of these inmates and COs alike in the building had fit the bill.

"Let me go and see what this guy wants," said CO Walker dismissing the two inmates in front of her. "Which one of y'all got food in your locker?" she asked.

The light-skinned inmate smiled, because he knew his friend had nothing in his locker and was basically starving! "Ms.Walker, I keep food!' the inmate boasted. "I got cold cuts, rolls and mad junk food!"

"Good,' she smiled. "Wash your hands and make me a sandwich with something to drink. And bring me a bag of chips."

She then walked away switching her ass, knowing they were looking at it bounce from side to side.

"Where you going?" asked the dark-skinned inmate.

"I'm gonna make my girl Ms. Walker a sandwich!" answered his friend.

"Yo, can I get a sandwich too?"

"Hell no! You stupid?!" remarked his friend walking off to make the sandwich for the CO, with his friend trailing behind.

CO Walker was 35 years old and had been working on Rikers Island for nearly 15 years. She had gradually watched how the prison's population had changed and had become gang infested. One of the first gangs in New York prisons were the Latin Kings. They were basically a group of Puerto Rican inmates who had become tired of being the victims of getting robbed, cut and stabbed, and felt it was in their best interest to band together and stop being victimized. But not to get it confused, not all Puerto Rican inmates were victims. Far from it! There were those who laughed at gangs and had reputations for getting extremely busy! Strangely, these were the ones who did not have racist attitudes and felt that if you did not get busy no matter what color you was, you deserved to get robbed and victimized. Later on in years, these same guys had become instant leaders of this gang to capitalize off of the numbers of them, and reap the benefits of what being a leader would bring. This gang became strong, and of course a lot of Blacks became victims of their assaults. But out of retaliation, a lot of Blacks formed their own sects of Bloods, Crips, Nubians, etc. After a while, it was no longer a race thing but what sect you claimed, and like the Puerto Ricans, Blacks that got extremely busy automatically received leadership positions. It was basically what the gangs figured their hands had called for. But also, the guys who did not belong to any gangs no matter their nationality who got busy, did not find themselves being victimized either.

CO Walker did not like the gang era. She preferred the days when it was only two groups: the gangsters and the cowards!

When she got in front of Mont-Mont's cell, she was surprise to see him with his shirt off doing push-ups. She had to admit he was definitely brolic and chiseled up! He got up from off the floor and stood in front of her like an African Warrior with his head held high. She knew instantly that he was definitely one of the gangsters she admired from back in the days, and she could tell that he still had it in him.

"What took you so long to get rid of them birds?" Mont-Mont asked. "You think I got all day?"

"Excuse me?" asked CO Walker with her hand on her hip and her lip turned upwards about to curse him out.

Mont-Mont smiled and said, "I guess you no longer have a crush on me, huh Valerie?"

She looked at him hard with her eyes squinted, as if that would help her memory. Then it hit her, and she couldn't believe her eyes! Her mouth dropped open and her eyes widened.

"Mont-Mont?" she asked not believing who stood in front of her.

"In the flesh!" smiled Mont-Mont.

She couldn't believe he was actually standing in front of her. He used to go out with her Puerto Rican friend Rosa when they were younger, but Valerie always had a thing for him and he knew it.

"I heard you was in a world of trouble," said CO Walker. "Oh my God! I can't believe I'm seeing you after all of these years. I heard you came home and I was trying to get in touch with you, but I can never catch up to you. Then I heard you was a part of that Bulldog thing. Oh my God! What's up!" she asked happily. "I am happy to see you! Not in jail, but happy to see you. Do you need anything? Are you alright? I'm a CO and everything, but fuck that! You'll always be my baby!"

"I'm straight," laughed Mont-Mont. "But then again, now that you mentioned it. You can bring me a 007 knife and some trees. You know how we do!"

"Boy!" she laughed. "I see you'll never change. But you my nigga, so you know I got chu!"

"Good! Now show me some love," he smiled with his arms held wide apart.

With a surprised look she asked, "Oh, you're not prejudice anymore?"

"What are you talking about?" he asked confused.

"Now you know you're stuck, on the Spanish thing," she teased with a smile.

"Nah, it's not like that," he laughed. "I love all women, but I do have to admit, Spanish women are willing to do what most Black women won't do."

"Well, maybe you've finally met the right Black woman," she smiled devilishly. "I just hope you can handle it!"

"We'll see," smiled back Mont-Mont with a bit of lust in his eyes.

Changing the subject he said, "You better get back to the birds, before they start running their mouths to your higher-ups! You know these niggas talk like bitches, and it ain't the same from back in the days."

"Yeah, I know. I was thinking the same thing to myself earlier," said CO Walker.

She wanted to stay in his presence and talk for the remainder of the day, but she knew he was right about the other inmates. However, she was already thinking of ways and places in the jail to spend with him. She had been working 16-upper cell block long enough, to know how to maneuver around jealous male COs and snitching inmates.

She quickly tongue kissed Mont-Mont as he palmed her ass. She then quickly exited from his cell. He had her panties wet from just a kiss, and she could not wait to do more with the man she always had a crush on.

Later that night, a group of inmates approached Mont-Mont in front of his cell.

"Yo par, you Scooby Doo?" asked one of the inmates asking Mont-Mont was he Blood.

Mont-Mont looked at the ten Blood members and busted out laughing. He could tell they were fresh off of the streets, and looked as if they were rehabilitating from smoking crack!

Mont-Mont still had his upnorth Attica size, and knew he could break every last one of them with his hands. However, this was the land of knives and razors! He couldn't wait to get the 007 knife from CO Walker, but in his possession he already had a nice and sharp jail made shank.

"Hell no, I'm not Blood!" answered Mont-Mont with his face screwed up in a gangster glare. "I'm BDC, nigga!"

"What's BDC?" asked the leader of the nine other Bloods.

"Bulldog Crew!" answered Mont-Mont.

You could see the fear in most of their faces when he made the statement. "Now if it's a problem," continued Mont-Mont, "we can do this fair." He looked at the leader of these Bloods and said, "You and two of your best gunmen meet me in the bathroom!"

Chapter 29

After watching the local news and reading the newspaper, L felt a bit better. Mainly because from what he gathered, all of the eye-witnesses he saw or read about, did not actually see who done the shooting in Manhattan that left six dead of which two were police officers. Of course the police speculated that he was a participant in the crime, but they did not have enough evidence as of yet to charge him. They figured being that Fats and Whitey were counted among the dead and Light was on the run for killing Moe-dog in broad day light, L had to play a part in at least the first crime.

L was keeping a very low profile only going into the streets at night when it was dark out. He and Tonya were back on speaking terms, but he still did not see much of her these days. Maybe he'd give her a call later on and see how she was doing, he thought as he got out of bed wearing only his flannel boxers. As he walked to the bathroom to take that urgent just wake up piss, he wondered why Big Lord or better yet the police hadn't come to his projects looking for him yet. They had to know where he lived. He already saw the story on the local news about the death of Moe-dog and his girlfriend Karen, but what surprised him most was when they splashed a big picture of Light across the television as the person responsible for the two killings. The news woman stated that it was several witnesses to the shooting, including the brother of the deceased young woman, who identified Maurice "Light" Jones as the perpetrator from a photo ray selection.

"Damn " L swore under his breath. He had been hoping that after the big Manhattan shoot-out, Light would have laid low. But now he had committed more murders and this time carelessly, because of his emotions. L tried calling him continuously to find out who these witnesses were, so he could try to help him clean up the mess he made, but Light's cell phone kept saying the party was not taking any calls. His mind raced to where he thought Light could be hiding, and he was genuinely concerned and hoped he would hear from his comrade soon. He already took all of his guns to his sister's house. He didn't want too many guns in his apartment, just in case the police did roll up. The only gun he kept was a .45 automatic.

As soon as L came out of the bathroom, the telephone began ringing. He picked it up on the third ring, and after clearing his throat he asked, "Yo what up, who's this?"

"What up homie? This is Mont-Mont."

"Oh shit," said L sitting down on the bed. "What's going on? Where you at?"

"Man," sighed Mont-Mont. "I'm on the motherfucking Island."

"You in jail?" asked L surprised as he sat up straight.

"Yeah man," answered Mont-Mont. "I got a few murder charges against me and two weapons possessions. I'll be able to beat the bodies though, 'cause I know they ain't got no witnesses."

Then changing the subject he asked, "But more importantly, what's up with the homie Light?"

"I ain't talk to him," answered L. "But I tried calling him though. I'm not getting any answer. They got my boy all fucked up all over the news!"

"Yeah I know," replied Mont-Mont sadly. "I just saw it. But homie check it right, I know we didn't see eye to eye on a few things but I got mad love for you. BDC forever! I'ma loyal nigga. And I'll die for niggas I love! I say that because, I talked to C-Allah earlier and he said the nigga Hook was pissing in his ear and in Light's ear about you. I heard he was saying a lot of bad shit about you. And I ain't bringing this to your attention to stir up shit, but I bring this to you because you have a right to know being that you're BDC. Hook is a cool nigga but he ain't Bulldog Crew from what I observe, so fuck'em!"

"Good looking out," said L. "But I ain't worried about that nigga Hook. Me and Light go too far back, and been through too much for him to listen to that big head motherfucker. It's a lot I wanna kick it to you about, but not over the phone. Before I hang up, give me your information and I'll get up there to see you. Do you need anything?"

"Nah I'm good," answered Mont-Mont. "I got a few people making sure I'm straight,"

"Well, I'll bring you some razors."

Mont-Mont laughed and said, "Nah, you know I don't do the razor thing, unless I'm going to court. I'm good homie. I had to check a few Blood cats, but they ain't want it. And I had to slap up this Spanish kid for running his mouth about me and this CO bitch I'm kicking it with at the moment. Anyway, you just take care of yourself and come check me when you get a chance. And yo, try to help the homie Light out, if you know what I mean."

"I'm two steps ahead of you," chuckled L. "But you know what?" he asked, and before Mont-Mont could respond he continued. "All of us got money, but we ain't got no real structure. No cause for some of the shit we do. We didn't even have to do some of the shit we do. And that's what bothers me. We ain't got no goals and that defeats the purpose of being crewed up! You feel me?"

"Yeah man," said Mont-Mont but not understanding at all. The bottom line was that he thought like Light and Fats and all that mattered to him was killing, getting more money, having sex and staying loyal to his team.

"I'm gonna call you back in the morning," said Mont-Mont not wanting to hear L's sermon about change. The last thing he needed was for somebody to blow his high from the blunt he just smoked before making the call. "When I call you in the morning, I'll give you my information then."

"Yeah, do that! One," said L hanging up the phone.

Mont-Mont wasn't so bad after all, he thought as he got up to get dressed. It was 7:00 PM on a Monday night, and L figured that he'd go to his sister's house and see what she and her husband were up to. He admired their relationship, and wondered if he possessed what it took and maybe one day have the same with Tonya. Ever since he'd been with her, he started to think about things he had never gave thought to before.

L walked over to his closet and grabbed a blue pair of Sean John jeans, a blue and white Polo shirt and a thin blue Polo jacket.

After getting dressed and putting on his blue Yankees baseball cap, he tucked his gun down into his pants and concealed it with his shirt. Just as he was about to walk out of the door, the telephone began ringing. He figured it was probably Mont-Mont calling back, but when he answered it he was surprised to hear the female voice on the other end of the phone.

"What's up, baby?" asked Tonya. "What was you doing?" L was smiling from ear to ear when he heard her voice. He missed her so much and wished she was in his presence right now, so he could hug and kiss her beautiful face and lips. She was all the things he had ever wanted in a woman, and though she was no little girl, she had an innocence about her that made him feel as though he had to always be around to protect her. Because of that, she always made fun of the little things he did. Like not introducing her to his friends, telling her don't speak to the girls in his building, and letting the guys in his projects know that if they so much as said hello to her he would have their heads! She would always joke that she felt so over protected, it was no need for her to keep up with her appearance anymore being that guys were scared to talk to her anyway. L was missing her smile, the way she laughed when he shuffled cards, and everything else about her as he hoped she would come over and spend the night with him.

"I'm not doing anything," answered L. "I was about to go to my sister's house, but I can put that off for another day. I would love to see you. Can you come through?"

"Not tonight," she answered, "because I'm spending time with Lisa at her brother Omar's house. She and I have to get up early in the morning and go see Pam."

"How is she doing?" asked L concerned.

Tonya paused for a moment and then said, "Everything is the same. She's still in the coma."

"I trust she'll come out of it, and again I apologize."

"L, you don't have to keep apologizing," sighed Tonya. "What's done is done. We just have to put it in God's hands and prays she comes out of it okay. Every night, we all do prayer together for her. Prayer works."

Then changing the subject she asked, "Do you miss me?"

L laughed and said, "Girl, I don't know what you've done to me, but you're constantly in my thoughts even when I'm sleeping!"

"I miss you too," she smiled. "And I'll see you soon. Go ahead to your sister's house, and I'll see you this weekend. You know, I saw your friend Light on the news. This beef they got doesn't make any sense. And even though Moe-dog and Gina broke off their relationship, she's distraught over what happened to him. We had a long talk and she said she knew it was coming, because of the way he was living. And when she said that, I thought about you."

"I didn't have anything to do with Moe-dog dying," said L.

"I'm not saying you did," responded Tonya. "But what I'm saying is, you're part of the streets and the reality is your own death may be around the corner. So how am I suppose to deal with that, if it were to occur? You know I love you."

Not having an answer for her question, L said, "Baby, we'll work through this."

After a moment of silence Tonya said, "I really love you."

"I love you too," smiled L.

"Hold on," said Tonya. "Bishop wants to talk to you."

Within seconds Richard was on the telephone.

"Bishop, what's up homie?" asked L hoping Richard would not keep him on the phone all night talking about the bible. When he was in Attica, Richard sent him so many letters containing bible scriptures, L remembered a lot of them by heart.. He agreed with some of them, but that whole Christian thing was something L was not ready for. Everything had its time, and to L, now was not it!

"How are you doing, L."

"I guess you can say, I'm maintaining."

"That's good. Did you see Light on the news?"

"Yeah, I saw him. I haven't spoken to him though. Actually, the only one I spoke to was Mont-Mont, and he's locked down on Rikers Island right now."

"What's going on with C-Allah?" asked Richard.

"I don't know," answered L. "I haven't spoken to him in a while either. I guess everybody is falling back for a minute."

"Everybody should've been fell back. And that includes the whole Bulldog Crew, Moe-dog, Whitey and Big Lord. This beef doesn't make any sense, and I hope you pull back from all of this street stuff, L. Especially being that you're the only one with some kind of sense!"

"Man," sighed L. "I didn't want no war with them niggas, and I still don't. But this shit is on, and you know I'm not letting anyone do anything to me!"

"I know man, I know. Trust me, I do."

They talked for five more minutes before hanging up.

L left his apartment and took the stairs, instead of waiting for the elevator.

"What's up, L?" chorused a group of young boys standing in front of the building.

"Ain't nothing," answered L as he continued stepping.

When he got near his car, a gunshot went off. He knew it had to be Big Lord, and was surprised to see that he was not hit being that the person shooting were no further away than 50 feet from him!

L took off running and pulled out his own gun, as the second bullet whizzed by his head! He spinned around and returned two shots from his own gun, nearly hitting the gunman in the head. But now was not the time or place to be in a shoot-out, so L fired two more shots and ran back to his building. But as he ran and looked over his shoulder, he was definitely surprised to see what he saw. The figure shooting to kill him was not Big lord as he expected. L's mouth dropped open when he saw Light jump in his car and drive away!

Chapter 30

Big Lord was saddened to hear about the death of Moe-dog. He warned him continuously about being seen so much in Vanderveer Projects. He understood he had a girl there, but it was never smart to deal with a project chick unless you were from the area, Big Lord argued on many occasions. Because he figured, if guys from the projects didn't know you, didn't like you, or was scared of you, they would quickly tell the police or the enemies your whereabouts. That's why Big lord made it a habit not to stay in any areas of the ghettos no longer than five minutes. When he did stay longer, he would be surrounded by his most loyal gunmen. But he knew deep down inside, they was scared of the infamous Bulldog Crew, and that's why he hired Moe-dog and Whitey because they was just as dangerous as the crew of gunmen he found himself in beef with.

Big lord knew Light was laying low due to his exposure in the news for killing Moe-dog and Karen, he heard C-Allah was also laying low but was trying hard to contact Light, and Mont-Mont was locked down on Rickers Island, so he figured it would be easy for him to catch L by himself in the Langston Hughs Projects where he lived. But first, he wanted to get the money man out of the way.

Hook was just like a lot of gangsters, thought Big Lord. He always had to be seen in the 'hood. He was very flashy; driving Bentleys through the Brooklyn streets, shooting dice on the corner taking re-up money from the up and coming hustlers, and having sex with the best looking women in the 'hoods; young and old. So Big lord figured it would be relatively easy to get Hook and wondered why no gangster had gotten him thus far!

As Big lord drove through the Brownsville streets of Brooklyn in his black Cadillac Escalade, he was surprised to see his ex-girlfriend Nicky coming out of a corner grocery store carrying a little girl in her arms. He pulled over to the curb and blew his horn to get Nicky's attention.

She squinted her eyes to see who was in the truck. Normally she would've just walked up to the vehicle, but she had her one year old daughter in her arms so she stayed where she was and wondered who was in the truck.

Realizing the situation, Big Lord stepped out of the truck and when Nicky saw who it was, she became so excited that she nearly dropped her baby. Big lord smiled and waved her over. He then got back in the truck and within seconds, she was sitting in the passenger's seat right beside him. She knew Big lord was a big balla, and figured now was the perfect opportunity to get back with him. She had just broke up with her baby's father, and figured if anyone could put her back on the map it was Big lord! She already heard the news about his girlfriend being shot and counted it as her good fortune.

"What's up baby?" she squealed happily as she leaned over and kissed him on the cheek. "Why I ain't see you in so long? What have you been up to? Remember, we went to Atlantic City? I'm saying, when are you taking me out again?"

She asked a thousand questions before he could say anything to her. Cutting her twenty one questions off in mid-sentence, Big Lord asked a question of his own.

"Who's baby is this?" he asked smiling and looking down at the cute little girl.

"Yours," she answered laughing. Then getting serious she said, "No, it's this bum ass wanna-be hustling ass nigga from East New York. He lives in Pink Houses and he ain't no fucking body!"

Big Lord could tell Nicky's mind was working as to who she could get to watch her daughter, while she freaked off and hung out with him. What hoes would do for money, he thought. But he had no time for Nicky or her game, so he figured he'd get straight to the point.

"Nicky," said Big Lord touching her hand and looking into her eyes, "you know Hook, right?"

"Who don't know Hook?" she responded.

"Did you see him?" asked Big Lord.

"I heard about y'all beef, and you know I'm not getting involved with that. I have a daughter to raise," she replied looking down at her sleeping baby girl. " I don't need the drama!"

"Come on," said Big Lord. "You know I would never put you in no drama. You know that! But I need to get this nigga! Nicky, you wanna see me die?"

Nicky looked real hard into his face as her eyes watered up a bit. She remembered all of the good times in the past that she and Big Lord had shared, and she illusioned herself to think that those times could be re-lived again. But then she looked down at her sleeping daughter again, and was not willing to get caught up in Big lord and Hook's beef.

"Nicky, once I get rid of this nigga, it can be just about me and you again," lied Big lord hoping she would fall for the game. He knew women in general were emotional by nature, so he figured he'd play on that and see what he can find out.

"Nicky, he'll never know you told me anything," continued Big Lord. "And after I take care of Hook, we can shoot to Cancun or somewhere. Just me, you, and baby girl there.

Big lord was willing to tell her anything to get some information about Hook. He had no plans of seeing Nicky, or her daughter ever again! He knew she and Hook knew one another very well, because from what he remembered they lived on the same block at one time, before he blew up. Also, if anyone wanted to know anything about Hook or anyone else in the street, Nicky was the one to talk to. It seemed as if nothing happened in Brooklyn that she didn't know about.

Big lord kissed her softly on the lips, looked into her eyes and with a smile asked, "Are we going to Cancun or what?"

Nicky was feening to get away from the dangerous and boring Brownsville streets. She licked her bottom lip as she looked at Big lord and debated what she should do.

She then thought about all the fun they would have in Cancun and with a smile asked, "What'chu wanna know?"

"Just his whereabouts," smiled Big lord.

"Well," began Nicky. "I seen Pookie get in the car with him not long ago, but Pookie gotta come back soon to hit his workers off. So, nine times outta ten, Hook's gonna drop him back off' cause Pookie's car is still parked in front of the spot," she pointed to a building across the street from where they were parked.

"Okay," said Big Lord. "Just lay low, and after everything is taken care of, we can roll out. You can start packing and I'll give you a call tonight."

"You don't even have my number."

"Oh shit," said Big Lord looking around inside of the truck for a pen. After finding one and writing her number down, he gave her a kiss and watched her exit from the truck.

But before closing the door, she asked with a smile, "Can I have some money?"

"Of course," smiled Big Lord. He knew it was coming. That's something he had never liked about street girls, they always asked for money, with none of their own. He pulled out a stack from his pocket and peeled off five one hundred dollar bills.

"Make sure you're ready when I call you," he said hoping she would hurry up and disappear.

"I'll be ready," she said closing the door and walking away.

Big Lord was parked right across the street from Pookie's spot and was amazed at Nicky's knowledge that he would have to come back soon to re-up his workers. Already he saw disappointed fiends leave the dope spot in search of their next destination.

Big Lord pulled out a brand new 16 shot nine millimeter as he looked around the area through his tinted windows. His cell phone began ringing and he was surprised to see Omar's home number on the caller ID. He hadn't talked to Omar since their big argument. He had a lot of love for Omar, but he didn't appreciate him interfering in his personal street business. Especially being that his friend was no longer down to put in work with him. He wondered why Omar was calling him. If he had a change of heart about things and was ready to get busy, Big Lord was willing to accept his apology, give him one, and accept his invitation to ride with him. But when he answered his cell phone it was not Omar on the other end, it was Lisa and he wondered why she was calling him being that he and her brother had a big fall out.

"Big Lord, how are you doing?" asked Lisa.

"What's up Leese?" asked Big Lord watching the area closely hoping that Hook and Pookie would pull up soon.

"I know you and my brother are going through y'all thing," said Lisa, "but I felt that I should still call you, and let you know what's going on. We're on our way to the hospital. Did anyone tell you about Pam?"

Big Lord's heart raced and pounded in his chest. He prayed Lisa was not calling to tell him that Pam had died. That was the last thing he needed to hear, but he braced himself for the bad news.

"No," he answered. "No one told me anything about Pam. Tell me what's going on."

"Well," said Lisa. "The bad news is that she'll be in the hospital for a while and the good news is she's out of the coma and she's talking and eve---"

"Word?!" yelled Big Lord excitedly,cutting her off in mid-sentence. "Yo Leese, good looking for calling me! I'm on my way to the hospital. I'll meet y'all there! I just gotta make a quick call."

Big Lord hung up the phone before Lisa could say another word, and he began dialing another number.

When he got the party he wanted on the other line he said, "Yo Sty, get a few shorties and strap'em up! I need you to take this information down. I want y'all to shoot over here, and kill this nigga Hook! I gotta move out. Something very important just popped up. You got a pen? Aiight. Come to Saratoga and ----"

$

Light was driving Kia's Honda Accord being that it was more down low than the expensive cars he owned.

"I'ma show these punk motherfuckers how gangster I am!" he said to himself as he drove out to the Nassau Hospital.

Light had no idea that Pam was no longer in a coma, but her present condition meant nothing to him anyway. He was going to kill her so Big Lord could feel the pain that he was feeling. Right now was all about get back, but he knew he couldn't just walk in the hospital and blow her away with the .44 Bulldog handgun or nine millimeter he carried. He had no silencer on any of them and knew one gun shot would have the hospital surrounded with police. It would be impossible for him to get away! But stashed in his car's compartment, was the very sharp scalpel he planned to use. He was already a wanted man so he didn't care who saw his face after leaving the hospital, he just needed to get in, kill Pam and get out. He had plans to cut her up pretty bad. He figured he'd cut her throat first before cutting off body parts.

Light was blinded with rage! Not only was he depressed over what happened to Fats, Kia and his daughter, but he was also upset that his attempt on L's life was unsuccessful. And was even more upset from the fact that L had almost killed him! He knew he should've approached L as if everything was cool and then killed him. But he shrugged it off, because he knew he would get L on a later date. He knew he was more dangerous than L, because he was willing to kill in front of a million witnesses if he had to. L would never take such risk.

Light figured he would also get C-Allah and Hook as well, when the opportunity presented itself. It was him against the world now, he thought as he continued driving to the hospital while listening to the same titled "Me Against The World" CD by the late great rapper Tupac Shakur.

He didn't even try to contact C-Allah, but he did try to get in touch with Hook. Unfortunately Hook was dodging his phone calls and visits because he felt that Light was too hot to be around. He did not want the police heat Light's presence would bring him. Light now knew that being on the run was similar to already being in prison with a life bid. No one wanted to look out for you, no one wanted to contact you to put you up on what was going on, and definitely no one wanted to assist you on a financial level! It was basically a life of isolation. You would have to associate with new people who did not know you was a fugitive of law, or you can bet your ass that they would get away from you as soon as possible as well.

Light already heard through the streets that Mont-Mont was locked down on Rikers Island. He then smiled at the thought of his comrade and wished he was out in the streets with him. Because he knew without a doubt that Mont-Mont would be down for whatever because his loyalty was to the death! No matter how crazy the plan, he would do it. He knew L would never consider going to the hospital with him to kill Pam. He was too stuck on Tonya, and just the thought of her convinced Light to kill her as well when the opportunity presented itself.

When Light pulled up to the hospital, he couldn't believe his luck. "Fuck Pam," he said as he watched Big Lord quickly pull into a parking space. He didn't know why Big lord was rushing, but it didn't matter to Light one way or another. He adjusted his guns and left the key in the ignition with the car still running, as he exited from Kia's car.

Normally, Big Lord was very observant when it came to his surroundings, but he was so happy to finally be able to speak to Pam since the incident, that he paid no attention to anything around him. He just wanted to see his future wife and that thought alone made him smile. But he didn't even get a chance to make it to the hospital's entrance when Light ran up on him from behind and pulled the trigger of his .44 Bulldog handgun blowing away the back of Big Lord's head! Blood and brain matter stained the sidewalk.

Light then ran back to Kia's car and drove away, as the hospital's confused security guards ran in different directions with the screaming terrified people that heard the gunshot, or those who witnessed the bold broad-daylight killing!!!!!

Chapter 31

Hook had just pulled up on the block, thirty minutes after Big Lord had left the scene. He and Pookie exited from Hooks' brand new silver Bentley Continental GT. He was styling and being boisterous as usual as he laughed and talked with his friend.

Pookie's name had definitely betrayed his appearance. He was 6 foot 2, dark-skinned and weighed over 250 pounds. The gold tooth in his mouth gleamed as he smiled and listened to Hook boasting about how rich he was.

"Them niggas is bums!" laughed Hook. "They call that shit they doing hustling?! I can feed their whole fucking projects for a year nigga!"

Pookie laughed as he spotted three dope fiends about to approach him. Before they could ask him anything, he said, "Yo, wait five more minutes and then y'all can cop!"

They walked a few feet away and waited impatiently to get their fix. It was getting dark outside and out of nowhere, more fiends appeared from the shadows waiting to cop their drugs.

Hook looked at his diamond infested Cartier watch and said, "Take care of business, and when you're done give me a call. I'm jetting out to Co-Op City to see some bitches I met."

"Hold up nigga," said Pookie. "I'm coming with you! I want some of that pussy too! I ain't never fuck no bitches from out there. Give me one minute."

He then called a light-skinned youth who was sitting in front of the spot over to the car. He pulled a brown paper bag from his jacket pocket and handing it to the youth said, "Take this inside, and tell Joe it's twenty thousand dollars worth, and if he needs more just give me a call on my cell."

The youth took the bag inside of the apartment building and after five minutes of his departure, Pookie nodded his head to two dope fiends and once they started walking towards the spot, the rest of those waiting followed suit.

Hook and Pookie was just about to get into Hook's Bentley, when a guy wearing a baseball cap pulled down to his eyes quickly crept up on the two thugs. They didn't see him or the silver nine millimeter in his hand until it was too late.

Hook grabbed for his own gun but was hit two times in the chest, as Pookie ran towards the building. When he reached the steps to the spot, he thought he was home free but that illusion died with him, when three bullets from the gunman's gun entered the back of his head.

The dope fiends that did not enter the building yet, ran to safety clutching tightly to their dollar bills. The ones that made it inside of the building before the gunfire erupted, nervously waited for the gunfire to cease. They just hoped the gunman did not enter the building firing his gun before they can get their fix! They've grown so accustomed to seeing murder being done to Blacks and Puerto Ricans, that none of them took it seriously anymore. They have grown numb, immune to the pain.

Hook laid on the ground still breathing but was too weak to reach for his gun.

"You should've stayed out of our fucking business!" said L angrily as he pulled the trigger again killing Hook with a bullet to the middle of his head.

L then quickly made his getaway. He knew the dope fiends would rob Hook and Pookie for their money and jewelry, before police could even get to the scene or anywhere near it. After all, this was Brownsville!

As L made his getaway, he saw a black van pull up and three young boys jumped out with Mac-elevens in their hands. They did not see L, but they saw Hook's car and quickly walked towards it with their guns aimed and ready to shoot.

When L got two blocks away, he jumped inside of a blue stolen Nissan Sentra. He had no clue as to who the young boys were who jumped out of the van, but one thing was for certain, they were coming to let some bullets fly.

As L drove away, he was kind of on edge until he pulled up and parked the car a block away from his projects. He wore black leather gloves, so he wasn't too concerned about leaving any prints inside of the car. Plus, he knew the car would be gone within an hour or so, once the neighborhood kids, or crack addicts discovered the abandoned car with the ignition popped out. L walked away from the car, leaving the door open. It would definitely be used for joy riding, or sold for some drugs.

As soon as L reached the front of his building, he stopped to greet the group of young boys standing out front.

"What up, what up, what up?" he asked with a smile

"What's up L?" they chorused.

"Niggas came through here looking for me?" asked L to see if they would put him on point to what was going on in the projects while he was gone.

"Hell no!" answered the youngest youth out of the three with his young face screwed up. "Niggas know not to come through here! The only ones that came through here was a few bitches. And they still in the building. So, we just waiting for them to come back down so we can push up!"

L smiled, pulled out a bank roll of money from his pocket and peeled off three hundred dollar bills handing it to the young boy.

"That's for the three of y'all," said L referring to the young boys standing in front of him. "When them bitches come downstairs, take them to the movies or something."

"The movies?!" said another youth. "Man, we taking them bitches to Pebbles Beach!"

All three of the young boys started laughing.

"Pebbles Beach?" asked L confused. "Where the hell is that?"

"The roof!" answered the young youth causing L to double over in laughter. These kids were getting crazier and crazier, he thought as he walked inside of his building and pressed for the elevator.

When the elevator reached the lobby and the doors opened, the four young girls the youths were waiting on, were getting off of the elevator as L was getting on. They looked at L and smiled openly flirting with him.

L smiled back and said, "Have fun at the beach!"

They turned around and looked at him confused, before the elevator door closed.

When the elevator opened up on the fifth floor, L stepped off of it with his gun in his hand. He knew he had a lot of enemies that wanted him dead, so he was always on point and ready for an ambush. That's why he was never routine. Sometimes he would take the stairs, sometimes he would take the elevator, and then there were times when he would take the elevator to the third floor and walk the remaining two flights up.

As soon as he walked into his apartment, the telephone was ringing off the hook. He walked into his bedroom and snatched it up as he threw his gun on the bed.

"Who dis?" he asked taking off his baseball cap.

"What's up? This Born-Self," said the voice on the other end of the line.

"What's up?" asked L wondering how the Franklin Avenue thug had acquired his phone number being that it was unlisted.

Born-Self was also dangerous, but L felt the thug was no real threat to him, because he had way too many bad habits such as: Being seen in clubs too much, hanging around too many other grimey thugs, and being in relationships with mainly boosters and credit card scammers. L knew being seen in clubs too much gave your enemies the opportunity to kill you, hanging around so many grimey thugs gave your enemies the opportunity to have them flip on you and kill you for money, and being in relationships with trifling hoes had always gotten brothers killed. He could even remember hearing about Born-Self setting up his own homeboy and having him killed over one of them foul ass bitches. L hated grimey niggas, and just thinking about it upset him.

"How the hell you get my number?!" asked L angrily.

Born-Self laughed and said, "Damn homie, be easy. I'm on your side. But to answer your question, I got it from that stupid bitch Tarsha form L.G. you use to fuck wit' awhile back. I'm just calling to put you on about some shit."

"Talk about it," said L calming down,

"Yo," said Born-Self, "you can't let my name get out as to putting you on point about this, but niggas from Kingsboro is planning on coming through your projects to get you over Moe-dog getting killed. I never liked that nigga anyway!"

"Who's suppose to be getting at me?" asked L.

"Turtle and dem niggas," answered Born-Self.

"Aiight," said L. "Good looking out,. I'll take care of it."

"No doubt," replied Born-Self. "Yo, get up wit'me. Come through later or something. I got bad ass Kim from the Plaza here at the crib and her homegirl Tamika from Van Dyke is suppose to be here in a minute."

"Nah, I'm good," responded L. "I gotta go, but I'll give you a call another time."

"But you don't have my number."

"Trust me, that won't be hard to get," said L hanging up the telephone. He would never be caught hanging out with grimey Born-Self, he thought to himself.

"The nigga gave up faggot ass Turtle," said L under his breath with a chuckle. "His own cousin."

A minute didn't even go by and the telephone began ringing again. L snatched it up and said, "Yo, who dis?"

"It's me!" answered Tonya angrily. "If you wasn't there, I'm sure you know what happened!"

"What?" asked L dumbfounded as to what she was talking about.

"You didn't see the news?" she asked.

"Nah," answered L. "I just got in.What's going on?"

"Turn the TV to Channel Nine!' she ordered.

L grabbed the remote and pressed it to the channel with the phone still to his ear. Being Tonya stayed silent, L heard just about everything the woman on the news said.

"We now take you back to the breaking news," said the news woman. "Police are still searching for the gunman that gunned down a notorious thug from the streets of Brooklyn in front of the Nassau Hospital, here in Long Island. The victim was identified as Shawn 'Big Lord' Moore. Shawn Moore's fiancé had just come out of a coma. Apparently, he was on his way to see her for the first time since coming out of the coma when he was viciously gunned down. The shooter in this case has been identified by police sources and witnesses as Maurice 'Light' Jones. He is also wanted for the double killing that left a young man and his girlfriend dead in the Vanderveer Estate in Brooklyn. If you have any information on this man, you can contact police at 5-7-7---"

L looked at the picture of Light across his television screen, and felt sick to his stomach. He couldn't believe what he was seeing. Even though Light had tried to kill him as well, he still had a lot of love for his friend, and had even tried to contact him continuously to see why they now had beef with one another. But it was still nearly impossible for him to touch bases with him.

"I don't believe this shit," said L into the phone as he sat down on his bed.

"We were at the hospital when it happened," said Tonya. "But we were in the hospital room talking to Pam when all of this had occurred. Pam doesn't even know what happened to Big Lord yet."

"She's out of the coma?" asked L.

"Yes, she's out of the coma," answered Tonya. "But it's going to be hard to explain to her what happened to her fiancé. I wonder how the guy Light knew Big Lord was on his way to the hospital."

A warning went off in L's head when Tonya made that statement to him. He knew it was Pam that Light was actually coming to get. Big Lord's presence just changed what he had planned. He also knew Light's killing spree was far from over.

"I need you to stay with me for awhile!" said L. "Tonya, this is very important!'

L knew he had to save Tonya's life, and the only way to do that was to have her close to him at all times!!!

Chapter 32

"Where is Big Lord?" asked Pam weakly while lying in her hospital bed.

Richard, Lisa, Gina and Tonya remained quiet, not wanting to be the one to give her the bad news about her fiancé. And Lisa had pleaded with Pam's parents, the doctors, and the nurses not to give Pam the bad news until she felt better physically. But today, Pam would not let up. She wanted to know where was Big Lord and why didn't he get to the hospital to see her yet. She's been out of the coma for two days now, and the bullet wound in her chest was healing nicely. She remembered a few of her ex-boyfriends in the past who had gotten shot would complain how the wound itched uncontrollably, whenever it rained outside.

Pam hoped that would not be the case with her, because she loved to sit at an open window when it rained and just think about things for hours! Plus, she thought about the days when she and Big Lord had made love in their back yard in the rain, and she looked forward to a few more of those episodes. However, Pam was just grateful to be alive. But what surprised everyone, was how calmly she took the news of who actually shot her. She even encouraged Tonya to stay with L. Especially being that he was the one who had saved her life. She just hoped Big Lord would see things her way and not do anything stupid, because she knew how he could be when he became angry. She heard stories in the streets of how he would torture his workers and friends, when he felt they betrayed him. So she could only imagine what he would do to his enemies! However, she personally only knew the big, gentle, caring, humorous, intelligent, loving and romantic side of Big Lord. But something always told her, that some of the things she'd heard about in the streets about him was true.

"Why do I have to keep asking y'all about Big Lord?" asked Pam.

"You tell her," Gina told Richard. "you're the preacher."

Normally, her statement would have been funny to everyone in the room, but this was a delicate and very serious matter.

"I'll tell her," said Lisa taking Pam's hand into hers. "Pam, I hate to tell you this but Big Lord got killed."

Pam's eyes shot wide open as she calmly asked, "What happened?"

She was too shocked about the news to cry or say anything further. His death hadn't really hit her yet. It didn't dawn on her that she would never see the only man she'd ever truly loved ever again.

"He got shot," continued Lisa, "by the guy Light from that Bulldog gang. But the police know he did it. He's on the news and everything, so he should be caught soon."

"He got shot at the house?" asked Pam.

"No," answered Lisa looking down at the floor. "In front of the hospital."

"Coming to see me?" asked Pam surprised.

"Yes," answered Lisa nodding her head up and down.

"When is the funeral?" asked Pam looking at Lisa.

Lisa continued looking down at the floor. She could not look into her friend's eyes for fear of what she would see. Pam's pain was hers as well, and she was not ready to face it in her best friend's eyes. Over the years, Big Lord had also been like a brother to her as well.

"The funeral is next week," answered Lisa.

"Oh," responded Pam.

Everyone watched her closely and waited to see her emotions but she did not show any. They were all worried about her, and hoped she would pull through all of this okay.

"I remember Divine got killed," Pam said out of the blue while glancing over at Gina.

She then looked at Richard stepping closer to her. "I'll get in touch with his parents and have a talk with them."

Tears began to fall from Pam's eyes.

Tonya was the only silent one in the hospital room. Because she still felt guilty being in a relationship with L; one of them who was there when her best friend got shot.

Gina took a napkin from her Gucci purse and wiped the tears away from Pam's eyes as they continued to fall. Being she went through the same pain of losing Divine, and even Moe-dog, she knew what her friend was feeling. Nothing had ever hit Gina like the death of her mother and Divine, and though she had broken up with Moe-dog before he passed away, she still felt scarred over his demise. It seemed as though everyone she had ever loved, was being taken away from her one by one.

"I need some more of that fucking Demoral," winced Pam referring to the strong medication the hospital had given her for the pain in her chest. But nothing could take away the pain of losing Big Lord. Her mind kept drifting back to him no matter how hard she tried to think about other things. She now truly felt what it was like to lose someone very close to you.

"I know Omar is fucked up as well," said Pam. "They were very close. Like brothers! Fuck that, I want him to get that nigga Light!"

"He ain't gonna do that," said Lisa with her head down. "Pam, you know he's not into that killing and stuff anymore."

"What?!" asked Pam angrily not understanding Lisa at all. "Yo, that was his man! It ain't like he gotta do shit personally! He can get one of them grimey niggas in the streets that he still cool with to do it!"

Gina sighed and said, "Omar and Big Lord had a big fall out before he died."

"For what?" asked Pam confused. As far as she remembered, they were like brothers and nothing could come between the two.

"They had a big argument," explained Lisa, "because Big Lord, Moe-dog and Whitey killed the guy Light's girlfriend, two other girls and a bunch of kids. It was real crazy."

"Get the fuck outta here!' said Pam angrily. "Big Lord would never do no shit like that. Yeah, he was no angel. But he wasn't no grimey ass nigga either."

She knew her deceased fiancé was dangerous, but what Lisa had just described she couldn't imagine Big Lord doing such a thing. Not to innocent women and kids.

Lisa sighed and said, "Pam, I don't know what took place. I'm just letting you know what's going on, because you have a right to know. None of this stuff makes sense."

Richard looked at his watch, leaned towards the hospital bed and after kissing Pam on the forehead he said, "We have to pick Dejanay up from Gloria's. Try to stay strong. We're praying for you, and if I can do anything for you, don't hesitate to ask. We love you and we'll be back to see you later on tonight. Do you need anything? Something to read or something?"

"No, I'll be okay," said Pam as her tears continued to fall from her eyes. "Y'all go on. I want Tonya to stay here so we can talk, being that she hadn't said a word since she'd been here."

They all kissed Pam on the cheek and forehead promising to come back later that evening, before leaving she and Tonya in the room alone.

"So, what's up?" asked Pam after they left.

Tonya dropped her head because she didn't know what to say. But then she courageously looked into Pam's eyes and said, "Pam, I feel terrible about what happened. And I feel it's my fault to a degree."

"It ain't your fault. Come here," said Pam slowly moving over on the big hospital bed so Tonya could lay down next to her.

Tonya sat her purse down on the small table, and slowly laid next to her best friend and they made small talk until Tonya's cell phone began ringing. She wasn't going to answer it when she saw it was L's number that showed.

But Pam knowing who it was said, "Answer it, I know who it is, and I wanna talk to him!"

$

"Are you going to the funeral?" asked Gloria sitting on Omar's desk in his office at the record label.

"Yeah I'm going," answered Omar. "As bad as I don't wanna go and see him like that, I believe I owe it to him. It'll be a slap in his family's face if I didn't show. But I don't want you to come. That's for sure!"

"Why not?" asked Gloria. She always listened to her husband and knew she was not going as soon as he suggested it, but it was a habit of hers to question his reasoning about things.

"Because I want to protect my family," he answered pointing to her and her stomach. "There's no telling how many gangsters from all over may be there."

"But you're going, and we," she pointed to her pregnant belly, "do not want daddy to get hurt or into trouble as well."

"I already thought about that," smiled Omar. "And that's why I'm traveling with a posse of legal guns. I'm talking P.O's, C.O's, a few gangsters that move kilos."

Gloria bust out laughing and said, "Please leave the rapping of words to the youngsters, or the rap group the O.G.'s."

"Shit," said Omar looking like he was in serious thought. "I might have to set up a meeting with them. Imaging me rapping with the O.G's. I'm saying, Puffy rapped with Biggie, Dr.Dre rapped with the boy Eminem and Jermaine Dupree rapped with all of his artists."

"Suge Knight, J.Prince and Russell Simmons never rapped with their artist," laughed Gloria.

Omar smiled and said, "That's because they can't rap."

"You're crazy!" she said. Then getting serious she asked, "Baby, do you think your celebrity status will ruin the funeral?"

"I also thought about that," said Omar sincerely. "But I'm starting to know how to deal with the crazy ass paparazzi. Plus, I'm not concerned about them. That day belongs to Big Lord."

"Baby," he said after a slight pause, "he put a lot of work in on them streets. But I believe in karma. I think he really crossed the line in God's eyes when he killed them innocent women and children. Look, everybody that played a part in that is dead!"

"But it wasn't God that killed Big Lord, Moe-dog and Whitey. It was the same Bulldog Crew of thugs."

"They're just tools that will be dealt with as well. You see the guy Fats is dead. And if the other two don't repent and ask for forgiveness, I think they're gonna regret it."

"Dang!' smiled Gloria. "You're starting to sound just like Bishop!"

"Get outta here!" laughed Omar. "Speaking of my little brother, he's preaching the funeral. So, he's rolling with me and my posse of hired killers. But on the serious side, I hope none of our old enemies decide the funeral is the place to settle the score. Because if so, there's going to be a lot of gunfire!!"

Chapter 33

"She's even beautiful when she's sleeping," L said to himself as he smiled looking over at Tonya lying beside him. He leaned over and kissed her on the forehead before rolling onto his back and staring up at the ceiling in deep thought.

He had a very serious discussion with Tonya late last night before going to bed. He knew she had made a lot of sense but he had no idea what would occur if he was to follow her advice. As he stared at the ceiling, he thought about her words to him last night. "So, what are you going to do?" she asked as they walked to his bedroom.

"What am I going to do about what?" he asked not really understanding the question.

"With your life," said Tonya. "Baby, this gangster life style you're living ain't gonna last forever."

L smiled and asked, "What else can I do? Deliver pizza? Work for minimum wage at one of them jobs out there?"

He then laughed and said, "I make more money in a day's work, than what most people make in a year!"

"I know," said Tonya nodding her head. "But it ain't all about money. You know I love you, and it doesn't matter how much money you make because I'm not with you for your money. Baby, if you was to work at a minimum wage restaurant mopping floors, I would still be with you. Because I know money doesn't make a man. And it doesn't make a relationship either. That's why things are messed up now, because women out here are putting money over their relationship, or they get good careers and instead of just helping their partners out they wanna act all high and mighty and compete financially with the person they say they love. And trust me baby, the love of money had killed many relationships. See, I'm not like that anymore. God showed me what it is to love. And I rather see you work a 9 to 5 job for regular money and live for at least thirty more years, than for you to get rich in the streets and possibly die within the next year or so. Or maybe get locked up for life in a stupid cell like an animal."

"I'm saying," joked L. "If I was to get life in prison, you will still marry me, right? We could still be together forever."

"No we can't," said Tonya seriously. "I'm not with that jail stuff. I've never been! Lisa, Gina and Pam could do it but never me. I know, because they all did it before. But I like to relax at home with my man on Valentine's Day, Christmas, and every other holiday and day of the year. It's not about me being against prison relationships or anything, I just can't deal with what I have to go through to see someone I love that's in there. All the searching and emptying out my purse just to get inside and visit, I'm not with that. I like my privacy. I love you and everything boo, but I can't do it!"

L smiled and said, "Don't worry about it baby girl, I ain't going back to prison anyway."

"You never been convicted, right?" asked Tonya with hope in her beautiful eyes. "I'm saying, you beat that case you had on appeal. So, won't you take the test and get a job as a Corrections Officer?"

L laughed so hard, he fell off of the bed. It took him a full two minutes before he was able to stop laughing and comment on what she'd suggested.

"Yeah I can see it now," smiled L. "The newspapers will read, 'A member of the infamous Bulldog Crew that is believed to be responsible for over sixty unsolved murders, wants to join the other side of the law. "Yeah, I can see it now," laughed L holding his stomach.

"You're responsible for over sixty murders?" asked Tonya wide eyed.

"No, only about two," lied L. "And I wasn't the one who pulled the trigger. I only carry guns to protect myself."

"Well," said Tonya, "I don't know. But I do know that I love you and I don't want you to die, kill nobody or go back to jail. Now, come give me some of that thug loving you're always talking about!"

L looked over at Tonya sleeping and smiled, as he got out of his bed. He walked quickly to the bathroom with no clothes on to release that important morning piss.

After brushing his teeth and washing up, he entered back into the bedroom. Tonya was still sleep and he thought about getting back in bed with her, but he knew if he did he would never make it to the grocery store to get the things he needed to buy.

L went to his closet and after putting on his underwear and tee shirt, he grabbed a pair of jeans and a white button up Polo shirt he had on two hangers. He always wore button up shirts and it had nothing to do with the Jay-Z craze almost everyone was following.

After getting dressed, he reached up on the closet shelf and grabbed his .44 Bulldog handgun. He hoped Tonya would still be sleep when he returned from the store. He wanted to cook and serve her breakfast in bed. But at the moment, he was out of eggs, cheese and bacon.

He placed his gun on the dresser and grabbed a comb, parting his giant unkempt afro straight down the middle. He then braided two big lop-sided braids on each side of his head and realized his scalp was as dry as his bedroom walls. He figured he'd let Tonya put his hair in corn-rows later on, being that she did not have to work until late tonight.

"At the least I can do is grease it up a bit," said L to himself as he walked to the bathroom to get some hair grease.

Tonya smiled to herself after hearing him talk to himself about his hair. She liked when he had his hair out. When he did, he had the whole Maxwell/Lenny Kravitz thing going on. And she wanted to laugh out loud when he put his hair in the crooked four braid style.

Tonya's smile quickly vanished when she saw the .44 Bulldog revolver sitting there on the dresser. She quickly got out of the bed and ran over to it. When she picked the gun up, she was surprised to feel how heavy and cold it felt. She remembered when she was younger how she would play with her ex-boyfriend's .38 revolver as he laughed and showed her how to use it. But this gun felt much heavier, and she wondered how L could carry a gun so heavy all day long.

Tonya opened the barrel and saw the six big bullets nestled snugly in the six holes waiting to be fired. She did not want L to get into anymore trouble by shooting someone, so Tonya quickly took the bullets out of the gun, closed the barrel and laid the gun back on the dresser like he had it, before running back to the bed and getting under the covers palming the six bullets in her hand.

L came back into the bedroom still rubbing the hair grease into his hair. He then grabbed the stack of money on the dresser and after pocketing it, he stuck the .44 Bulldog revolver into his waistline and pulled his shirt down over it so it wasn't too noticeable. He knew he had to keep his gun on him at all times. Not only for his enemies, but also for Light who he still, in a strange way, considered to be his friend.

He grabbed his keys off of the dresser and headed out of the apartment. As he walked to the store, he thought about the conversation he had with Pam when he called Tonya's cell phone that day when she was visiting at the hospital. He was never a nervous person, but he did feel funny talking to Pam on the phone. After all, he was there when she got shot, and was also down with the guy who killed her fiancé.

"Hold on," said Tonya that day. "I'm at the hospital, and my friend Pam wants to talk to you."

L's heart beat started to increase and he understood why. He had never talked to someone after being a part of shooting them, or even someone they loved.

"Hello," said the weak childlike voice on the other end of the telephone.

"Hello, how are you doing?" asked L.

"At the moment I can't even answer that question," answered Pam. "I've been through so much, I don't know whether I'm coming or going. I'm going through a lot."

"I understand," said L. "I know an apology do not cut it at all, but I do apologize to you. And if I knew you were peoples, this whole thing would've never happened. Things was never ever suppose to get out of hand the way they did. And again, I apologize. I also heard about your fiancé, and I send my deepest condolences to you."

"No you don't" said Pam causing L to get real quiet by her statement.

"Let's be real," continued Pam. "If your friend didn't kill him it would've been you, because I doubt you would have let him kill you. Because if Big Lord didn't get killed, he would have gotten all y'all for the shit y'all did. Especially the dummy that shot me, that's locked up."

L knew she had spoken the truth but was surprised by the calm manner and tone she spoke. Anyone else would have been screaming on him and crying, she just did it in her own way.

"Well," said L not knowing what else to say. "I hope you get better soon."

"I will physically," responded Pam. "But only time will tell if I get better emotionally. And .....thank you for saving my life. Here is Tonya."

L thought about that whole conversation as he walked pass a group of young boys as he headed to the store. They were standing near the corner talking to a group of girls. It was only 9:30AM and it seemed as if everyone was already outside on this warm morning.

"What's up L?" said a group of guys as the group of girls they were talking to greeted him as well, trying to flirt with him using their sexiest voice.

"Aiight, aiight,aiight," greeted L as he continued walking. When he turned the corner and got half way down the block, he noticed two tall dark-skinned guys he never saw before walking towards him with their faces screwed up and looking at him.

L reached for his gun but when he saw the police badge around one of their necks, he turned around and ran back the way he came. A blue van screeched to a stop and a bunch of homicide detectives jumped out of the van's side door.

When L had first saw the detective he initially thought they were maybe Big Lord or Moe-dog's peoples but they were cops and he thought fast on how to get out of the area.

He pulled out his gun as he turned the corner. He knew at least one shot from his .44 Bulldog would make the cops take cover giving him the opportunity to get away. He shot two times over his shoulder but all he heard was a click. He tried again as he ran pass the group of guys and girls he earlier passed, but again his gun did not shoot.

"Drop the gun!" yelled a detective running twenty feet behind him ready to shoot.

L was no dummy. He was not going to die like this, so he dropped his gun, threw his hands in the air and waited for the detective to tackle him. He was glad that a lot of people were outside, because had they not been, he knew the police would not hesitate to shoot an unarmed Black man, especially him.

The detective finally caught up to L and tackled him, as his partners also caught up with their guns drawn. Three of them put their knees in his back while one of them slapped the handcuffs tightly on his wrist.

"I got the gun!" yelled one of the detectives. "You're under arrest."

"For possession of a weapon so far," said the officer that handcuffed him.

L knew it was only the media attention dealing with the situation with Light that prompted the homicide detectives to arrest him. Because homicide detectives never came to arrest a person just for a gun possession.

"We come for questioning, and come up with a fucking gun! That's what I like about this job!' laughed another detective as they threw L in the police van and drove away to the precinct.

Chapter 34

Omar was surprised to see so many big time drug dealers all out in the open at Big Lord's funeral. Especially being that the Feds were probably in the cut somewhere snapping pictures. He knew most of the dealers from when he was in the game, and they quietly acknowledged his presence and complimented his success at being able to make the transition from selling drugs, to becoming a legitimate successful businessman in the recording industry. He had come a long way from selling crack cocaine and cutting heroin with lactose. In the past, he would have been delighted to speak to some of the drug dealers in attendance that he hadn't seen in so long. But the times have changed. He was no longer one of them.

Omar looked around the big church and shook his head sadly from side to side as he looked at the many gangsters that was in attendance. Most of them had beef with one another and it was no doubt in anyone's mind that things could indeed get ugly! They were all there to pay their last respects to Big Lord, but their eyes never left those of their enemies. No one wanted to meet or share the same fate as Big Lord, so there was probably more guns inside of the church than there were bibles! Not a person there wanted to meet their early demise like the thug they all had come to pay their respects to.

Omar was flanked by ten legally armed bodyguards. He didn't care about the image of being a gangster and street. In his eyes, he was passed that stage. He had a family to live and provide for, and was not willing to risk everything over an image. But that did not mean that his morals and principles had changed. He still did not condone snitching, betrayal or anything against the rules of being a man.

When Richard approached the altar to preach the service, the few gangsters who recognized who he was looked on in surprise at the changed young man. They remembered the war years back that he had with Shameek, Rashien and T-Bone who were all dead. They remembered that it was Omar and Big lord who took him under their wing and put him in the game years ago before he became and ordained minister.

As they thought these things, Omar was thinking the same thing as he looked at his young brother-in-law about to preach the service. He knew about the bodies Richard had caught back in the days before he turned his life back over to God.

“Damn, this funeral is gangster!” Omar said under his breath. “Even the preacher caught bodies at one time.”

“Shawn ‘Big Lord’ Moore was a good man,” preached Richard. “We can all attest that none of us are perfect. Even when a man ran up to Jesus and asked, ‘Good teacher, what must I do to inherit eternal life?’ in Mark 10:18 Jesus answered, ‘Why do you call me good? No one is good-except God alone.’ Brothers and sisters, I remember a few of you from my past that are here today,” said Richard looking at a few familiar faces in the church, “and you all can testify that at one time I also was one of the streets. One of this world! But I tell you all today, I am now truly a man of God. I am controlled by the spirit because of the spirit of God lives in me. Brothers and sisters, this here,” Richard pointed at his body, “is only a shell. Shawn Moore is no longer in that body. His spirit has been lifted back to the creator, and only he can judge Shawn’s sins, as well as his good deeds. We will all face judgment and I tell you the truth, not everyone who pray is going to Heaven. Only God can judge.

Some of us in this church right now are still living like the devil. I'm also talking about those who are aware of their sins, but still won't repent and ask for forgiveness. I said earlier that Shawn 'Big Lord' Moore was a good man. I said it because I knew him personally and saw a lot of good things he had done. But there was another side to him as well. A side that was truly the work of the devil! And like his good deeds, he will be judged for his bad ones as well. Don't look surprised! Before I agreed to even preach this service, I had a long talk with his parents. I told them if they wanted a preacher that did not know their son and only preached how good of a man and innocent he was, then I was not the man to preach this service. As a man of God, I can only preach the truth. His parents understood my position and devotion to God, and agreed that I was indeed the one to preach this here funeral. And I preach all of this because Shawn 'Big Lord' Moore should not die in vain. There are those of you here that are doing the work of the devil. So, understand that Shawn 'Big Lord' Moore's body is here not only for you to see him 'one last time' or to 'pay your respects', but it is here as a testimony of what is to come of all of us if we don't repent, ask for forgiveness and change the way we live."

Everyone in the church turned around in their seats when two fat white New York State Correction Officers entered the church escorting a youthful looking muscular black man in handcuffs.

Omar recognized the guy in shackles as Big Lord's older brother Born Magnetic. He was brought down to the funeral from Green Haven Correctional Facility wearing tacky looking State issued clothing.

Born Magnetic and the two white male officers sat in the back of the church. Born Magnetic's mother stared back at her oldest son with a weak smile as his father looked ahead and listened to every word Richard preached.

"Romans 8:1 states, 'Therefore, there is no condemnation for those who are in Christ Jesus, who do not live according to the sinful nature but according to the spirit, because through Christ Jesus the law of the spirit of life set me free from the law of sin and death. For what the law was powerless to do in that it was weakened by the sinful nature, God did by sending his own son in likeness of sinful man to be a sin offering. And so condemned sin in sinful man, in order that the righteous requirements of the law might be fully met in us, who do not live according to the sinful nature but according to the spirit'."

A lot of women in the church eyes were stuck on the very handsome Richard as he preached, but a handful of them kept glancing back at the even more handsome and healthy looking Born Magnetic. But of course, the majority of them kept trying to get Omar's attention being that he was a rich record industry celebrity. Some of their favorite artists was signed to Omar's 'Untouchable Records.'

Omar looked at some of the gangsters in the church eye-balling one another, and wondered how the funeral would play out. He wanted to get out of here but didn't want to leave Richard or Big Lord's parents behind, so he sat back as comfortably as possible. He quickly looked in the back of the church and could see the fear in the two white officers faces. He knew had they knew beforehand that it would be so many gangsters at this funeral, it was no way they would have allowed Born Magnetic to attend his brother's funeral.

Omar quietly chuckled at the scared officers, and then he turned back around and listened intently to Richard preach.

"Those who live according to the sinful nature have their minds set on what the nature desires; but those who live in accordance with the spirit have their minds set on what the spirit desires. The mind of sinful man is death, but the mind controlled by the spirit is life and peace; the sinful man is hostile to God. It does not submit to God's law, nor does it--"

This was the first time Omar had heard Richard preach and he was truly impressed. Especially the way Richard quoted the scriptures word for word without even opening up a bible! He thought about having Richard talk to the children at Kendu's Youth Center, and just as fast as that thought came to him, he then thought about Big Lord. He wished things had turned out better, and he hated the fact that he and Big Lord had parted ways on such a sour note. He had a lot of love for his fallen comrade and often wondered had he done the right thing. But the crazy thing was that, Omar could not cry for the death of his friend and wondered why. Maybe because throughout his life, he saw so many of his closest friends die in the streets over nothing, that he might have become immune to the pain, he thought to himself.

"And if anyone does not have the spirit of Christ, he does not belong to Christ," continued Richard. "But if Christ is in you, your body is dead because of sin, yet your spirit is alive because of righteousness. And if the spirit of him who raised Jesus from the dead is living in you, he who raised Christ from the dead will also give you life to your mortal bodies through spirit who lives in you. Therefore, brothers, we have an obligation- but it is not to the sinful nature, to live according to it. For if you live according to the sinful nature, you will die; but if by the spirit you put to death the misdeeds of the body, you will live, because those who are led by the spirit of God are sons of God. For you did not receive the spirit of sonship.' Now let us all come and see the body of Shawn 'Big Lord' Moore for the last time on earth. Let's keep him in our hearts and minds and pray that he is accepted by God to rest in Heaven."

Everyone in the church stood up and walked to the front of the church to peer into the coffin at Big lord and say their last words to his body. Men and women openly wept as others hugged one another for comfort.

"I knew deep down inside it would end like this," said a voice behind Omar as he looked at his friend Big Lord.

Omar spun around to see the voice belonged to Big Lord's brother Born Magnetic. He hugged Born Magnetic tightly as the two scared white correction officers looked on.

"Born, how much time you got left?" asked Omar.

"Another year before I see my fourth parole board," Born Magnetic answered. "That dumb ass governor ain't letting niggas go! But it's my last board anyway."

"Good," said Omar. "When you come home, leave the streets alone. I got a spot for you at the record label, if you wanna ride with me. I need good dudes."

"I'm with that!" said Born Magnetic. "I'm not putting myself back in a position in the streets to end up like my brother, or to give these crackers more years of my life!"

"That's right," said Omar. "Here comes your moms and pops. Take care of yourself, and get my number from them and call me collect when you get back upnorth."

Omar walked away and caught up to Richard.

"You preached a good sermon today," he said smiling.

"Thanks," responded Richard. "I hope my words changed someone's life, considering there's so many gangsters in here."

"Word," replied Omar. "I'm going outside to get some air. Yo, Mr. and Mrs. Moore is calling you. I think they want you to meet Big lord's older brother, Born Magnetic."

As Richard approached the mourning family, Omar and his team of bodyguards headed outside of the church with almost everyone else.

When Omar stepped outside, he saw Mercedes Benz, BMW's, and other expensive cars ride by the church very slowly. He knew some of them was Big lord's comrades as well as enemies, that did not want to be seen but wanted to pay their respects, or those who wanted to just see who came to the funeral.

Omar had been to many gangster's funeral. Some was shot up, some was disrespected by laughter at the deceased, and some of the bodies was even spit on! But the worse one he remembered was when gangsters came into a funeral and turned the casket over depositing the body on the floor, before all mayhem broke loose! But also there were those that went smoothly. He just hoped the remainder of Big lord's funeral would turn out okay.

Chapter 35

"Everything is okay," sighed Gloria hanging up the phone. "Omar said they are on their way here."

"Good!' said Lisa relieved that everything turned out okay. She knew how crazy Brooklyn's funerals could get. The drama was never over until the person was buried in the ground, and at times it didn't even end there.

"What's up?!" Gina asked Lisa. "You gonna deal the cards or what? She said everything is alright!"

"It's my deal," said Tonya shuffling the cards.

They were playing spades. It was Tonya and Gina against Lisa and Gloria, and Lisa and Gloria were up two games to nothing.

Gloria sat down and cut the cards, and Tonya began dealing. "I don't know why Omar didn't want us to go to Big Lord's funeral," said Gina. "It's not like we didn't know him! Damn, it's like ever since Omar left the streets alone, he's paranoid about everything!"

Gloria looked at her like she was crazy.

"See, that's the problem with you young girls," she said. "Y'all don't know shit. The more money people get, the more jealous people get, and wanna take what's yours. Including your life! So, my husband is only protecting us."

"True dat, true dat," said Lisa nodding her head.

They all bust out laughing.

"She's a nut," said Gina through her laughter. "First, she is the downest bitch I ever met, then she moved downsouth only to come back looking and talking like Shirley Ceasar, and now she's temporary back in New York mode sounding like Lil' Kim."

"Don 't ever compare me to…..her!" said Lisa with her lip upturned and rolling her eyes causing all at the table to laugh.

"Stop it," said Gloria defending the female rapper. "I like Lil' Kim. She's a stand up bitch. Plus, she used to be in L.G. where most of you know, that is where I'm from," she smiled.

"Can we play cards?" asked Tonya with an attitude. "What are y'all bidding?"

"What's wrong with you?" asked Lisa.

Gina laughed and said, "Her boyfriend L cursed her ass out for almost getting him killed!"

"What happened?" asked Gloria.

"This stupid bitch here," laughed Gina, "took all the bullets out of his gun, knowing he got beef with damn near the whole Brooklyn. And when he went outside, the police snatched him up. It could have been one of his enemies!"

"The police is one of his enemies," said Gloria.

Everyone except Tonya laughed.

"I got five books," said Tonya ignoring them.

"You got five?" asked Gina wide eyed while looking at her own hand. "Bitch, we taking Boston!"

"Board," said Lisa not bothering to ask Gloria if she had any books.

"So, what the police say?" Gloria asked Tonya while throwing out a four of club.

"I didn't talk to the police," answered Tonya. "I talked to L. I gotta go to court next week and bail him out."

"What's his bail?" asked Lisa.

"Ten thousand dollars. He told me to wait until he go to court to see if they drop it, but if not get him out," answered Tonya shrugging her shoulders. "I don't care, it's his money."

"I know that's right," laughed Gina. "Because your cheap ass ain't bailing nobody outta jail with your own money!"

"You got some nerve talking about somebody being cheap," Tonya told Gina. "Divine left you a few millions, and you ain't buy nothing new besides clothes since he passed away."

"Yep," said Lisa laughing.

"Bitch, what are you yepping about" asked Gina. "I don't see you spending none of that money your husband left the game with either!"

"True dat, true dat," laughed Tonya.

"Y'all stuck!" laughed Gloria throwing an Ace of spade on the table to add to the three books she already collected.

"Damn!" yelled Gina. "I can't win shit with this bitch!"

Everyone laughed.

"I made my five books," said Tonya. "You're the one that didn't make yours."

"That's it for me," said Gina standing up.

"I'm going to put on some music," she said walking towards the big stereo system.

"Don't turn it up too loud," said Lisa. "Little Divine and Dejanay is upstairs sleeping."

"They won't hardly hear it from upstairs in this big ass house your brother and Gloria got," said Gina looking through the large CD collection.

"Put on the latest Usher CD!" yelled Gloria.

"Let me do this," responded Gina. "Before Bishop comes back and beat us in the head all night with that church shit!"

Lisa threw a nasty look her way and said, "There's nothing wrong with Church music. And my husband's name is not Bishop, it's Richard Timothy Brown, Jr!"

"He'll always be Bishop to me," laughed Gina.

"True dat, true dat," said Gloria causing everyone to laugh.

"Hold up!" said Tonya getting out of her chair quickly and looking at her watch. "Y'all got me missing the Gangster Larry Show. I gotta see that!'

"It's on now?" asked Gina as she stopped looking through the CD collection.

"Yes," answered Tonya walking to the next room. Even with her being a Christian, she was hooked on the show. Not only did Gangster Larry keep it real, but he was also very comical.

Tonya laughed just thinking about him. All the time he'd been on the air, he had only one serious show. That was when he married his childhood girlfriend De De, and even that episode was funny as hell. Because De De who looked as beautiful as ever, stood next to Gangster Larry who was wearing a black three piece suit, black Timberland boots and a blue and red bandanna! But what took the cake was when, De De demanded that he cut off his braids before they married. Because she hated men who wore braids. In her own words, she stated that it made them look like "little bitches!" The viewers often wondered who was more gangster; Larry or De De!

"I'm going to see who's on there," said Gina walking towards the big livingroom.

"Who's Gangster Larry?" asked Gloria.

"Come on, you gotta see this guy," said Lisa getting out of her chair and leading the way. "He's similar to Dave Chappel, but as Gina would say, 'he's more gangster.'"

When they entered the livingroom, Gina and Tonya was already laughing at the television host. Gloria and Lisa sat across from them and stared at the giant sized television. They couldn't believe their eyes. Gangster Larry had his first balled up and stood over a seated hair braided West Coast rapper that almost everyone considered gangster when he was part of a notorious record label ten years or more ago.

"You're a bitch nigga!" said Gangster Larry through clench teeth. "Now say I'm a bitch, and I'll break your jaw!"

The rapper knowing about Gangster Larry theatrics smiled, waved him off and said, "Ain't no need for that cuz. It ain't about jaws getting broke, or niggas getting smoked. I'm pass all dat! I just wanna have fun and stack that scrilla. Dig?"

Gangster Larry looked at him hard, sucked his teeth and said, "Boy, you're lucky we're on the air. 'Cause if we wasn't, I'll smack the shit out of you!"

The audience and the rapper laughed, as Gangster Larry sat back down in his chair.

"Now," said Gangster Larry. "Being that all you punk ass rappers wanna be gansta and from the streets, I'ma ask you some questions the streets wanna know."

"Bring it on cuz," smiled the rapper while drinking from a pimp cup. This was like no other show he'd ever been o n.

"First off," began Gangster Larry. "From what I hear, you are married with children. So, why are you playing this pimp image to the public if you're really just a family man?"

"Yeah, I'ma family man," smiled the rapper, "but that don't stop the pimping cuz."

"So, I take it that you pimp your wife to then. Well, how much money do the bitch bring in a night?"

"Oh shit!' said Gloria wide eyed with her hand to her mouth not believing the content of this show or the host.

"My wife ain't no hoe!" the rapper said almost losing his cool. "She don't have to be on the stroll, I take care of her!"

"So, you're the hoe?" asked Gangster Larry as the audience laughed at the rapper.

"You need to watch your mouth!" said the rapper. "I could never be a hoe!"

"You could never be a hoe, huh?" asked Gangster Larry with a very rare smile. "Okay, let's take a look at this thing, and we'll let the audience decide what you are. You have a wife that does nothing because you take care of her. You're on a record label that takes majority of the money after you sell a million albums. You have a clownish looking street pimp you pay as your so-called spiritual advisor, who pimped your ass from the streets to the award shows in Hollywood. So now I ask the audience, what is he?"

"A hoe!!!" shouted most of the audience who weren't the rapper's fans.

"So again," said Gangster Larry with his face screwed up. "I proved time and time again, that majority of rappers are frauds! They talk that pimp shit, but they're not pimps! They talk that gangster shit, but are far from gangsters. And they talk that big balls hustling shit, but majority of them are broke! Do not believe those videos!"

"I'm very far from being broke," smiled the rapper taking a sip from his pimp cup.

"Who cares?" asked Gangster Larry. "You're still a hoe, so just be a good hoe."

The audience laughed.

"So, do you have another album coming out?" asked Gangster Larry.

The rapper laughed, shook his head and said, "You're off the heezy for sheezy! But I dig your style and your show. Yeah, I got another album coming out this year. It's called 'The big dog is bazack.' I also got a few porno films the people can get. And my record label will be one hundred percent independent soon, so there will be no more hoing for these major labels and punk ass distributors."

"I like you!" smiled Gangster Larry. "Even though the only rappers I listen to from the West Coast is E-40 and C-Bo. But I always liked you. I'm feeling you!"

He then looked out at the audience and said, "Pick up his new album when it hits the stores, and all you horny fucks out there, pick up the porn tapes the man has. Next week, I'll have your favorite retired rapper straight outta the streets of Brooklyn, New York. Damn, I hope Shyne hurry up and come home. He might be the only believable motherfucker rapping! Y'all have a good motherfucking night!"

The credits rolled as Gangster Larry and the rapper shook hands and chatted amongst themselves, as one of the rapper's old classic songs played causing the audience to stand out of their seats and dance.

"Now, that boy is crazy!" laughed Gloria.

"Shoot," said Tonya. "he took it easy on that rapper. I'm telling you, usually he is a mess!'

"Y'all should get the O.G.'s to go on there," laughed Gina.

"Hell no!" responded Gloria. "Me and Omar is not promoting them on that show! Them O.G. boys is crazy too! It'll probably be a shoot-out on that stage! Trust what I'm telling you. They all did time before. And like Mary J.Blige said, we don't need no more drama!"

Before Gina could reply, the telephone began ringing.

"That might be Omar," said Gloria quickly walking over to answer the phone.

After a minute of talking, she came back smiling and said, “That was Pam’s doctor. She’s being released hopefully next week, so we’ll have to pick her up that Thursday morning!”

Chapter 36

"I feel like Osama Bin Laden right now," Light said to himself as he loaded up one of his nine millimeters. He thought about going to Big Lord's funeral to shoot it up. But then he realized there would probably be police all over the area.

Light heard through the streets that Hook had been killed, and he wondered who killed him. He never knew Hook to have a lot of enemies. He also heard in the streets that L, Mont-Mont and especially C-Allah, was trying to make contact with him. He knew he was wrong for trying to kill L, but what was done was done, and he wasn't about to cry over it now. So, the beef was on! He knew it would be no problem getting in touch with C-Allah, but he was in no mood to deal with C-Allah's funny ways of doing things. One person he felt he could count on was Mont-Mont, but of course he was now locked up. He wanted to go and visit him, but he knew it would be impossible for him to get off of Riker's Island without getting arrested, even if he did use a fake ID. He even thought about finding out when Mont-Mont was due to go to court and ambushing the Rikers Island bus to get his comrade out of there. He knew if he had L's assistance he could pull it off. But even if he made amends with L, he knew he would not be down for such a daring attempt. Maybe if it was Fats, Tommy Guns or Big Dave they were planning to break out, he would be down, but not for Mont-Mont. He knew L didn't like him that much. Also, he was sure C-Allah had heard about him shooting at L by now, so he doubted if C-Allah would trust him either. So getting in touch with him was also a waste of time.

Light threw the fully loaded nine millimeter on the bed with six other loaded guns.

"When them fucking pigs come for me, I'll be damned if I go out like faggot ass Sadam Hussein!" Light said to himself.

He was hiding out in Far Rockaway Queens, at Fats' mother's house. No matter what he was wanted for or who was after him, he would always be welcomed to come back and stay with Ms. Carol. She worked nights at the hospital, so most of the time Light was home by himself. He had always been a son to her after the death of his biological mother.

Light slept in the guest room, and he loved the very quiet neighborhood his adopted mother lived in. Not many people hung out on the block. It was a perfect little lay low spot, and like L, Light only hit the streets when it got dark outside. Being on the run was costly, so he was glad that he was always financially straight since Divine had started the Bulldog Crew. Light figured if he ever needed money it wouldn't even be a problem for him to go out and rob a rich drug dealer or something. Like three months ago when he needed more bullets for his guns. He knew Hook's little brother Ronnie and his crew always kept an assortment of guns and ammunition. The only problem was that they had never gotten along, and if it wasn't for Hook, Light would've killed Ronnie long ago! But now Hook was dead and he and Light's friendship had ended on a sour note anyway, so Light headed out to Brownsville one night to see what he could get from Ronnie.

Like always, Ronnie stood in front of his house telling war stories and talking tough to three of his soldiers and two young girls.

Ronnie stopped talking as he wondered who the light-skinned girl with long hair walking his way carrying a Gucci bag was.

His soldiers wondered the same thing, being they had sex with most of the girls in the area already, and wouldn't mind knocking off something new. But when Light got up close and stood in front of the small group, they knew they were outsmarted and it would had been suicide for any of them to reach for their gun. Behind the female handbag, Light was holding a .40 Caliber handgun and they all caught a glimpse of it.

"Nobody move and nobody get killed!' said Light as he pointed the gun at the group and used his other hand to retrieve the guns Ronnie and his soldiers carried in the waist of their pants. He put all the guns in the Gucci bag he carried and after searching the two girls and not finding anything, he was totally satisfied.

"Who's in the house?" Light asked Ronnie.

"What the fuck is you doing, Light!" asked Ronnie with his face screwed up. "You know if my brother Hook was alive, you wouldn't be doing this shit!"

"I'ma ask you one more time," stated Light calmly, "and if you don't answer me, you'll see your brother Hook to tell'em all about it."

"Nobody's in the house," answered Ronnie.

"Open the door and let's all go inside," ordered Light.

Ronnie thought for a few seconds before pulling his house key out of his pocket. The two young girls were terrified, and Ronnie's soldiers didn't know what to do. They had never been caught off guard like this! They had to admit, it was a smart move on Light's part to dress up like a female. He had no facial hair and the expensive female clothes and wig he wore had thrown all of them off. Even the two young girls.

They stepped into the house and Light made everyone bunch up together on the couch in the big spacious livingroom.

"Is the guns in the same place?" Light asked Ronnie.

He remembered Ronnie showing off his guns to him in front of Hook, and he kept them in a big card board box inside of his bedroom closet.

"Yeah," answered Ronnie with his face still screwed up.

"Let's go!" Light ordered the group while waving his gun. "The party is upstairs! Let's go!"

They all walked up the stairs, and Light made sure the two young girls walked in front of the guys and of course he walked in the back behind Ronnie. He didn't want anyone to get any funny ideas.

When they entered the big bedroom, Light made all of them sit on the bed. He opened the closet door and instead of one box, there were three. He quickly pulled all three of the heavy boxes out of the closet. He pointed his gun at the group as he opened the first box. Inside were all the guns he saw before when Ronnie was showing them off. In the next box, were guns that had to belong to Hook. There were .44's, .45's, nine millimeters with silencers and an assortment of other high powered weapons. The last box contained stacks of hundred dollar bills filled to the top!

"You only came for the guns, right?" asked Ronnie. "Light, take the guns and be out!"

"You're right," said Light smiling and looking deranged with the long black wig hanging off of his head.

"All I came for is the guns and ammunition," said Light. "But you know what, Ronnie? I never liked your ass."

Light then pulled a nine millimeter with a silencer out of the box and after checking to make sure it was loaded, he opened fire on the small group sitting on the bed. They all screamed and used one another as shields to get away but was cut down by gunfire as bullets entered heads, chests, legs and everywhere else. The scene looked horrific with all six bodies layed out all over the bed with blood everywhere!

'All I came for is the guns and ammo," Light said to himself with a smile, "but I might as well take everything else this punk nigga had."

He then threw the gun back into the box and proceeded to carry the boxes out to the car he came in that was in Fats mother's name. He had to make three trips to the car with the boxes, but when he went back to the house for the fourth time, he walked quickly to the basement. He opened the door and a three month old black pitbull puppy came running up the stairs.

"Come on Blackie!" said Light with a smile. "You know I can't leave you here."

Light hadn't left Ms. Carol's house in three days and he wondered what was going on in the streets of Brooklyn. He thought of who he could call to get some information, before heading out that way. He did not want to walk into a trap. He then smiled when a booster from Nostrand Avenue named Sharay came to mind. Sharay was the streets, and would know everything going on in them. Most importantly, she had always wanted to get with Light. But Kia was always the obstacle that stood in her way.

Light had Sharay's home phone number in his cell's phone, and when he dialed the number he hoped she would be there and not running the streets.

"Hello?" asked a female's voice on the other end.

"May I speak to Sharay?" asked Light.

"This Sharay. Who dis?"

"It's me, Light."

"Oh my God!" yelled Sharay excitedly. "What's up baby. Yo, where you at? What 'chu doing? When you coming through?"

Light laughed and said, "Slow down baby. First things first ma. What's going on out there?"

"Jomo from East New York just got shot, Hook's little brother got killed, Little Mel from Fort Greene got bagged by homicide police, and of course you know your ex-homeboy L got locked up not long ago."

"L?" asked Light. "What he got locked up for?"

"I heard he got bagged for a gun. I don't know yet but I can find out, because my sister is a police in the same precinct they took him to. And you know, the police is everywhere looking for you! I heard they had you on America's Most Wanted, but you know you can't believe halfa' these niggas out here! Anyway, what's up? When can we get together and chill?"

"We can do that," smiled Light. "Just give me a few days, and I'll call you back so we can meet up somewhere."

"Okay," blushed Sharay. "If you get my answering machine, leave a number and I'll call you right back. And if you need me to do anything, I got'chu! You know I love you nigga!'

Light laughed and said, "Aiight, I'ma holla. Take care of yourself, and keep that thing tight!"

"I will," lied Sharay. She was waiting for her boyfriend to come over to her house now, so they could have sex. She loved her boyfriend but without a second thought, she would cut him off for Light. Even with him being on the run for a triple homicide!

"Make sure you call me," said Sharay.

"I will," said Light before hanging up the phone.

Blackie came into the room carrying a cat's skull in his mouth. He was only six months old now, but he looked full grown. He had a very big had, reddish eyes and his chest was huge!

Light only walked him at night. He would also let him have fun by killing big stray alley cats and stray dogs. Ms. Carol would always joke that she didn't know who was more crazier; Light or Blackie!

Light pet Blackie on the head and said, "Come on boy, drop it like it's hot. I'm about to take you out for your walk, so you know you can't walk out of the house with that. But I'll let you have a little fun tonight."

Like he understood everything his master said, Blackie dropped the cat's skull and stuck his huge tongue out, fiending to commit a killing worse than his last one.

Fats would've definitely loved Blackie, Light thought to himself as he picked up Blackie's leash off of the floor.

Chapter 37

"What took y'all so long to come and get me?" asked Pam. "I've been waiting for like two hours! I'm feening to eat some real food for a change. I'm tired of this food here."

"The traffic was slow," explained Gloria. "It was a big accident and they took forever to clear it."

"Stop crying, we're here!" laughed Gina.

"About time!" said Pam.

"Here's your clothes," said Tonya handing Pam a brand new outfit and a pair of Prada shoes.

"I'm not wearing those!" said Pam looking at the shoes in Tonya's hands. "Every bitch I know got those!"

"Girl, just put the shoes on!" said Gloria angrily causing Lisa, Gina and Tonya to laugh. "You act like we got all day. I gotta meet up with my husband."

Pam took the clothes and shoes from Tonya and then asked Lisa, "Where's Dejanay?"

"We left her and little Divine at Omar's with Richard," answered Lisa. 'Oh yeah, Omar went by your house last night like you asked, and he located Big Lord's safe in the basement and got it opened for you. He said he'll come over tomorrow and have a new one put in. And he said he cleaned up the house, because it was a mess! Here's the keys," she handed Pam the ring of house and car keys.

"Thanks," said Pam as she continued to get dressed.

When she was done, without even looking back at the small hospital room she occupied for the last four months, she said, "Come on, let's get outta here!"

They all got inside of Gloria's blue Range Rover and headed towards Pam's house.

"Where are we going?" asked Pam. "Take me to get something to eat before we go to my house. That hospital food was worse than the gunshot!"

They all laughed and was glad to see that Pam did not lose her sense of humor despite everything that had happened to her.

"We're two steps ahead of you," smiled Lisa. "We cooked yesterday, and had Omar drop the food off at your house last night when he was there. We just have to re-heat it."

"Damn," said Pam. "Y'all had Omar working real hard at my house. I hope he didn't discover anything else in the house besides the safe….like my panties or something."

"Girl!" yelled Gloria almost swerving off of the road causing everyone in the truck to laugh.

When they pulled up in front of Pam's house, everyone noticed how she slightly hesitated to get out of the truck.

"Everything is okay," said Lisa rubbing Pam's back and shoulders. "We'll stay here with you as long as you want us to."

"I'm alright," said Pam opening the truck's door and stepping out. She looked at the new red Mercedes Benz parked in her driveway and then looked at Lisa and asked, "Who's in the house? Whose car is that?"

Lisa nervously glanced at Gina before answering Pam's question. "That's your car. Big Lord bought it for you, hours before the incident happened with you."

Pam showed no emotions as she walked pass the car and up to the front door of her house. She opened the door and they all stepped inside.

"I got time," said Gloria looking at her watch. "I'll go and re-heat the food," she said walking towards the kitchen.

Gina turned the stereo on and the sounds of Usher's song "Burn" came through the speakers.

After the food was heated up and they all ate, they talked and laughed until Gloria looked at her watch and announced that she had to go.

"What's up, who's going and who's staying?" asked Gloria.

"No disrespect," said Pam, 'but y'all can all roll."

"No you didn't!" said Gina with her lip turned up and her hand on her hip.

Pam laughed and said, "no, it's not like that! I just need some time to myself in this house, and I know y'all wanna stay and comfort me but I'm okay. Go take care of the things y'all gotta do, and give me a call or come back through later tonight."

"Okay," said Lisa. "I'll be back tonight, but if you need anything before I come give me a call."

"And I'm coming with her!' said Gina playfully rolling her eyes.

"Me too!' smiled Tonya. "I just have to take care of something real quick." She knew she had to hurry back to Brooklyn to go pick up the money to bail L out of jail.

"Whoever's going, come on," said Gloria walking to the front door and opening it. She waved good-bye to Pam with a smile and walked to her truck.

Lisa, Gina and Tonya all kissed and hugged Pam promising to come back later. As soon as they exited from the house, Pam went over to the stereo and turned it off. She then stood there and looked all around her livingroom. Everything was just as it was before the incident. She hesitated about going up the stairs to her bedroom at first, but then found the courage to make it up the staircase.

She pushed the door open slowly and stepped inside of her bedroom. The incident came back to her in a flash, and everything looked the same. The only thing different about the bedroom, was there was no blood stains on the bed or the floor. She remembered bleeding heavily on both. Maybe Omar or Big Lord cleaned it up, she thought to herself.

Pam peered inside of the open walk-in closet and saw that the safe was still open and of course empty! She made her way back downstairs and decided to go down into the basement.

As she walked down the stairs, she realized that this was actually the third time being in the basement since she and Big Lord had moved into the big house. She cut the lights on and the first thing she saw was Big Lord's workout equipment. He had the whole Universal set and coming out of the wall was a pull-up bar and next to it a dip-bar. She looked on the floor and noticed something like saw dust with foot prints in it. She followed the trail and it led to a big dresser tilted to the side, and behind the dresser was a safe in the wall that was left ajar by Omar.

Pam looked inside of the safe, and couldn't believe her eyes. Inside of the safe was at least twenty million dollars! She had never saw that much money in her life! She knew the Bulldog Crew would have loved to get a hold of what she was looking at. But what she didn't know was that the Bulldog Crew had never made it down to the basement. Light and his boy Mont-Mont was checking the kitchen, when L came running down the stairs and breathing heavy said, "We gotta get outta here!"

"What's up?" asked Light standing up from looking in the lower kitchen cabinets, as Mont-Mont pulled his gun back out.

"I just called the ambulance for her," answered L, "and they should be here in a minute!"

"Fuck you do that for?" Light asked confused.

"Because," continued L, "my girl was on her answering machine. Homegirl upstairs, is Bishop and Omar's people!"

"Oh shit!" said Mont-Mont knowing that he messed up by shooting Pam.

Light thought for a moment and then said, "Aiight, let's get the fuck up outta here!"

The money in the safe had Pam's undivided attention. She didn't know what to do with all of this money. So she decided to keep four million of it, and give the rest to Big Lord's family. She hoped the police wouldn't be snooping around her house trying to find out more of what happened to her, or asking anymore questions concerning Big Lord. As soon as she came out of her coma, two white detectives stood over her hospital bed with a pen and pad in their hands asking a thousand questions. "The person that shot you, what did he look like? Do you know him? What did he say? Was he alone? Who is Big Lord? What do he do for a living?"When they asked Pam the last question, she pretended to be in even more pain than she actually was in.

"Please, please," said a white doctor saving her from the interrogation. "You'll have to question her at a later date. Now is not the time. It is much too soon!"

The two detectives looked at one another and walked out of the hospital room without saying another word.

Pam thought she heard the door bell, so after walking back upstairs and locking the basement door, she went to the front window to look out. At first she didn't know who the crowd of people were outside of her front door holding balloons, flowers, teddy bears and bowls of food, until she saw her mother's smiling face and her dad standing next to her. Pam took a deep breath and opened the door. It looked as if the whole Fort Greene Projects stood out there. But this was all Pam's family: Father, mother, brothers, sisters, uncles, aunts, and her many cousins.

"My baby!" her mother yelled out being the first one to step into the house and hugging her. After her father hugged and kissed her, everyone else did the same. She had a tightly knit family, and appreciated that fact, being that not many families had that closeness anymore. She knew most of her cousins, and appreciated that they came to visit her in the hospital. She remembered when she was in her coma, she had a dream she'd found $500 in the hospital . The dream seemed so real, that when she came out of her coma she told her little ten year old cousin Hakeem that he could keep the money.

"I don't see no money," said the little boy.

"It's right there in my Gucci bag," said Pam pointing weakly to an empty chair.

"It's no bag there," said her mother.

"It is!' said Pam sure of herself. "I found the money and put it in my bag! Where is the money?!"

"Don't worry, we'll get it," said her father knowing his daughter could not have found any money, because she couldn't even get out of bed yet. So he figured he would have a talk with her doctor and see what he had to say concerning his daughter's mental health. Later on, the doctor explained that many patients experienced the same kind of actions after being in a coma.

"Cousin Pam," said one of her little cousins. "Can we go downstairs and play?"

"No," answered Pam. "The door is locked because there's work that has to be done down there. But y'all can play in the backyard, just don't get in the pool."

The little girl smiled and told a gang of other cousins, "Come on, she said we can play in the backyard, just don't get in the pool!"

"What's up sis?" asked Pam's brother Aaron after handing a sweet potato pie to another cousin. "I was worried about you. It's good to see you're okay. When it first happened, I was ready to get Big Lord myself!"

Pam didn't even respond to what her brother had to say concerning Big Lord or the whole ordeal. She loved her brother to death, but he always let the wrong things fly out of his mouth. Plus, she wanted to laugh in his face when he mentioned doing something to Big Lord, because she knew just as he did, that he wasn't even in big Lord's league.

Pam was happy to see her family, however, at the moment she needed time to be alone in her home to get herself together. Everything happened so fast, and she was still mourning the death of her fiancé Big Lord. Her family did not understand how much she loved him. She hated the fact that she could not attend his funeral. She debated, argued and pleaded with the doctors to let her attend the funeral, but they did not feel she was physically or mentally ready to be released from their care yet.

Pam looked in the kitchen at her family laughing, talking and fixing plates of food, but she could not eat another bite after already eating with Tonya, Gina, Lisa and Gloria. As her brother continued to ramble on about nothing, she wondered how long her family would be staying. She loved them all, but she needed her time and space to mourn the death of the only man she ever truly loved!!!

Chapter 38

L wondered if he would perhaps run into Mont-Mont as he waited to be transported to the Brooklyn Supreme Court. The two of them were in different buildings on Rikers Island, but it was common to run into inmates from different building on Rikers Island as well as the borough jails that was still open, in the court's pens. However, L had a red ID card which meant that he was labeled a violent slasher/stabber. Only inmates with a history of stabbing or cutting someone had a red ID card, or those who simply got caught with a razor or other kind of weapon. The worse thing about being labeled a predicate slasher with a red ID was that, when you went to court you sat in the pens as well as the court room shackled up. Also, you wore thick like Styrofoam mittens on your hands when being escorted to the pens to prevent you from cutting anyone else. L knew even if he ran into Mont-Mont, he would not be in the same pen with him being that Mont-Mont was not labeled as a predicate slasher/stabber as of yet. But he would still be able to see him.

In the building L was in, he was being treated like a king in 2-Upper. He stayed on the telephone by using other inmates pin numbers, instead of eating the jail food the other inmates was forced to eat, L ate food from the streets that was brought in by two male COs that lived around his way. He was also in a semi-relationship with a female CO, and an inmate in his housing unit did all of his laundry for two packs of cookies and a pack of kool-aid. Infact, the CO he was involved with was the cause of him and Tonya getting into an argument on a visit, because the CO braided his hair for him on the down low. L was surprised Tonya even came to visit him on Rikers Island being that she talked so much against jail relationships. But he knew love would change the most stubborn person, and he knew she was in love with him just as much as he was in love with her. The female CO meant nothing to him. He couldn't see himself getting into a serious relationship with someone who played a part in holding him captive. He had nothing against those that did, but to him, the female COs were only trophys to show off to the other inmates what his hands called for. When Tonya saw his hair neatly braided in a designed style, she had a fit.

"Who in the heck did your hair?!" she asked angrily. "And don't say one of your friends, because no guy can do hair like that unless he's a homo!"

"Oh shit!" laughed a girl sitting at the next table with her boyfriend, who overheard Tonya's statement to L.

"Mind your fucking business!" the guy she was visiting said angrily. "You talk too fucking much about shit that don't concern you!" Had it been someone else, they guy would have not cared what his girlfriend said, but he wanted no problems with L or anyone else that was down with the notorious Bulldog Crew. The word was already out, that they wouldn't hesitate to kill you or your loved ones! Everyone heard the stories.

L laughed at Tonya's comment and said, "You've been watching too much TV about jail. A homo can never touch my hair. And there are guys in here that are not queer that do know how to braid hair. But to answer your question smart ass, a female CO from out my way did it for me on the low."

"What else did she do for you on the down low?!" she asked with a frown on her pretty dark-skinned face.

L laughed and said, "Nothing, I swear!"

The Brooklyn court bus had finally arrived to the court, snapping L out of his thoughts of Tonya that day on the visit. A

Black male CO went inside the court building to drop their weapons off after pulling up into the court's compound.

L sat on the bus shackled up in a small cage separated from the other inmates sitting in the back of the bus. He had a red ID because they were still holding a few cuttings he did years back against him, before he went upstate.

L looked out of the bus window and thought about the heated conversation he had with Tonya when he first got arrested and sent to Rikers Island. "You took the bullets outta my gun?!" asked L angrily.

"Yes," answered Tonya. "I'm tired of all of this killing going on. Y'all guys have to grow up."

"What the fuck is you talking about?! You could've got me killed! That's some real stupid shit you did. I'm glad it was the police that rolled up on me, instead of Light or one of my other enemies. I sure as shit, would have been dead!"

"That ain't my fault that y'all out here killing each other for nothing!" Tonya yelled with tears coming down her face. "I'm sick and tired of it!"

"I don't wanna hear that shit," L said angrily. "Just go back to my apartment, and take some money out of my closet and bail me outta here."

"How much is your bail?" asked Tonya wiping her tears away. This was the first argument she and L had gotten into.

"Ten thousand dollars," answered L, "but wait until I go back to court. They might drop it. But if they don't, then get me out."

L hated the fact that he screamed on Tonya. He knew she only did what she thought was right. But he was just upset justifiably, because her actions could have gotten him killed. But at the same time, her taking the bullets out of the gun made his case weak.

Because the gun was not operable, and he was glad about that. L then thought about the dream he had last night that seemed so real! Big Dave appeared to him in his dream and said, "Listen homie, don't say anything, let me do the talking! First off, I know you miss me. But I'm okay, so is Tommy Guns, Divine and Fats. But this is very important! Remember what me and you talked about, when Light, Fats and Tommy Guns were out of state in Florida? I had told you that this day may come, and you cannot be afraid to confront it! And you cannot be stupid to over look it, because if you do you will truly be sorry. Bulldog Crew is over! BDC is like an empty bag being blown around on a windy day. Wake up homie, and do what you must. You do know where to go, we talked about that as well!!!!"

When L woke up, he remembered every work Big Dave had spoken to him. Now he just hoped he would be able to pull off, what he knew he had to do!

When the CO came back to the bus, all of the inmates were escorted into the court building and were put in a few bull pens where they waited for their names to be called to see the judge.

L was put in a cell alone, because he was a predicate slasher/stabber. But being that he was in the cell by himself, the male CO took the mittens off of his hands.

When L was finally called to see the judge, the first person he saw when he entered the court room was Tonya looking as beautiful as ever. His lawyer Mr. Kriss greeted him with a smile as L sat down next to him

The judge was a white elderly gentleman, and being that he was occupied looking at a few papers on his bench, L slightly turned around when he heard Tonya whispering to him.

"Why the heck they got you shackled up like an animal?" she asked angrily.

"Because to them that's what I am," answered L. "But don't get upset, I'm okay baby girl."

"I'm going to try and get your bail reduced," said his lawyer Mr. Kriss. "This is a meatball case; a gun with no bullets. They're dragging this out, mainly because of your alleged affiliation with this Bulldog Crew gang."

When the judge lift his head from the papers, the District Attorney stood up and said, "I'm District Attorney Robert Russell and I speak on behalf of the people, against the defendant Lamont Williams. He was arrested of possession of a weapon in the third degree and I suggest that bail remain at ten thousand dollars, until a deal is made or a trial date has been set."

"Your Honor," said Mr. Kriss. "There will be no deals, and I seriously doubt this case even makes it to trial. How can my client's bail remain at ten thousand dollars when he was arrested on a case that can easily be a misdemeanor; a gun with no bullets."

"I agree," said the judge. "His bail should not remain so high."

"But your Honor," complained the fat white DA. "This here defendant is part of the Bulldog Crew gang that has rocked our city with violence!!"

The judge's face turned pale at just the mention of the Bulldog Crew. He was well aware of the Bulldog Crew's actions, according to what he heard through the media.

"Alleged!" said Mr. Kriss. "My client is no part of any kind of gang, especially that of this so-called Bulldog Crew."

"Bail remains at then thousand dollars!" said the judge angrily. "Next court date is set for----"

Mr. Kriss smiled and whispered in L's ear, "Don't worry about it, I'll have this case thrown out soon! Your girlfriend is a very smart woman. She kept your ten thousand dollars, and took ten thousand of her own money out of her bank account and kept the receipt, so there shouldn't be any questions when she bails you out today!"

L turned around and smiled at Tonya as she returned his smile. It would be a few hours before he would be bailed out of prison.

Chapter 39

L tucked his nine millimeter as well as his .44 Bulldog handgun into the waist of his pants. He then threw on a light dark blue Nike jacket to conceal the bulges. He looked in the mirror and was satisfied with his appearance.

As soon as he was released from Rikers Island, he took a nice hot bath, ate a big dinner Tonya cooked and then made love to her all night long. But now he was glad that Tonya was spending the entire day with her friends, because he didn't want to try explaining where he was going at 10:30 at night wearing dark color clothing.

L looked in the mirror one last final time before heading out of his apartment. He made it down to his car and drove out to Queens, as he listened to the banging Sub-zero mix tape on CD. It was one of the best mixed CD he had in his collection.

When L finally arrived in the area, he wasn't surprised to see how quiet the block was. He could see that the area hadn't changed much since he visited many years back. He got out of the car and pulled his baseball cap down to his eyes. He walked to the house and rung the bell, as he grabbed both of his guns, but no one came to the door. He knew of nowhere else to go so he rung the door bell again and when he got no answer he went and sat on the stoop to think about his next move. He figured he'd wait for a while before heading back to Brooklyn. While he waited, he thought again about the dream he had of Big Dave talking to him. The dream seemed so real, he expected to see his friend again when he woke up. His words were clear and L understood everything he was told. Most of the dreams he had were forgotten as soon as he got up in the morning and brushed his teeth. But this one would not go away, and L turned Big Dave's words over and over again in his head all morning.

L looked at his watch and decided to come back tomorrow night. Just as he stood up off of the stoop and made his way to the car, he noticed a young woman walking a dog coming his way. Something about the young woman had caught his attention though. He knew he did not know her, but it was just something so very familiar about her even at the half block distance they were from one another. Then it hit him! He noticed the walk. L quickly ducked behind a parked car and waited in the dark.

Light didn't see L get off of the stoop. He was too busy making Blackie drop the dead black cat he had in his mouth. When he was 15 feet from his hide-away home, he heard the shot as the first bullet him square in the stomach. He was still able to pull the nine millimeter out of the red Gucci bag he carried but it did him no good because L kept firing.

The second bullet hit Light in the neck. Blackie saw his master fall to the ground and when he focused in on L, the dog attacked like a demon possessed. He ran at L full speed with bloody sharp teeth bared.

L could have swore he hit the dog three times, but the dog showed no signs of slowing down. Just before the dog was able to close in on him, L pulled the .44 and pulled the trigger blowing away parts of Blackie's head. He then quickly walked over to Light and with tears streaming down his face said, "I'm sorry man, you know I loved you!" before shooting Light in the head with the .44 Bulldog handgun killing him instantly.

L ran to the car, jumped inside and quickly drove away. He could see lights in people's homes coming on, and he knew the police would be in the quiet neighborhood in no time. He wasn't worried about someone catching his license plate numbers, because the plates he had on his car was stolen plates he took off of another car, and he doubted the plates were already reported stolen being that he took them not even an hour ago.

As L drove on, he thought about the conversation he had with Big Dave many years ago. Big Dave sat in L's apartment and out of the blue said, "Yo L, you know I love you, right? I would never cross you and that's word on everything I love. We Bulldog Crew for life! But Light and Fats is off the hook. It's really the nigga Light. Fats just go along with everything he say being they like biological brothers. I'm not saying we should flip on them niggas, because I would never suggest doing that to my closest comrades. But if a day ever came where one of them flipped on one of us, don't hesitate to kill'em! Because they'll kill you. And you know it's one person they'll always trust, and that's Fats's mother Ms. Carol being that she raised both of them, and I believe that's where they'll always go back to."

L drove into Jamaica Queens with tears still falling from his eyes. He then pulled over and took the plates off of the car and threw them in a sewer before putting his own plates back on.

Chapter 40

Mont-Mont knew L was the one who killed Light as soon as he heard about his death on the local news. Especially, when the news reporter said the fatal shot came from a .44 Bulldog handgun.

Mont-Mont felt L had betrayed the team, and vowed to get revenge for the death and betrayal of Light. But today he would have to focus on his own fate!

He sat in the bullpens with a group of other inmates waiting for his name to be called. He had on a very expensive blue three piece suit, a white shirt, blue tie, and blue and black alligator shoes. He was now on trial and couldn't wait to get it over with. Plus, last week they re-arrested him on another homicide that occurred in Brooklyn involving a Jamaican drug dealer.

"Lamont Hall!" yelled the Black male CO that came to escort him to the court room.

""Right here!" yelled Mont-Mont as he stood up and approached the bars. The CO opened the cell, handcuffed him and led him to the court room.

All year, Mont-Mont had been traveling back and forth from Rikers Island to Brooklyn Supreme Court for court appearances that led up to his trial. The first person he saw when he entered the court room was his lawyer, Mr. White.

In the court room, sat a bunch of supporters for Mont-Mont; mostly Spanish women from his Harlem neighborhood. The District Attorney was a very attractive white woman, and she looked at Mont-Mont with disgust as she watched him sit next to his lawyer. The judge was also a white woman and she was ready to get the trial started. The fourteen jurors; 12 and 2 alternates, sat in the jury panel and waited impatiently to get on with the trial.

"Okay, let's get this case started," said Judge Faye. "What is your witness's name?"

"My witness your Honor," said the DA, "name is Darnell Washington."

The young boy Mont-Mont hadn't saw in a year and a half, entered the court room and walked to the front of the court with a slight limp as he approached the bench.

"Mr. Washington," said Judge Faye. "Come up the steps, stand along side the chair, face the clerk and raise your right hand."

After being called as a witness on behalf of the people, Darnell Washington was sworn in by the clerk of the court.

"Please have a seat," said the clerk.

"Speak into the mic," said Judge Faye, "and give us your full name please."

"Darnell Washington!"

"Okay, you may now inquire," Judge Faye told the DA.

"Thank you Judge," said the DA. She then looked at the witness and said, "Good morning Mr. Washington. Mr. Washington, where do you live?"

"100 Hart Street," answered Darnell.

"Here in Brooklyn?"

"Yeah, right here in Brooklyn. Bed-Stuy!"

"Okay, I'm going to direct your attention back to June 10th of last year. Where was you at 7:15 AM, on this particular day?"

"I was being robbed on Tompkins and Willoughby."

"Do you see the person that robbed you in this court room today Mr. Washington?"

"Yeah, he's right there," said Darnell pointing at Mont-Mont.

"Let the record reflect that the witness has pointed out the defendant. Okay, then what happened Mr. Washington?"

"After him and his friends robbed us, a gangster that died that they called Light was wit'em. Light shot me and my man Tim in the legs. And when we fell, he told him," Darnell pointed at Mont-Mont, "and another dude to kill us. That's when he," Darnell pointed at Mont-Mont again, "shot my friend Tim in the head and killed him. The other guy he was with shot two times near my head just barely missing me. I guess it wasn't my time to go."

'Damn C-Allah!' Mont-Mont thought angrily. He thought both of those boys were dead. All week he'd been calling C-Allah but could not reach him. He now knew C-Allah left town and left him out to dry.

"What the defendant and his friends do after that?" the DA asked with a smile.

"His friends were already in the car," answered Darnell. "But like I said, that's when the other guy shot at my head but missed me."

"What happened next?"

"They all got in the car and drove away."

"Are you sure without a doubt, that the defendant is the one who killed your friend on that morning?"

"Yeah, that's him!" Darnell answered angrily. "I'll never forget his face!'

"No further questions your Honor," said the DA smiling from ear to ear. She knew this case would definitely make her a celebrity district attorney.

"The defense may now cross examine," said the Judge to Mont-Mont's attorney.

"Thank you your Honor," said Mr. White getting out of his chair approaching the witness box.

"Mr. Washington," said the lawyer, "you've stated to the court that my client and his friends robbed you. May I ask, what did they rob you of?"

"A lot of money!" answered Darnell.

"About how much money was taken from you?"

"They took about sixty thousand dollars from us."

"Wow!" exclaimed the lawyer. "That's a lot of money. In fact, that's more than what most people in this court sees in a year! Where did you get so much money from?"

"Selling drugs," Darnell answered with his face screwed up. "I'm not gonna lie. Me and my peoples made a lot of money selling all kinds of drugs, but that ain't got nothing to do with your client killing my friend."

"Did you see my client shoot your friend?"

"Yeah, I believe I answered that already! But again, yeah I saw him shoot Tim."

"Did you see the gun?"

"Yeah, I saw the gun. It was a big revolver. It could've been a .357, but most likely it was a .44 Bulldog they're known for using. Or what they always used."

"How do you know they always used a .44 Bulldog?"

"You don't watch the news?" asked Darnell causing a few police officers in the court room to laugh.

"Objection!' said the lawyer. "To hearsay and media misinformation!"

"Sustained!' said the Judge. "Jurors, disregard the last thing the witness said. Defense continue."

"Okay," said the lawyer looking at Darnell. "You named two kinds of guns. A .44 Bulldog and a .357 I believe. How do you know so much about guns? Do you have any?"

"Yeah, I know about guns. I had some before."

"Have you ever shot someone before?"

Darnell smiled and said, "I'm not on trial."

"Anyway, I'm sure you was scared when your friend was killed, right? I know I would be. But do you think just maybe, you was so frightened that you did not actually get a good look at the gunman's face?"

"I was scared, I admit that. But I'm one hundred percent sure that your client is the one that murdered my friend Tim in cold blood!"

"Okay, but you admit that you are a big time drug dealer?" asked the lawyer.

"I never denied that," answered Darnell.

"No further questions," said the lawyer in defeat walking back to his chair. He knew things did not look good at all for his client Mont-Mont, and hoped things could get no worse.

"The prosecution has no more questions for the witness either," smiled the female DA.

"The witness may be excused," said Judge Faye.

Darnell Washington walked by Mont-Mont glaring at him and it took everything Mont-Mont had inside of him not to grab the young boy and snap his neck!

After Darnell left the court room, the DA said to Judge Faye, "Please give me two minutes to get everything together your honor."

The Judge nodded and while the DA went through her papers, Mont-Mont turned around and was surprised to see C-Allah walk into the court room.

"Where the fuck you been?!' Mont-Mont whispered angrily. "Yo, kid, a nigga you fucked up and left alive just testified against me!"

"Word?!" asked C-Allah in surprise. He then looked at the closed court room door, shook his head and sat down.

"Okay I'm ready," said the DA causing Mont-Mont to turn back around in his chair.

"Okay," said Judge Faye. "You may call your next witness."

"Your Honor," smiled the DA. "I now call Detective Kenneth James to the stand."

Mont-Mont could not believe his eyes when C-Allah walked by him and approached the witness box!

"Detective James," said Judge Faye, "come up to the steps, stand along side the chair, face the clerk and raise your right hand."

After being sworn in by the clerk of the court, C-Allah sat down.

"Speak into the mic and give your full name and occupation please," said Judge Faye.

"My name is Kenneth Oshea James," answered C-Allah, "and I am a special homicide detective with the special Task Forces of CECO. I wish I can give you more details on this new task force, but I cannot do so for security reasons."

"I understand," said Judge Faye. She then looked at the DA and said, "You may now inquire."

"Thank you Judge," said the DA as she stood up and slowly approached the witness box. "Good Morning Mr. James."

"Good Morning," smile C-Allah.

Mont-Mont knew he was dead, and when he noticed two young white women and three black women in the juror's box lusting after the young handsome detective, he knew it was a wrap!

"Detective James," asked the DA, "how long have you been with this confidential special task force?"

"Well, it's relatively new," answered C-Allah. "But I've been with them from the beginning which is now three years today. It's been put together under the Terrorist Act."

"I see. Detective, I'm going to direct your attention back to June 10th of last year. Can you tell the court what you was doing on that day?"

"Of course," smiled C-Allah. "I was working undercover on the murders that the notorious Bulldog Crew had committed. And believe me, there were many!"

"How many would you say?"

C-Allah whistled and said, "I'll say they're responsible for at least 80 unsolved murders."

"Objection!" yelled Attorney White. "It is not proven that my client played any role in those murders! And he is not on trial for those unsolved cases!"

"He will be," smiled C-Allah causing a few jurors and the DA to smile.

"Sustained!' yelled the Judge. "Disregard the statement of the 80 murders as well as the witness's last remark! Prosecutor, continue with your questioning."

"Okay," the DA told C-Allah, "continue the story."

"As I said before," continued C-Allah. "I was working undercover. I along with the defendant and two other Bulldog Crew members, put a plan together to rob a few drug dealers. When we was able to get the victims; Timothy Green and Darnell Washington out of their Mercedes Benz, they were robbed of all of their drug money which came out to sixty five thousand dollars plus jewelry. Both victims were shot in the legs by the leader of the Bulldog Crew, Maurice 'Light' Jones. Me and the defendant Lamont 'Mont-Mont' Hall, were then ordered to execute the two victims. Maurice 'Light' Jones and John 'Fats 'Zimmerman got back into the car. Leaving myself and the defendant Lamont 'Mont-Mont' Hall alone with the victims. It was then that I saw the defendant pull out a .44 Bulldog handgun and fire two shots into Timothy Green's head execution style. He then laughed and got back into the car with the other two Bulldog Crew members, leaving me alone with Darnell Washington. As a police officer, I cannot just go around killing people, so I fired two shells into the ground to make it look as if I had killed the victim."

The Spanish women supporters for Mont-Mont, openly wept because they knew he would never come home again based on the testimony the officer was giving.

"Okay," said the DA, "let me ask you this. Did anything block your view of you possibly not being able to see the defendant kill Mr. Timothy Green?"

"No," answered C-Allah. "I saw him pull the trigger that day …… and on many other occasions. Especially, when he killed the young kid Timothy Green."

"No further questions your Honor," said the DA walking back to her chair.

"Defense may cross examine," said Judge Faye.

Mont-Mont's lawyer Mr. White looked as if he didn't even want to stand up. But he hesitantly approached the witness and began with his cross examination.

"You stated that you saw my client shoot Timothy Green," said the lawyer. "Are you sure of that?"

"I'm positive!" smiled C-Allah.

"Have you ever killed anyone while working undercover on this 'Bulldog Crew' investigation?"

"Objection!" yelled the DA. "That question has nothing to do with this case!"

"Sustained!' said the Judge.

"No, it's okay," said C-Allah. "Yes, I have shot and killed people during this investigation, but of course it was always in self-defense. And as a police officer, I am justified to do so to protect the innocence of society," he said looking at the women in the juror's box.

"Well let me ask you one more question," said Mr. White already knowing that he lost this case. "I'm sure there were many killings as you say, that happened after this case. I would like to know, why then was no one arrested when this case had occurred? I mean, you did say you've witnessed a murder. Why wasn't anyone arrested then?"

C-Allah was quiet for ten seconds before answering.

"Because we messed up," he said. "We wanted to get all of the Bulldog Crew members at one time. But it was one member that we concentrated on but we could not catch him doing anything or saying anything, so it was difficult to charge him with the act of doing anything or conspiracy. And none of the Bulldog Crew members ever mentioned him doing anything. It was very hard to get him, because he didn't like me or trust me. His name is Lamont 'L' Williams, and he has eluded us thus far. And later on, before we were able to snatch up the other Bulldog Crew members they were already dead or running from the law."

"No further questions," said Mr.White walking back to his seat.

"You may be excused," Judge Faye told C-Allah after the DA had stated that she had no more questions as well.

C-Allah got up and proceeded to walk out of the court room, but he was not prepared or fast enough for what happened next when he got near the defense table where Mont-Mont sat.

Mont-Mont spit a razor out of his mouth and with the speed of lightning he slashed C-Allah all in his face and neck. Before the DA could run, Mont-Mont caught her by the hair and cut her face up with six swift motions as well. He would have made it to the juror's box if the police officers weren't fast enough. But they tackled him and beat him senseless as they applied the handcuffs on his wrist so tightly, it cut off his blood circulation in his hands. But Mont-Mont didn't care. He figured he was dead already anyway!!!!!

The End!!!

EPILOGUE

L and Tonya had a baby girl they named Aaliya. L now knew how precious life was and realizing that he had something to live for, he moved downsouth to Atlanta, Georgia taking Tonya and his baby girl with him.

Mont-Mont was sentenced to 75 years to life in prison for three murders that C-Allah had testified against him on. He was also going back and forth to court for killing an inmate up in Clinton Correctional Facility, as well as for cutting C-Allah and the female District Attorney that retired. Presently, he had ten years to do in the box at South Port Correctional Facility.

Omar and Gloria are doing very well. They had made the Forbes list for being one of the year's richest young Black entrepreneurs. They also opened three more youth centers to keep children out of the streets. Gloria gave birth to the baby girl who she and Omar named Kenya and she is presently pregnant with a boy she and Omar had planned to name Kendu.

Big Lord's brother Born Magnetic was finally home and doing well under Omar's guidance of business learning before using some of the money Pam had given to he and Big Lord's parents, to start his own thing.

Richard, Lisa and Dejanay went back downsouth. And Pam and Gina continued to always be there for one another and both were presently in happy relationships with legitimate businessmen. They had enough of being with 'limited time on earth' bad boys!!! Neither wanted to relive that pain again, especially Gina!!!!!!

A POEM OMAR WROTE TO THE CHILDREN AT KENDU'S YOUTH CENTER CALLED

"CHILDREN ARE THE FUTURE

I believe children are the future, Remember that song?
Remember that saying?
The singer sings it, the teachers, the politicians,
and everyone who gives a positive speech say it.
I believe the children are the future,
but what do the future have in store for our children,
besides them being killed by racist, trigger happy
police men who enjoy killing Blacks and Puerto Ricans,
no matter what age they may be?
In their racist, blinded vision, he or she is still…
a nigger!
I believe the children are the future, but the future doesn't
Look too bright when you have children becoming
Bloods and Crips,
Latin Kings and Ne'etas
Loading up clips,
Killing other children because they've never been loved.
Or their parents are so busy working just to survive,
That they don't have time to listen to their children cries…..
For help!
And the TV and the music they listen to are filled with
So much violence, but they can identify with it because
In the neighborhoods they see it everyday!

The prosecutor, the judge, the CO that won't budge,
The police, the politician, and the parole board,
they do not want to see a peaceful world.
Peace was never profitable for them,
I'm sure you understand, their jobs would be useless,
un-needed or as the prosecutor say when they aim to shoot
your appeal down,
meritless!
So they charge children as adults, but never charge adults as
children, and I wonder why,
When everyday we see men thirty years old acting five.
So the system is designed for political reasons and to
Make money,
"CASH RULES EVERYTHING AROUND ME .... CREAM!!!"
The system will always exist and generate billions of dollars,
because children\n are the future!
I believe children are the future,
The cute little four year old girl, that forces you to smile,
And say, "Ooh, she's so cute!"
But at what age will she become a bitch?
How long will it take to convince her that she ain't shit,
And you can make her happy with material things if she
Sucks your dick?
The cycle repeats, so realize that the last woman you called
A bitch, was once that cute little girl that forced someone
To say, "Ooh, she's so cute!"
I believe children are the future,
Even I was once that teen-aged child
That did something terrible to another teen-aged child,
Because I could not see that children are the future.

One child gone, one child in prison,
Until I become a man,
And other children in prison asked themselves the question,
"Why should I change? The parole board, the employers,
And the rest of the world will always see me as a criminal.a"
So they say, "Fuck Change!"
And they remain…..children.
I believe children are the future,
It may come a time when police shoot an unarmed man,
Forty one times,
But they will not get away,
Because a child that grows up to become revolutionary,
A true thug,
That truly believes in justice even if he has to bust slugs,
Will straighten it out because he may believe,
That children are the future!!!!!!

A NOTE TO THE READER

I hope you enjoyed this book. It was not written to glorify violence in any way. It was to show that the negative actions in the streets that we call the 'game' is fruitless and unrewarding.

There are too many single parent households, too many unnecessary murders and too many followers of the wrong things.

I would like to say, just as with Kia, her friends and the children, the violence we call the game is ruthless and sometimes snatches away life from innocent women and children, because there are ignorant individuals playing something called 'The Game' that they don't even know the rules to. Most don't even know how to play! And after years of searching for the definition of this thing that we call the 'game' that have took away so many of our people's lives, I finally was able to find the definition.

THE GAME MEANS ....GENOCIDE
AND
MORE
EFFECTS!!!!!!!

WAKE UP!!!!!
LIFE IS NOT A GAME!!!!!!

COMING SOON!!

HATERS ANOMOSITY

"LET OTHERS HATE BE YOUR MOTIVATION"

A STORY BY:MIZ

Order Form

Pen Cushion Publishers
PO Box 85
New York, NY 10116
(718) 844-0686
www.pencushionpub.com

CHECK ONE:

Bishop.................................$14.95
The Bulldog Crew.....................$14.95

ADD:

Sales Tax..............................$1.05
Shipping and Handling................$3.20
Total...................................$19.20

MONEY ORDERS ONLY

rchaser Information

me ____

dress____

y ____________________ State _____ Zip __________

ntity Ordered?

Orders shipped directly to Correctional Facilities, Pen Cushion Publishers will deduct 25% of the sale price.

hop................................$11.21
s Tax..............................$ .78
pping and Handling..............$ 3.20
al..................................$15.19